Romancing *Yesenia*

The publisher and the University of California Press Foundation
gratefully acknowledge the generous support of the
Ben and A. Jess Shenson Endowment Fund in
Visual and Performing Arts, established by a major gift from
Fred M. Levin and Nancy Livingston, The Shenson Foundation.

Romancing *Yesenia*

*How a Mexican Melodrama
Shaped Global Popular Culture*

———

Masha Salazkina

UNIVERSITY OF CALIFORNIA PRESS

University of California Press
Oakland, California

Suggested citation: Salazkina, M. *Romancing* Yesenia: *How a Mexican Melodrama Shaped Global Popular Culture.* Oakland: University of California Press, 2024. DOI: https://doi.org/10.1525/luminos.196

Library of Congress Cataloging-in-Publication Data

Names: Salazkina, Masha, author.
Title: Romancing "Yesenia" : how a Mexican melodrama shaped global popular culture / Masha Salazkina.
Description: Oakland, California : University of California Press, [2024] | Includes bibliographical references and index.
Identifiers: LCCN 2023054054 (print) | LCCN 2023054055 (ebook) | ISBN 9780520400757 (paperback) | ISBN 9780520400764 (ebook)
Subjects: LCSH: Yesenia (Motion picture)—Influence. | Motion pictures, Mexican—Influence—History—20th century. | Motion pictures, Mexican—Soviet Union—History—20th century. | Socialism and motion pictures.
Classification: LCC PN1997.Y456 S235 2024 (print) | LCC PN1997.Y456 (ebook) | DDC 791.43/72—dc23/eng/20230105

LC record available at https://lccn.loc.gov/2023054054
LC ebook record available at https://lccn.loc.gov/2023054055

33 32 31 30 29 28 27 26 25 24
10 9 8 7 6 5 4 3 2 1

CONTENTS

Acknowledgments   *vii*

Introduction   *1*

Prelude: The Soviet Stardom of Lolita Torres   35

1. *Yesenia* in Mexico and the Soviet Union   63

2. Mexican and Soviet Womanhood, circa 1970   83

3. Between Mexican *Cursilería* and Russian *Poshlost'*   112

4. The People, the Gray Market, and the Ballroom Gown   139

Coda: *Yesenia* in China and the Arrival of Telenovelas
   in the Socialist World   172

Notes   *179*

Index   *213*

ACKNOWLEDGMENTS

This book began with a *MUBI Podcast* episode on *Yesenia*—this experience and others' reactions to it ultimately convinced me to go down this rabbit hole, and what a fun time it has been.

I am grateful to Yulia Glushneva, Laura Zoe Humphreys, Ilona Jurkonytė, Rielle Navitski, Sarah Ann Wells, and Agustín Zarzosa for selflessly reading a full draft of this book and offering extremely helpful insights that reshaped many of my arguments. Roger Gathmann, as always, has been a crucial interlocutor. Kaveh Askari, Maria Corrigan, Kay Dickinson, Alejandro Kelly, Ilya Kliger, Jie Li, Mariano Mestman, Joshua Neves, Elena Razlogova, Viviane Saglier, Rachel Sandwell, Samhita Sunya, Joan Titus, and Eric Zolov have offered encouragement and suggestions on specific parts and/or overall conceptualization of this project. Additional research by Ilona Jurkonytė, Muxin Zhang, and Xin Zhou has been invaluable. Tess McClernon's work on the manuscript and Egor Shmonin's on the illustrations and cover has made this process so much easier. I am also grateful to Miguel Errazu and Sidharta Yair Manzano Valenzuela at the Hemeroteca of Mexico for helping me locate the materials there, which proved to be crucial for my analysis. Thank you, Miruna Achim and Arturo Ramírez, for all the warmth and laughter that made my trips to Mexico even more special—and I am definitely writing my next book on Una Paloma Blanca!

I was lucky and honored to have Eliot Borenstein and Ignacio Sánchez Prado as the readers for this manuscript, as their own work has shaped much of my own thinking about popular culture. It has been a great pleasure working with Raina Polivka, Sam Warren, and the whole team at the University of California Press— again, thank you for all your help.

At home, of course, this book would not have been possible without Luca Caminati's endless patience and unconditional support, and Vini's good cheer.

Writing this book was also inflected by two losses, both painfully untimely—of Ana López and Katerina Clark. In so many ways, this is a tribute to both of them.

The publication of this book has been supported by the Social Science and Humanities Research Council of Canada.

Introduction

A 2005 Russian made-for-TV documentary, *Kiss Me Stronger or Operation Bésame Mucho* (*Tselui menia krepche ili operatsiia Bésame Mucho*, Maksim Vasilenko, 2005), begins with a reconstruction of the 1976 attempt at hijacking a Soviet airliner. Officially, hijackings and other terrorist activities were not supposed to take place in a country of developed socialism, so stories of these and other such events were persistently suppressed in the Soviet media. And yet, as the film reveals, contrary to what one might expect, this particular attempt lacked the political motivation that characterized the spree of international hijackings that reached a pinnacle in the 1970s. Unlike most Soviet citizens who attempted to escape to "the West" via Europe or the US, this hijacker bizarrely demanded that the plane take him to Mexico so that he could finally meet the composer of the song "Bésame Mucho," Consuelo Velázquez. In the film, this episode becomes an occasion for early-2000s Russian musicians, producers, and cultural critics to reflect on the song's enormous popularity, extraordinary emotional charge, and enduring resonance in the Soviet Union. The escapist romantic sensibility embodied in "Bésame Mucho," all the interviewees in the film claim, felt at once exotic and familiar. It provided an exotic imaginary destination, tapping into the sense of a continuous longing for escape that characterized the everyday affect of life under the Soviet regime, while resonating with local vernacular musical traditions that survived the impositions of official communist culture. Rather than waning over time, this particular sensibility found new outlets in post-Soviet culture, and thus, the critics interviewed in the film affirm, the "phenomenon of 'Bésame Mucho' transformed into the phenomenon of Latin American telenovelas."[1]

Indeed, when the TV documentary aired in 2005, Latin American serials had reached a distinctive cultural ascendance across the former Socialist Bloc, from China and Eastern Europe to Cuba—competing for airtime with the kind of cultural-analysis-cum-sensationalist-fare that this documentary itself epitomizes. And just like the story of the airliner hijacking that sets the documentary's narrative into motion (deviating as it does from conventional characterizations of "the West" as an alternative to Soviet society), the popularity of Latin American romance, from its musical to television forms, calls attention to a different and wholly unexpected global trajectory of media fandom. *Operation Bésame Mucho* inadvertently highlights its affective power as unpredictable, unruly, and potentially subversive—albeit in ways that also defy conventional understandings of Cold War politics and dissent. After all, wasn't it the Beatles (or the Scorpions, depending on which US media source you prefer) that brought down the Berlin Wall?[2]

In all these aspects, the focus of this Russian TV documentary surprisingly resonates with discussions that emerged in the North American cultural sphere in the past decade, foregrounding the unanticipated force of popular culture produced across the Global South and increasingly consumed all over the world (as the title of one recent book suggests).[3] From Latin American telenovelas and Latin pop, to Bollywood, Nollywood, Japanese anime, K-pop, K-drama, and Turkish *dizi*, the immense popularity of these cultural products circumvents and, in many cases, rivals Hollywood and other entertainment behemoths of the Global North. As such, it re-diverts the conventionally anticipated directionality of entertainment media's global flows and the modes of its consumption.

Scholars have traced the origins of these new global media flows to the beginning of globalization and to the neoliberal restructurings of the entertainment industries that took place throughout the late 1980s and 1990s, in conjunction with technological developments.[4] It is therefore assumed to be a relatively late twentieth-century phenomenon, born of the global media over the past forty years. In the post–Cold War world, audiences' habits and preferences have been radically altered as they opened up to popular forms from distant parts of the world. Bishnupriya Ghosh and Bhaskar Sarkar have theorized this cultural phenomenon as "the global-popular"; its impact is undeniable, its politics ambiguous at best.[5]

The emergence of this essentially neoliberal global culture thus appears to fold neatly into a deterministic post–Cold War historiography. But could longer genealogies of the global-popular be constructed to challenge this reified conventional historiographic understanding? How would it alter our conceptualization of global media circuits and their origins? And could such earlier histories change how we think of the continuities and ruptures, as well as the politics and ideologies, of the global-popular today? This book considers one such historical precedent: the unexpected and mostly unexamined popularity of the Mexican film *Yesenia* (Alfredo B. Crevenna, 1971) in the Soviet Union. Set during the Second Franco-Mexican War, this unassuming movie melodrama was based on a successful television series, itself an adaptation of a popular women's romance graphic novel, a genre that was extremely common in mid-century Mexico. Screened in the Soviet Union in 1975, *Yesenia* became the highest-grossing film in the history of Soviet film exhibition, unsurpassed by any movie, foreign or domestic. Based on ticket sales alone, it was seen by an astounding 91.4 million viewers in only the first year of its release.[6] *Yesenia*'s popularity in the Socialist Bloc, largely unbeknown to its Mexican producers, continued for decades as the film migrated from cinemas to television screens and video. Boosted by its success with Soviet audiences, the film enjoyed a similarly spectacular exhibition history in China in the late 1970s, when the country was opening itself up to more international media, paving the way for other Mexican and Latin American production broadcasts on Chinese television in decades to follow.

Approaching this period retrospectively, cognizant of more contemporary developments in the global media, I conceive of this episode in film history through the framework of television culture as well as fashion and music industries whose combined impact, I argue, shaped both the film's Mexican production and its subsequent reception within the Socialist Bloc. I also argue that *Yesenia*'s popularity carved out a crucial node within the global circuit of cultural and industrial networks, further enabling Latin American media's transcontinental reach. The longer history of this circuit began with the reception of Argentinian tango and Mexican boleros in the 1920s, expanding to Mexican Golden Age film classics and Argentinian musicals in the 1950s and 1960s, and to Mexican historical melodramas in the 1970s that circulated in the Soviet Union and China, and culminating in the triumphant march of the Brazilian telenovela *The Slave Isaura* (*A Escrava Isaura*, Globo, 1976, hereon *Isaura*) through European, Cuban, Chinese, Soviet, and Algerian television screens in the 1980s. Sold to 104 countries, *Isaura* is widely understood to be the most dubbed show in the history of television, with accumulative worldwide viewership in the billions. Its international success signaled the rise to global power of Brazilian and Mexican TV conglomerates Globo and Televisa, opening the floodgates to the Latin American telenovelas that came to dominate the TV screens of the former Socialist Bloc in the 1990s. Thus, in 1991, Soviet viewership of the Mexican telenovela *Los ricos también lloran* (Televisa, 1979–80) considerably surpassed that of the contemporaneous US soap opera juggernaut *Dallas* (1978–1991), when both were broadcast on television in the last months of the Soviet Union's existence.[7] This process accelerated further in the early 2000s, pointing not only to audiences' already-formed preference for Latin American melodramatic media but also to the potential for a truly global fandom for melodramatic serialized television originating from Turkey, South Korea, and India today.

With this broader backdrop in mind, this book focuses on the reception of Mexican melodrama in the 1970s as a crucial transitional moment whose culture and politics have informed our global-popular present in hitherto unattributed ways. The four chapters analyze different facets of *Yesenia*'s production, international circulation, and reception, maintaining a dual focus on the Mexican and Soviet cultural and political milieux of the 1970s.[8] Because the titular protagonist is a young woman raised in the Roma community, Yesenia's Mexican identity in the film is mediated through transnational markers of the Romani culture, in particular music and dance associated simultaneously with Spanish/Andalusian and Eastern/Southern European origins. The book argues for the centrality of the figure of "the gypsy"—and of "gypsy music" and "gypsy fashion"—as the space of mutual articulations and negotiations of the sentimental cultures and forms of affective and political belonging and non-belonging in the Soviet and Mexican contexts of the 1970s.

However, to set the stage for the exploration of this history, the book's prelude offers a snapshot of an earlier moment of the late Soviet 1950s, when post-Stalinist liberalization allowed for a powerful entry of foreign influences, setting in motion many of the cultural dynamics of the subsequent decades. This new cultural opening and popular enthusiasm over all things foreign included the influx of Latin American cinema and music, epitomized by the popularity of Argentinian actress-singer Lolita Torres, who became an idol for Soviet audiences. Although it constitutes a distinct case study, placing Torres's Soviet stardom as a starting point for the book's narrative draws out some of the key aspects governing the Soviet reception of Latin American melodramatic media in their historical development, tracing their transformations from the period of hopeful exuberance of the 1950s to the global crisis of the 1970s.

What ultimately guides my analysis of *Yesenia* as an early instantiation of a global-popular icon is the way it brings into relief some of the key social, cultural, and political conflicts of its era: namely, the gradual transition in the 1970s from versions of state socialist, nationalist, and internationalist formations to the early emergence of neoliberal ideologies on the global scale. Although rarely considered in relation to each other, both Mexico's and the Soviet Union's twentieth-century histories were rooted in the experiences of their respective revolutions—revolutions that ultimately were incomplete at best or, at worst, totally failed in their original ambitions for a truly emancipatory social transformation. Without undermining the continuous practices of organized state violence and repression, both the Soviet Union in the period of late socialism and Mexico in the last decades of the Institutional Revolutionary Party (PRI)'s rule could perhaps be described as *dictablanda*—a "milder" kind of dictatorship (especially as compared, in the Soviet case, to its Stalinist past, or, in Mexico's case, to the military dictatorships of the countries of the Southern Cone): a single-party institutional political hegemony that emerged through the reification of the earlier radical revolutionary rupture.[9] In both the Mexican and Soviet cases, the impending collapse of the system was inseparable from the advent of global neoliberalism in the 1980s. And yet, I argue, in its transitional nature the 1970s was a period not yet overdetermined by the impending neoliberal globalization, containing instead multiple possibilities for political and cultural development, however unrealized. In my analysis, discussions of aesthetic tastes and the material conditions for their reproduction provide necessary entry points into broader historiographic questions, and their transnational context suggests their relevance beyond local specificities.

Inseparable from aesthetics and material infrastructures are the affective registers triggered by the global-popular sensibility associated with *Yesenia*, characterized by the excess of feeling, sentimentality, and sensuality. While projecting conservative models of gender and sexuality, such melodramatic expressions speak to the overwhelming shared feelings of social and political injustice that both countries' progressive elites (whether associated with the state or the intelligentsia) failed to address. Melodrama in both contexts carved out a socially legitimized space for articulating such sensibilities, and its contemporary critical discussions themselves reflect the historical shifts this book investigates. However, melodrama—whether understood as a specific genre or as a cultural, aesthetic, or affective mode—is not the primary object of this book. I largely understand melodramatic sensibility and the cultural works that embody it—whether films, graphic novels, TV series, or songs—as enabling producers, consumers, and critics to stage particular social conflicts and leverage their positions (including, but not necessarily, counterhegemonic ones). In the case of the cultural flow of Latin American melodramatic media in the socialist world, it gave rise to new transnational communities of feeling. Such imaginary sentimental communities, however, did not necessarily fully rely on either universalist or pre-constituted cultural affinities. I argue that they functioned, instead, as an avatar of a new shared form of global populism, one that that went against the grain of official ideologies and the taste criteria of the intelligentsia in both countries. This new form, I argue, was tied to changing models of femininity and consumer culture, linked to informal and DIY production and circulation practices that reflected and reshaped conflicting notions of individual and collective agency in both Mexico and the Soviet Union. These consumer practices, in turn, both reflected and were triggered by transnational circulation of media at large, and melodramatic media in particular.[10]

Certain genres of music were crucial for this global melodramatic media sensibility. "Bésame Mucho," with which we started, is indeed a perfect case in point: the Mexican bolero that became the most recognizable Latin standard of the postwar period worldwide, used frequently in film soundtracks from this period (from the 1940s well into the 1980s), ubiquitous and yet with a fanbase that, on the extreme end, would hijack a plane to meet its maker. As we'll see, in the Soviet Union this was equally true both of Lolita Torres's renditions of Luso-Iberic songs and of the Russian and "gypsy" romance songs (*romansy*) whose resurgence accompanied *Yesenia*'s reception and whose aesthetic regime, I argue, further resonated with that of Latin popular romantic music.[11]

The connection between music and melodrama (formally underscored by their shared etymologies—*melos* means music), in terms of aesthetics and affect as well as the intertwining of the film and music industries, has a long history, in which "melodrama became more and more closely identified with an auditory imagination that conditioned the responses of listeners to melodramatic scenarios in lyrics and music."[12] Similar to their Indian and Egyptian counterparts, sound technologies and practices in Latin America historically were integral to the establishment of the melodramatic cinematic ethos.[13] Music production specifically was embedded in the story of the success of the leading Latin American film industries of the twentieth century (Argentina, Mexico, and Brazil), and this relationship is reflected in the development of specific genres (for example, *cabaretera* in Mexico), the thematic and narrative function of songs in many films, and the formation of stardom.[14] This crossover continued on television, illustrated by the fact that in the early 2000s, Televisa, the largest producer of Mexican telenovelas, formed a joint venture with EMI, one of the four largest international record labels. In turn, the process of "standardization of ways of feeling and expressing, of gestures and sounds, dance rhythms, and narrative cadences" produced by the melodramatic media (as discussed by Jesús Martín-Barbero and Marvin D'Lugo, among others) had broad transnational impact far beyond the inclusion of songs in film soundtracks or the films' diegetic narrative structures, to extra-cinematic everyday realities.[15] Both Mexican boleros such as "Bésame Mucho" and *romansy* in the Soviet 1970s formed part of the sonic background that shaped the experiences of cultural producers, audiences, and critics alike through what Anahid Kassabian has referred to as "ubiquitous listening."[16] Thus, although *Yesenia* was not a musical, its cultural reception extended to this broader field, constituting a crucial part of its intermedial environment.

THIS BOOK'S THREE LEITMOTIFS

Intermediality is integral to the three most prominent aspects of the story of *Yesenia* as recounted in this book. The first of these leitmotifs is focused on the distinctive media circuit linking Latin America to the Socialist Bloc. Falling largely outside the dominant European- and US-centered industry networks, this linkage provides a new perspective on the history of global media circulation, its "flows and counter-flows," to use Daya Kishan Thussu's famous formulation.[17] This circuit was shaped in the period between the 1950s and the 1980s, until eventually it largely merged with (or was partially subsumed by) the dominant globalized music and TV market. During its existence, however, this circuit developed its own particular infrastructure, geography, common points of reference, its own distinctive temporality, and a different notion of what constitutes a global media capital.[18] This book develops out of the premise that in its many iterations, global media production and consumption today reengages historical memories and continuing affective attachments to earlier intimacies—including those of global melodrama (whether Latin American or, increasingly, its other regional variants)—across nations of the former Socialist Bloc, intimacies that were enabled by this distinctive circuit.[19] Taking cues from Latin American cultural critics such as Martín-Barbero, D'Lugo, Ana M. López, and Matthew Karush, and placing their work into conversation with that of scholars of Soviet media Alexander Prokhorov, Elena Prokhorova, Lilya Kaganovsky, Eliot Borenstein, Christine Evans, and Kristin Roth-Ey, I approach this transnational circuit as defined through a melodramatic sensibility mutually constituted across media such as radio, recordings, TV, and cinema.

Despite its undisputed scale and cultural impact, one reason why the history of Latin American popular media consumption in the Socialist Bloc has been largely ignored is that it disrupts many of the established scholarly narratives around transnational circulation dynamics and affective communities constituted by them. Within much of the scholarship on transnational popular media, the historical viewerships of Latin American film musicals and melodramas (and, subsequently, of telenovelas) have been presumed to be primarily regional.[20] For the first decades of its existence, such media has been associated with lower-class audiences, and almost exclusively with Hispanophone communities in the Americas.[21] The rise in worldwide popularity of Latin American telenovelas in the late 1990s, which positioned media conglomerates such as Globo and Televisa as global leaders and secured their market presence throughout much of Asia and the Middle East as well as in the Western Hemisphere, changed such assumptions. Most scholars, however, have understood this shift to be predicated on an overlapping series of ruptures resulting from economic globalization and technological changes of the period.[22]

Similarly, the "Latin Pop Explosion" that began in the North American market of the late 1990s has been linked simultaneously to the growth of the domestic market share of Latinx and to the "World Music" turn within the industry as an extension of the same process of neoliberal globalization.[23] The continuing tie-ins between music industries and audiovisual media as constitutive of Latin media's global popularity, however, have continued to be explored in scholarship only in the context of the Americas.[24] Their continued presence within the former socialist sphere was largely ignored. Given the ongoing isolationism of the cultural histories of the former Socialist Bloc and the geographic ghettoization of postsocialism as an Eastern European phenomenon, we still have not picked up on the continuities between the global media circuits of the Cold War era and the transnational cultural traffic afterward. Following the examples of Michael Denning's *Noise Uprising: The Audiopolitics of a World Musical Revolution* and Andrew F. Jones's *Circuit Listening: Chinese Popular Music in the Global 1960s*, this book seeks to reconstruct a specific historical transnational circuit—articulated in particular through its local reception in the Soviet Union—as one possible prehistory of contemporary global media circulation.[25]

My interest, therefore, is not merely in investigating cultural reception, but in probing the character of the circuit itself. With all its distinctiveness, its Soviet–Latin American iteration, I argue, should not be thought of as either a historical anomaly or a cultural curiosity. The phenomenon of transnational film and popular media circulations bypassing the Global North is historically anything but exceptional. The distribution of Mexican, Indian, and Egyptian popular cinema (as well as Mexican and Brazilian telenovelas) in the Soviet Bloc relied at least in part on their already established international success, albeit on a regional scale. However, because of the Soviet Union's position outside of Western media markets, the geopolitical and economic motivations of its media distribution networks, and the realities of its socialist intellectual property regime, its global media circuits followed a distinctive trajectory for much of the twentieth century. Tom Lamarre's discussion of regional television in an East Asian context provides another useful conceptual frame for such a materially grounded analysis: as he reminds us, merely by virtue of its existence, "distribution produces something in its own right . . . a complex set of social functions."[26] Understanding such functions is even more crucial in instances where the shared geography constituted by these networks does not "correspond with received territories and geographies but entails a sense of affective possession, emerging in conjunction with the mapping of the transmedial onto a geopolitical domain. Its 'where' is between media and nations."[27] Indeed, a peculiar sense of deterritorialization emerges throughout this book, and it is especially evident in the discussions of specific cultural forms— *Yesenia* providing a particularly telling example, with its pseudo-Romani protagonist and Franco-Mexican nineteenth-century settings offering a loose sense of cultural (mis)identification for the Soviet audiences, setting in motion a series of affective displacements.

The second, albeit interconnected, story this book tells explores this media circuit as a vehicle for intersecting sexual politics in the Soviet Union and Mexico in the 1970s. As has often been the case historically, the melodramatic regime enabled continuous renegotiations of gender norms through the new structures of feeling conveyed via film, TV, and music. I understand these particular renegotiations as part of the process leading up to the veritable explosion of sexual norms in the late Soviet period and their quick reification into the extremely reactionary gender regime of the post-Soviet era—a shift that intersects with a more globally recognizable neoliberal postfeminist ethos that became dominant everywhere by the 1990s, impacting in particular the more economically and politically vulnerable subjects.[28]

Changing gender and sexual norms, in the Soviet Union as elsewhere, were inextricable from the increasing role of consumer culture—especially the fashion and personal care industries—which, in turn, both inflected and were inflected by entertainment media. This further amplified the import of shadow economies and black markets, which fueled much of late Soviet consumer culture.[29] The increasing prioritization of profits within the Soviet film apparatus that shaped the exhibition of foreign cinema in the 1970s was itself a reflection of the broader acceptance of a consumerist logic that was seeping into national life. At the same time, this logic was tied as much to the emerging global capitalist consumer culture as it was to the latent informal (or semiformal) economies, which relied on social, interpersonal, and kinship bonds.

These Soviet developments were not unlike the 1970s Mexican state's attempts to negotiate between global internationalist imaginaries and (highly nepotistic) commercial structures as governing its own film exhibition policies. At the same time, informal economies—from street vending and popular markets to various forms of domestic DIY practices—similarly constituted major spaces of consumer culture in 1970s Mexico, selectively integrated with the state economic priorities of import-substitute industrialization. This book shows how changing gender norms co-constituted these broader social and economic processes, and how much, in turn, these changes were inseparable from media both at the level of representational models and in its material networks. In pursuing this gendered line of analysis, I build on the extensive work of cultural historians and anthropologists of the Soviet Union: Gail Lapidus, Lynne Attwood, Alexey Golubev, Natalya Chernyshova and Anna Rotkirch. Feminist scholars Marta Lamas, Eli Bartra, Gabriela Cano, Jocelyn Olcott, and Anne Rubenstein, and cultural historians and critics José Agustín, Eric Zolov, and Louise Walker, similarly guide my exploration of the Mexican context.

Ultimately, placing the Soviet-centered developments side by side with the radical changes in Mexican society reveals the broader transnational dynamics of the complex politics of the global 1970s. It demonstrates how the demands of the sexual revolution of the global 1960s were recuperated by mainstream cultural actors and reshaped—as well as being reshaped by—conservative models of femininity. While the rhetoric of sexual agency combined with the increasing sexualization of women posed a challenge to traditional feminine roles, this contradiction was successfully mediated through a consumerist logic. And yet, for the majority of women in both countries during this period, its realization remained largely aspirational—as the realities of informal economies effectively blurred the distinction between production and consumption, creating a much more complex interplay between individual and collective agency and identity. I demonstrate how the 1970s in both Mexico and the Soviet Union formed a crucial transitional moment of mediation between traditional models of gender essentialism, the rise of feminist consciousness, the continuing relevance of communal ideas, and the emerging neoliberal postfeminism that would culminate in the subsequent decade. Bearing in mind Latin America's own "peripheral" status vis-à-vis Eurocentric histories of twentieth-century feminism, the transnational and comparative aspects of this process offer a provocative counter-history of the women's culture and politics of that period, as constitutive of the popular media circuit this book reconstructs.

This geographic and cultural juxtaposition is at the center of the third and final story nested in the book's narrative. My overall argument here is that for much of the Cold War period, cultural modes originating in what we now tend to refer to as the Global South, which relied heavily on affective identification in the form of melodrama, consistently proved to be more emotionally accessible to socialist audiences than their European or US counterparts. This affective translatability readily allowed for the creation of global cultural icons via their projections on big and small screens—from Raj Kapoor and Mithun Chakraborty, in the case of Indian cinema, to Lolita Torres and the protagonist of *Yesenia* (and, subsequently, those of the many telenovelas) in Latin America. Originating from the peripheries of the global world order and centering on characters from backgrounds marginalized by class, ethnicity, and race, yet determined to follow their passions in a way that transcended their organic communities, these media texts simultaneously legitimized the status of the outsider while ultimately integrating them into the mainstream (narratively, often via the melodramatic trope of mistaken identity). As such, these icons offered complex negotiations between the private and public spheres, mediating between conservative, state hegemonic, and popular vernacular ideological formations. By the 1970s and into the 1980s, these media texts functioned as informal sites of cultural intimacies, offering an unintended alternative to state-supported internationalism, cosmopolitan universalist humanism, or radical Third-Worldism, all of which had largely lost their cultural and political currency for the majority of the common people, whether in Mexico or the Soviet Union.

Without flattening the significant differences between Mexico and the Soviet Union, and acknowledging the uneven dynamics of their political and cultural relationship, I argue that what allowed for such points of intersection were the global dynamics of political and social developments in the 1970s. Further following Ghosh's insights, I understand these articulations of melodramatic global icons as arising with particular force during moments of social transformation and crisis. In the case of *Yesenia*, this period was marked by the aftermath of the global 1960s and the traumas of state violence in Prague and Mexico City of 1968. Aimed at eliminating internal dissent and motivated by maintaining their respective geopolitical positions, both the massacre perpetrated by the Mexican state on the student demonstrators at Tlatelolco and the Warsaw Pact invasion of Czechoslovakia led by the Soviet Union threw into deeper crisis their respective imaginaries of the revolution, eroding all vestiges of state legitimacy in both countries.

The powerful affective dimensions of such seemingly incongruous transnational communities were first foregrounded by Brian Larkin in his work on "Indian Films and Nigerian Lovers."[30] While I argue that these affinities were determined by the dual logic of uneven development and ambiguous relationships to "the West" as a cultural and geopolitical construct, their imprint cannot be ascertained within conventionally construed North-South or East-West binaries. Nor do they fold neatly into the liberal versus authoritarian divide, instead constructing distinctive—and distinctively uneven—expressions of agency. These affinities have much in common with the sentimental communities described by Lauren Berlant in the

2008 book *The Female Complaint*, with an important caveat: they were predicated on a series of displacements and deterritorializations resulting from an ambiguous foreignness of the very cultural forms that shaped them. As such, their function is best described by Ghosh as "a repertoire of popular cultural practices that rely on dispersed mass media flows from 'elsewhere' as their 'clay,' as the raw semiotic material for their expressive performances of the popular."[31]

The "elsewhere" of these sentimental collectivities, despite melodrama's appeals to the universal, is inscribed in imaginaries that are recognizably geopolitically specific yet highly ambiguous, where the very notion of clear national or regional identification gets dispersed. This logic accounts for why it was the artless Yesenia—a nineteenth-century Mexican "gypsy" whose displacement of cultural and national identity is very much at the core of the film's drama—that touched audiences in the Soviet Union and China, and not the iconic heroines of the Mexican Golden Age melodrama performed by María Félix and Dolores del Río, whose national belonging is firmly sutured into their films' narratives and aesthetics. At the same time, it had to be a Mexican—and not a Hollywood, French, or even Japanese—film that produced the very ambiguous deterritorialized foreignness to which socialist audiences so ardently responded. The geopolitical contours of these shared affects reflect the ambiguous Cold War status of Latin America vis-à-vis the Socialist Bloc, where both functioned in some ways as "a different West," one that was at once less alienating than Europe or North America and yet reflected their shared, broadly "Western" cultural models and aspirations. Building on work by, among others, Carlos Monsiváis and Ignacio M. Sánchez Prado, I argue that this North(East)-South(West) interplay is articulated in Soviet and Mexican overlapping theorizations of the taste regimes that, wittingly or unwittingly, simultaneously affirm European cultural models and underscore the impossibility of their adaptation to local vernacular forms.[32]

As I demonstrate the importance of fashion and consumer culture in mediating the models of femininity that emerge in the transnational reception of *Yesenia*, I argue that, similarly, the cultural intimacy and mutual recognition that emerged from it participated, at least in part, in both countries' transitioning to what just a decade later would crystallize into globalized neoliberalism. Thus, in many ways both Mexican and Soviet affective communities in the 1970s unwittingly pre-negotiated the local conditions of the emergent neoliberal world order (symbolically embodied both by the collapse of the Soviet Union and by Mexico's coercion into the General Agreement on Tariffs and Trade, which prepared its way into NAFTA) that would come into fuller effect over the course of the 1980s.[33] This dynamic would become fully legible in the subsequent reception of Latin American telenovelas, but we can read this process retroactively, manifested already in the 1970s. Again, unsurprisingly, the stamping of neoliberalist hegemony on the countries outside the capitalist core was made particularly visible by the changing contours of gender representation and gendered modes of consumption.

And yet, while the iconicity of figures such as Yesenia is not entirely subsumed by the logics of the corporate industries that produce them (as would implicitly follow from a conventional Marxist approach), they are too deeply imbricated in the cultural industries to be easily translatable into an alternative political agency for its subaltern audiences. Shaped through a volatile transitional period when "an internal frontier appears between the institutional system and the 'people,'" the political impulse in such expressions of the global-popular is, indeed, highly ambiguous.[34] These new and uncertain configurations of polity are also inscribed in the notion of fandom as distinct from the kind of audience formations imagined by the nation-state and by socialist media producers: these active spectators often express their agency in unruly ways that fall beyond the didactic logic of hegemonic modernizing cultural institutions.[35] The push-and-pull of cultural industries and their local vernacular mediations produces, at best, forms of political potentiality and, at worst, the ugliest versions of conservative populism.

Looking back at this transitional moment of the 1970s and its popular cultural manifestations through a transnational lens lets us glean its instability and mutability, revealing not the inevitability of neoliberalism but instead the multiple and frequently incompatible social forces at play. For all these reasons, and many more besides, the history of *Yesenia*'s circulation and reception, with all the pitfalls of mis-recognition that are at the core of the very notion of cultural intimacies as I understand it, presents itself as a rich field for cultural analysis.

OUTLINE OF THE BOOK

Given these broader historiographic goals, after this introduction, the prelude sketches the rise to Soviet stardom of the Argentinian singer-actress Lolita Torres. It places her celebrity in the Soviet Union in the late 1950s to 1960s within the larger context of the emergence of new notions of glamour and consumption that were inscribed into the socialist discourses of the Thaw period, musical performance and reproduction practices, and shifting definitions of folkloric versus popular culture. In highlighting the creation of libidinal transnational intimacies via stardom, interjected with complex negotiations of markers of foreignness within both Soviet and Perón-era Argentinian performance cultures, the prelude aims to draw out the book's major thematic threads and key dynamics.

Chapter 1 shifts to detailing *Yesenia*'s production and exhibition, placing the film's distribution in the Soviet Union as part of the intensification of Soviet-Mexican political and cultural diplomacy in the 1970s, which brought the two national film industries into closer contact, as well as the changes within the Soviet film apparatus that enabled the wide exhibition of Mexican popular cinema. I briefly describe *Yesenia*'s complex intermedial history, emblematized by its adaptations from highly successful serialized graphic romance novels (*historietas*) to a telenovela, to a film, to yet another telenovela, within the context of the rise of the Mexican TV media giant Televisa.

Building on the centrality of intermedial women's culture, chapter 2 places *Yesenia* in the dual context of the significant transformations of gender politics of the 1970s: the growth of an institutionalized feminist movement in Mexico and the demise of the institutionalized ideals of women's liberation in the Soviet Union. By analyzing women's magazines and the reemergence of film melodrama in Mexico and the Soviet Union respectively, I argue for the impact of the discourses and practices associated with the sexual revolution on gender essentialism within mainstream mass cultures in both countries.

Chapter 3 turns to a discussion of aesthetic models that came to define, shape, and characterize the overlapping transnational space of women's cultures in both countries. I place two culturally specific iterations of kitsch—Mexican *lo cursi* and Russian/Soviet *poshlost'*—in dialogue with melodramatic modes and women's culture, and the vernacular music of boleros in Mexico and *romansy* in Russia. The chapter further traces these aesthetic and affective regimes in the cinematic subgenre of "gypsy melodramas," which form the context for *Yesenia*'s production and transnational reception: their genealogy in Mexican cinema, their 1970s iterations on Soviet screens, and in particular their intersecting modes of representation and their patterns of exoticization and racialization.

Chapter 4 investigates the same cluster of cultural and ethnic signifiers in 1970s costume drama and fashion in both countries (some of *Yesenia*'s most enduring traces are visible in the names of dresses, hairstyles, wigs, burlesque dancers, drag queens, clothing shops, and beauty salons). The chapter explores the intersections between the mass-produced imaginaries of fashion and glamour on the one hand and informal cultural production and consumption practices on the other. The conclusion of the chapter returns to the opening episode of the book, tracing such DIY and "pirated" practices in the context of the Soviet reception of "Bésame Mucho" and its inclusion in the soundtrack of a Soviet melodrama that became the country's most successful export to Mexico, *Moscow Does Not Believe in Tears* (*Moskva slezam ne verit*, Vladimir Men'shov, 1979), just a few years after *Yesenia*.

The book's coda briefly sketches out *Yesenia*'s reception within yet another global socialist context: China in the late 1970s and early 1980s, where it was screened as part of the first Week of Mexican Cinema in Shanghai in 1979, subsequently giving rise to several revivals of the film, sponsored by official media channels. As such, it opens up a considerably broader geography of a late socialist/postsocialist circuit of Latin America's melodramatic media, one that ultimately demands separate further investigation.

While much of the book's narrative is focused on the details of these case studies of circulation and reception, the remainder of this introduction offers critical reflections of a more speculative nature. While directly tied to the arguments of the subsequent chapters, thus referencing them where appropriate, it is intended both as an overview of different aspects of the conceptual framework I propose and as a consideration of its implications beyond the specifically Soviet-Mexican context explored in the rest of the book. As such, it offers a snapshot of a broader context for understanding the distinctiveness of the global circuit activated by Soviet media circulation, focusing on cinema and music. This is followed by a more in-depth discussion of the historical dynamics of East-South transnational affinities and their complex relationship to the Euro-American culture, as well as the emergence of a different notion of the popular out of such contexts. Finally, the introduction concludes with some brief considerations of discourses on melodrama as both primary and secondary sources for exploring some of the key issues at stake in the book and their potential implications for the study of melodrama beyond the field's canonical emphasis on Hollywood.

ASYNCHRONICITY OF TRANSNATIONAL STARDOM AND FANDOM IN THE SOVIET UNION

One of the unique aspects that shaped the circulation of Latin American popular culture in the Soviet Union was the particularity of its media environment and the status of foreign film stars within it. While the conventional Cold War discourses in the West created the impression of the Socialist Bloc as autarkic, reinforced by the late socialist and early postsocialist critics' lamenting their experience of cultural isolation (primarily from Hollywood cinema and British and American counterculture), scholarship by, among others, Alexei Yurchak, Kristin Roth-Ey, Eleonory Gilburd, and Rossen Djagalov has offered us a considerably more nuanced vision of the cultural landscape of the Soviet relationship to all things foreign during the last decades of the country's existence.[36] The picture becomes even more complex when we place the Soviet mediascape's relationship to foreign cinema and international stars within a comparative context.

In the US, commercial exhibition in the mid- to late twentieth century consisted almost exclusively of domestic products, with foreign films being largely limited to "art cinema" circles while the industry famously invested in its global expansion.[37] Foreign stars tended to be integrated within Hollywood productions, contributing to the perception of diversity within American cinema, rather than perceived as representatives of other national film industries.[38] In Western Europe and Britain, Hollywood similarly occupied the largest share of foreign cinema on local screens—with the other strong film industries (such as those of France, Italy, and Britain) representing a certain percentage.[39] Despite the fact that Japan and India were the leading film producers in the world during that period, films from those industries were absent from US and Western European movie repertoires—with the exception of a few directors like Akira Kurosawa or Satyajit Ray, whose films formed part of the film festival circuit. Latin American screens (except for Cuban ones after 1959) were dominated by a combination of Hollywood, Mexican,

Argentinian, and, to some degree, Brazilian commercial cinema.[40] While French movies (as well as early Soviet and German films) were an important part of the noncommercial circuit, Italian genre films ("pink neorealism" and comedies) were particularly visible and beloved by Latin American audiences, thus forming a more diverse cinematic geography.[41]

In the Soviet Union, exhibition (like all other aspects of the film industry) was centrally controlled by the state and consisted roughly of a mix of half Soviet, half foreign films. According to numbers quoted by Marina Kosinova, in a typical year the exhibition schedule included 130 Soviet titles, seventy from other socialist countries, twenty-five to thirty from capitalist ones (a category that included Japan; only about six or seven were from the US), and thirty from "developing countries" (including India).[42] But the actual percentage of foreign films on Soviet screens was higher and their reach was broader: because entertainment films from "capitalist" and "developing" countries were considerably more popular with the audiences and thus brought higher revenues to movie theaters (and, ultimately, the state) than domestic productions, the print run of their copies was higher—including print copies made in 16mm, making screenings possible in small venues around the country (from clubs in the countryside to mobile cinemas).[43] If an average Soviet film was seen by 390,000 viewers, an average for a foreign film (taking into account those from other socialist countries) was 424,000—while many regularly reached between one and three million viewers.[44] Most of the Indian and Egyptian films, as well as the less numerous US, French, and Italian genre movies, reached twenty-five to sixty-five million viewers, *Yesenia* holding the record with over ninety-two million tickets sold in the first year.[45] Once we add the informal practice of screening popular foreign films instead of the officially designated Soviet or Socialist Bloc films to generate further profits for individual theaters (which would not be reflected in these official statistics) as well as the practice of screening these films on television for many decades, we can imagine the scale and reach of foreign film exhibition in the Soviet Union.[46] Their affective and cultural impact was therefore enormous even before the advent of video, which drastically changed the late Soviet mediascape as it did in the rest of the world.[47] Thus, what may at first appear as isolated cases of the popularity of specific Latin American films, songs, or series, acquires a different dimension when we take into account the scale of their reach and impact.

The other, connected, dynamic in Soviet exhibition and reception of foreign cinema was its peculiar temporality, which goes counter to all the norms of film exhibition in the capitalist world. Because foreign films were bought for a flat sum, with no royalties but with exhibition rights for long periods (which could be further extended—although it was probably as common to simply violate these agreements), it turned out that most of the films the Soviet Union purchased were older and thus considerably cheaper and/or minor films with known stars, which were also marked down. And these films—many of which were already some ten years old at the moment of their first Soviet exhibition—would continue their exhibition run for several decades. The practice of watching older films in theaters was also common for Soviet cinema—in fact, the revenues from "second runs" of Soviet films in theaters regularly exceeded those from the new releases.[48] Within the more elite, cinephile cinema culture—taking place through such venues as festivals and weeks of foreign cinema—retrospectives (whether of national cinemas or specific auteurs) were an especially common exhibition format.

These practices generated a distinctive temporality of, especially, international stardom: the idiosyncratic socialist symbolic economy did not fully recreate the capitalist logic of constant renewal, with its emphasis on the newest releases and contemporaneity and its constant production of new stars and tentpole films. Given the highly controlled nature of information flow (with virtually no independent access to foreign media) and relative lack of international travel opportunities for Soviet citizens, the disconnect (or anachronism) of Soviet reception was not apparent or, frankly, even relevant to most Soviet cultural consumers. Because, as we'll see, an unusually large number of imported films in the Soviet Union were historical dramas and literary adaptations, the question of the contemporaneity of their representations—including such markers as dress and hairstyle, cars, and music— was even more opaque. Thus, the popularity of the international stars of the 1940s, 1950s, and 1960s—Jean Marais, Louis de Funès, Gina Lollobrigida, as well as Raj Kapoor and Lolita Torres—continued in the Soviet Union into the 1980s. This was furthered by the unusual synergy between film exhibition in cinemas and on television. Because both industries were state owned, and thus they were not in competition in the same way as their counterparts in most other countries, cinema officials extended broadcasting rights for newly released films to television "fairly quickly and cheaply, which meant that even more people got to watch these films on TV soon after they had run in cinemas."[49] Moreover, the broadcasting rights tended to be granted for extended periods, which meant that most of these films continued to be shown on television for decades (apparently, either this was included in their original distribution purchasing rights or else such nuances were simply disregarded).[50]

At the same time, against the phenomenon of commercial film production and exhibition cycles both reflecting and generating fashions and trends, in Soviet cultural reception broader generational identities (as well as, to some extent, specific subcultures) accounted for choices of movie and music icons, thus allowing for their extended cultural relevance. And Latin American stars—cinematic, television, and musical—played a crucial role in this process, acquiring increasing cultural importance in particular as a site of acquisition of "sentimental education" within a Soviet culture whose official position was oriented toward collective and social—not private or intimate—forms of existence.[51] Their popularity came to define a period— sometimes marked as part of a generational identity, other times easily expanding into decades. Such overlapping processes created a particular scene of cultural reception, where the popularity of earlier stars still exercised a strong pull, despite their anachronism (especially vis-à-vis the sites and dates of their original production).

In other words, in disproportion to both their synchronic and diachronic domestic successes in Argentina and Mexico (respectively), Lolita Torres became one of the icons of the late 1950s through 1960s, and Yesenia of the mid-1970s through early 1980s. Each period was characterized by significant cultural and political shifts as the project of developed socialism traced an arc from hope to collapse.

But this peculiar—extended and overlapping—temporality is also what allows us to inscribe the Soviet reception within longer cycles of transnational circulation and the transformation of Latin American media, as was typical especially for the telenovela genre. The full cycle of remediation of most telenovelas through their various transmedial remakes likewise extends their relevance through several decades. Many telenovelas originated as radio plays or graphic novels, then were repeatedly adapted and remade into television shows and movies, many of which were transnational, such that their life spans could be well over half a century. This is the case with early juggernauts like *Simplemente María*: the original 1967 Argentinian telenovela was based on Celia Alcántara's romantic novel of the previous decade; it became internationally known via its 1969 Peruvian version; and it was remade by Mexico's Televisa in an even more internationally successful 1989 version, which became enormously popular all over the former Soviet Union in the 1990s. Similarly, *Corazón salvaje*, based on a 1957 novel by another woman romance writer, Mexico's Caridad Bravo Adams, has been made into two movies and four telenovelas to date, and its adaptation in 1968 was especially popular in China in the late 1970s to early 1980s. Such an extended temporality is fully exemplified by the transmedial history of *Yesenia*, which started as a historieta in 1965 (or in 1942, if you consider versions that came out under a different title), was made into a telenovela in 1970 and then into a movie in 1971, and was remade again as a telenovela in 1987—thus making its protagonist a cultural icon in Mexico for several generations. Reinserted into a new national reception context in the Soviet Union (and subsequently in China) allowed it to function as a *global* icon, "as an 'aperture,' an opening (in an optical system) into a *there*—the ever-receding ground of history," in Ghosh's understanding of the term.[52] History, as it emerges from this transnational analysis, is anything but a simple linear progression, and is itself subject to multiple uneven and overlapping temporalities, false starts, and incomplete processes—both reflecting and shaping my objects of study.

TEMPORALITIES AND GEOGRAPHIES OF THE SOCIALIST MUSIC CIRCUIT

A similar distorted temporality (as compared to the Western-capital cultural-media production cycles) and a distinctive geography are characteristic of the global music circuit engendered by Soviet socialist distribution and reception of foreign music. While its primary international export was classical, foreign mainstream popular music was considerably more present in the postwar Soviet culture than what could be accounted for by the usual emphasis on the unavailability of American and British rock. Both its geography and its function, however, were very different from the English-language-dominated, US- and UK-centered global popular music market of that period. Although the Soviet recording company *Melodiya* was the second largest record manufacturer in the world by 1970 and released a fair number of international popular music records, as part of a state-controlled, noncompetitive socialist market its stars and hits were not generated through record sales.[53] Radio, movies, television, and (from the 1960s) popular press outlets such as *Krugozor* magazine (which included a flexi disc with songs featured in it) and music events (concert tours and international music festivals) were much more constitutive of taste making for popular music. As a result of such institutionally and media-centered construction, rather than the quickly changing hit-parade charts generated from music sales, international music stardom in the Soviet Union was also subject to longer cycles and uneven temporalities.

The geography of the Soviet circuit of international popular music, especially from the early 1970s on, was also quite similar to that of popular film imports. This book's prelude explores the reception of Latin American music in the immediate post-Stalinist period in the context of the success of Argentinian musicals and global folkloric revivals. By the early 1970s, however, the international popular music scene in the Soviet Union came to be increasingly more in sync with its Southern European circuits (France, Spain, Italy—even Greece), at least in part due to the organized international music events, promoted by European institutions and media, that were broadcast in the Soviet Union.[54] Thus, performers like Yves Montand, Mireille Mathieu, Dalida, and Joe Dassin, Demis Roussos, ABBA, Boney M, Ottawan, Baccara, Julio Iglesias, Raffaella Carrà, Toto Cutugno, Al Bano and Romina Power, Ricchi e Poveri, and Adriano Celentano were all extremely popular in the Soviet Union in the 1970s and 1980s, thanks to their television and movie appearances. Most of them toured the country with concerts as well. In addition to the Eurovision and Intervision song contests (the latter overlapping with the Sopot International Song Festival in Poland), the Sanremo International Music Festival in Italy played an important part in the creation and promotion of this particular music circuit, which extended to the Soviet Union—but also, importantly, to Latin America. As Laura Podalsky has shown, Italian *musicarelli*—musical films from the 1960s that were developed in response to Sanremo's growing influence, some of which were also shown in the Soviet Union—shaped both Spanish and Latin American (Argentinian and Mexican) perceptions of youth culture and their transnational film and music productions from the 1960s on.[55] In short, while the Soviet foreign popular music canon of the 1970s and 1980s looks very different from the North American or British one, it was actually part of a distinct circuit that extended, especially through Spain and Italy, to Latin America.

However, one crucial difference between the circulation of music and of cinema, at least until the 1980s, is in the modes of reproducibility and the relationship to forms of ownership. Until the spread of video technology, films could only be seen in theaters or on movie screens set up elsewhere, but for much of the twentieth century, popular songs could be purchased as records. Even more importantly, those records could be reproduced and thus continuously reenter circulation. Songs were also subject to new performances and often new recordings, whether covers by local artists or, informally, by nonprofessionals (the latter assisted by continuing sales of sheet music). Given the radically different copyright regimes, these practices were considerably more common in the Soviet Union than elsewhere well into the 1970s, thus creating additional modes of music circulation. Moreover, bootlegged copies—both of songs that were released by the Soviet recording companies and, especially, of foreign ones that were officially scorned by the Soviet regime—were widespread throughout the socialist world as early as the 1940s. These were first (re)produced on discarded x-rays, later on reel-to-reel magnetic tape decks, and finally on cassette tapes.[56] This informal music circulation had its own temporality, responding not so much to actual scarcity (given that the actual volume of record manufacturing in the Soviet Union was quite massive and fairly varied) but rather to the ebbs and flows of the official ideological control of popular music. Most famously, the informal circulation focused on jazz and rock and roll—but the practice also extended to recirculating older forms of vernacular and romantic Russian music, in particular their emigré performers, which at various points have been deemed ideologically unacceptable by the Soviet establishment, as well as recordings of local, "unofficial," guitar-playing singer-songwriters (*bardovskaia pesnia*).[57] The anachronistic, belated temporality of the circulation of those musical forms, as we will see in chapter 3, resonates in a particular way with the cultural function of Latin American romantic musical traditions, such as Mexican bolero (of which "Bésame Mucho" is a fine example) and its Soviet icons.

Given this complex media temporality, the nature of the cultural icons at the center of this book, emerging in periods of historical transformation, is largely transitional. They mediate, I argue, between national-popular and global-popular formations, as well as between socialism, however broadly conceived (as I include here Argentina's 1940s–1950s Perónist worker-populism, in the case of Lolita Torres, and Mexico's 1960s–1970s one-party institutionalized revolutionary *dictablanda* in the case of Yesenia), and, respectively, the liberalism and neoliberalism that have emerged in the subsequent decades. I see these icons as concrete manifestations of the emerging media and cultural infrastructures of global distribution and circulation. In this earlier period, predating the accelerated neoliberal globalization of the 1990s, they acted less as networks than as *relays*—in the sense that Kaveh Askari uses this term in his work on Iran, where it "evokes circulation but with an emphasis on sequence, interruption, and incremental agency over top-down or seamless transparency."[58]

What interests me, however, is the relationship between the shifting—and, to use a term that Peter Schmelz employs as paradigmatic for the late Soviet period, increasingly *polystylist*—late Soviet culture and the emergence of certain forms of specific universalism and popular/populist consciousness during this period.[59] Slavoj Žižek and some other scholars see in these late socialist forms a perfect container, as it were, not only for postmodernism but specifically for postsocialist globalized consumer culture at large. Thus, Matthew Jesse Jackson, in his study of unofficial Soviet art, argued that late Soviet culture "crystallized aspects of postsocialist globalization" and could therefore "be understood as an anamorphic projection of a beckoning postdemocratic polity."[60] Tempting as it may be to arrive at such provocative conclusions, my analysis shies away from such a deterministic view of history. While I trace in both Mexican and Soviet cases some early manifestations of later developments, the full subsumption of these cultural forms under the categories of, respectively, globalization and postdemocratic polity risks negating their (geo)political particularities by absorbing them into the very "globalized" Western categories they seek to oppose. As such, the anachronisms and cycles of deterritorialization and reterritorialization this book traces are much closer to the understanding of hybridity advanced by Néstor García Canclini and to Alexei Yurchak's discussions of internal deterritorialization within late Soviet culture—both finding a symptomatic expression in the highly charged and problematic figure of "the gypsy" in *Yesenia* as a point of affinities between Mexican and late Soviet sentimental communities.[61]

TRANSNATIONAL AFFECTIVE COMMUNITIES
AND CULTURAL INTIMACIES

This book's argument rests on the speculative hypothesis that central to the reception history of *Yesenia* in the Soviet Union was the experience of mutual recognition between the Socialist Bloc and the so-called Third World at large, and between the Soviet Union and Mexico in particular, a recognition that extended beyond the contours of this particular case study. It is crucial, however, that such transnational affinities and cultural intimacies be understood in the plural. There was certainly no single, overarching way in which they were experienced, nor were they shared by everyone at the same time, nor did they ever lead to a sense of unity. Instead, they emerged for different groups of people at different times, depending on their particular historical circumstances, cultural and social formations, experiences, beliefs, and needs—criss-crossing the longer history of the official relationship between the Second and Third Worlds in the turbulent twentieth century more generally.

Furthermore, this plurality reflects the different scales and registers implied in such sets of relations. At the same time, one could perhaps speak of the affective resonances between the Second and Third Worlds at large. At a different level, there were also distinctive affinities between the Socialist Bloc (inclusive of both Eastern Europe and the former Russian Empire) and Latin America. And yet, at a different granular level, we can detect parallels between the situations across Soviet and Mexican cultures and politics of the 1970s, which could be speculated to trigger a further sense of mutual recognition, whether acknowledged or not. In my discussions throughout the book, I tend to oscillate among these levels, dwelling most closely on the third, specific to Soviet-Mexican milieux of the 1970s, but it is here that I hope to tease out some of the broader historical and conceptual complexities of all three.

There were, of course, plenty of historical reasons for mutual recognition between the former subjects of the Russian Empire and of Latin America. As Gražina Bielousova asserts, the construction of Western proto-Orientalist imaginaries vis-à-vis Latin America and the Caribbean and vis-à-vis Eastern Europe and Russia became codified around the same time, and their structuring discourses were likewise strikingly similar. Despite their respective geographic positions (which are actually "West" in the case of Latin America and "North" in the case of Russia), European discourses on both are structured by the already established vocabulary of the Orient—the tropes of "Oriental despotism, Oriental splendour, cruelty, sensuality."[62]

This opposition between "Western" rationality and "Oriental" affective excesses came to be frequently reignited in the second half of the twentieth century in the context of the Cold War. Latin America was repeatedly constructed by the US as a "danger zone" particularly sensitive to communist—assumed to be Soviet—pressures, underscoring their shared irrationality, reengaging the simultaneous tropes of submissiveness and predilection to violence, so characteristic of Orientalist discourses. Such mutual interpellation was predicated, at least in part, on shared experience of demands for "civilized" subjectivity as conditions of entry into the developed world (or "the West")—and the inevitable denial of such entry. Positioned outside of such rational and civilized subjectivity, both postcolonial and postsocialist subjects to this day are always in excess (speaking too loudly, standing too closely, using too much body language), never processing "good taste" (dressing too garishly, favoring outrageous design in everything from cars to houses), incapable of good organization (never on time) or polite debate in the public sphere (arguing, gesticulating, and yelling too much), of civic-mindedness (not respecting the law, not caring for the environment), codependency in personal friendships and familial relationships (dedicating too much time to socializing with friends or family), lacking in appropriate boundaries (borrowing money, asking for favors), and accepting of various forms of corruption. The infamous reliance on informal networks that characterizes both formerly Second and Third World countries itself alludes to something even more profound that is also shared: lack of trust in the law, the state, and the institutions.

These markers—themselves deeply melodramatic in their affective and transpersonal excess—function at once as interpellations of Orientalist epistemologies and, at the same time, as profound shared affinities that can perhaps best be understood as what Michael Herzfeld termed *cultural intimacies*, albeit in a transnational and even transcontinental context: "a recognition of those aspects of a cultural identity that are considered a source of external embarrassment but that nevertheless provide insiders with their assurance of common sociality," offering "rueful self-recognition," which runs contrary to the official representations.[63]

Such transnational affects, as Rahul Rao has argued, are not necessarily always counterhegemonic—in fact, they "could serve *both* progressive and reactionary ends, often at the same time."[64]

At the same time that they are constructed as "the other" of the democratic, rational, and liberal (Cold War) West, the cultural identities of both Latin America and the Soviet Union/Eastern Europe are further complicated by an uneven relationship to their own colonialist legacies as manifest in internal differentiation of skin color or tone, caste, and regional, religious, and, of course, indigenous identities that resulted from their settler-colonial and imperial heritage.[65] As a result, such transnational affinities entailed their own iterations of racialized and Orientalized "otherness"—as we will see clearly in this book in the case of the shared projections of the figure of "the gypsy."

To varying extents, these mixed Orientalist and colonial legacies found expressions in geopolitical hegemonies impacting much of the postcolonial world, in certain critical moments in the histories of anticolonial movements contributing to the construction of solidarities between the postcolonial subjects and those of the Socialist Bloc. The more explicitly political of them, however, concentrated on the shared (or desired) experience of a revolution. The Russian Revolution raised the possibility of a radical reversal of power whereby the previously "backward" nation could become a political and, at least in some respects, economic superpower (insofar as it was able to raise its population from poverty, invest in massive industrial modernization projects, and distribute aid to Africa, Asia, and Latin America to broaden its sphere of influence). Such political affinities were based on the genuine sense of proximity to the revolution as a possibility of radical transformation—and for that reason, in the case of artists and intellectuals, such affinities often manifested in enthusiasm for the early Soviet avant-garde as the perfect embodiment of art's role in this process.

But for most socialist subjects in the turbulent 1960s—when for many Third-Worldists true revolution, following the Cuban and Vietnamese models, seemed just within reach, or even inevitable—revolution itself quickly became a reified object, endlessly commemorated and continuously emptied of any genuine transformative, let alone emancipatory, feeling. Moreover, the condition of "combined and uneven development" for both the socialist world and much of the postcolonial world was further complicated by the experience of "incomplete" revolutions—ones that failed to provide a profound sociocultural restructuring, uniformly resulting in the hegemony of the state—both "real" (through its practices) and symbolic (through its ideological weight). Mexico, which underwent a series of revolutions in the course of its history, offers a particularly striking example here. But even Third-Worldism, which arose as an alternative not only to capitalism and imperialism but also to the nation-state model and Soviet-style state socialism, in many ways followed the same pattern. As Jeffrey Byrne demonstrates through the example of Algeria, by the 1970s, Third-Worldism had been "transformed from a transnational mode of cooperation that evaded and subverted the authority of the colonial state into an international collaboration that legitimized and zealously defended the authority of the postcolonial state."[66]

Beyond the more radical articulations of Third-Worldist solidarity, there was also a shared cosmopolitanism of socialist and leftist Latin American intelligentsia, which was mutually inclusive. This is particularly evident in the literary sphere, from histories of translation of Latin American writers in the Socialist Bloc and of Soviet and Eastern European ones in Latin America to individual relationships forged through the network of writers' conferences and workshops during this period, each of which engendered a "global sense of commonality and solidarity that both surpassed and questioned the official narratives about East-South interactions."[67] The communist cultural sphere, as Kyrill Kunakhovich has persuasively argued in the case of Poland and East Germany, functioned during communist times as its own distinctive version of a public sphere. Within it, an outsized role was played by artists, intellectuals, and other members of the intelligentsia, who continued to negotiate with the state, making implicit but often conflicting claims of speaking on behalf of "the people" in articulating their respective visions of cultural policies, practices, and aesthetics.[68] Something quite similar could be said about the Mexican cultural sphere, especially in the 1970s, a period during which the illusion of autonomy from the state became particularly apparent.[69]

At the same time, however, the sense that this all-important cultural sphere actually excluded most of "the people" it was supposedly representing was becoming quite palpable in both countries—furthering the rifts between not only different classes but different cultural formations. Sentimental communities such as those enabled by the circulation of Latin American media both demarcated those differences and created an alternative affective sphere whose cathectic power depended on the continuing sense of exclusion from economic and symbolic privilege both nationally and globally as the shared experiential horizon of "the popular"—a term to which we will return shortly.

Ultimately, behind many of the affinities among the (post)socialist and postcolonial subjects are mutually recognizable historical traumas. From the militarization of social organization as an inevitable consequence of the anti-imperialist and national liberation struggles, to aggressive, state-run industrial modernization as an attempt to break out of the conditions of economic and geopolitical "backwardness" imposed by the imperialist and colonial legacies, to the weight of everyday experience of bureaucracies, these many aspects of socialist and postcolonial subjects' relationship to the state imposed their violent logic on the everyday.

And, paradoxically, while the project of solidarity between the socialist peoples and those of the "Third" or "developing" world was itself part of the (pro)socialist state ideologies, the actual affinities between the people were rooted, at least in part, in the recognition of the complex relationship of simultaneous complicity and resistance to that very state power, thus in some ways mirroring such state ideologies and refracting them. The development of elaborate ways of bypassing, avoiding, and sometimes resisting the state, its practices, and its ideologies formed a pragmatics of these affinities, elaborated in a vast informal sphere of economic, political, and fundamentally cultural activity as a defining shared feature of the global (post)socialist world and the Global South. This informal sphere reflected communal sociality in its many forms, coinciding neither with the official (socialist) state organization ("the people" or "the party") nor with liberal democratic and legal structures (the Habermasian "public sphere"), nor even with the kind of distinctive cultural sphere discussed by Kunakhovich. And furthermore, by the 1970s, even in the Soviet Union this informal sphere of shadow economies and cultural activities was already increasingly hard to disentangle from the flow of global capital.[70]

Indeed, from the perspective of liberal democracy and law (let alone that of global capitalism), these informal spheres are understood as further proof of the very backwardness and unruliness of the postsocialist and postcolonial world. They constitute the realm of "the multitudes"—whose existence, depending on your political views, is seen either as a major threat to our current world order or as its only salvation. Exacerbated by the events of 1968 that brought the crisis of the state's legitimacy to a head (the Prague Spring for the Soviet Union; the Tlatelolco massacre for Mexico) and followed by the numerous crises of the 1970s (the oil shock, hyperinflation, and borrowing by Third World countries to maintain state structures), the transition period to global neoliberalism was marked by pronounced segmentation and lack of social cohesion. In both self-understanding and imposed theorizations, this furthered the rift between "the people" (as an operative term within the socialist state) and what theorists have since variously termed "the subaltern" or "the multitudes."[71] The identity of the latter could not—or could no longer—be mapped out through either class structure or strong identification with the nation-state, the two major models that had provided cohesion under the earlier logic of socialist internationalism but that were now unassimilable. In contemporary political theory, these two polities—"the people" (united by their class and/or national identity) and "the multitudes" (no longer organizable through either)—have increasingly come to stand in direct opposition to each other as distinct alternatives for the Left's vision of political mobilization.[72] In this crucial transition period of the 1970s to 1980s in both Second and Third Worlds, however, the split between these two distinct imaginaries became apparent, leading to palpable anxiety among the intelligentsia and cultural elites aligned with the nation-state or the internationalist agenda alike.

The global-popular affects of melodrama of the 1970s speak more clearly to those disorganized multitudes—as such, they were generally at odds with conventional ideological positions dictated by the Communist Party or the Mexican state apparatus and increasingly imbricated in the emerging neoliberal and consumerist paradigms. Yet these new affinities nonetheless embedded the long-standing shared orientation toward communal good and what we may call "the commons," as opposed to the individualistic values and ideologies linked to personal fulfillment, more associated with Western liberal modernization. The twin sources of this communal orientation were vestiges of older (premodern) worldviews and the modern revolutionary ethos. Communal values were a crucial part of socialist aspirations, whose formation involved, among other intellectual and political sources, the recuperation of traditional (precapitalist) forms of social and cultural organization within a modern and centrally controlled economic system. Within both Russian and Latin American nineteenth-century intellectual history, these notions were grounded in the specificity of regional and local forms of governance (indigenous forms of land ownership in the case of the Americas; the peasant community, *obshchiny*, in the Slavophile traditions)—in both cases filtered through Occidental liberal philosophies. What such transculturation offered was a distinct form of universalism—not an acceptance of the universalism of the European Enlightenment, but a mediation between its orientation toward egalitarian inclusivity and particularities of local self-understanding.[73] As such, as Sánchez Prado argues in his discussion of the position of Latin America vis-à-vis the notion of the Global South, it also produced a somewhat distinct form of entanglement with these European legacies.[74] In both cases, the geopolitical self-understanding of such positionality vis-à-vis the global allows for resonances in the respective figurations of the relationship between the individual and the community. Such shared understanding relies not on the universality of the individual subject, but rather on the transcendent role of *communitas* not merely as superseding individual subjective interests but as integral to and constitutive of them.[75] This remained a consistent part of socialist subjects' self-understanding, even in the face of their disillusionment with the regime and their sense of the betrayal of these values by the political elites. This recognizably collectivist ethos was particularly persistent among the popular classes, even into the 1970s and 1980s.[76] Mutual recognition of these values is evident, for example, in the explanations given by Soviet audiences for their love of Indian popular cinema in the 1950s and 1960s (as documented by Sudha Rajagopalan), as much as in the more contemporary Cuban post-Soviet generation's nostalgia for Eastern European and Soviet animation, which defined their childhoods in the 1970s and 1980s (as discussed by Aurora Jacome, among others).[77] A similar sense of mutual recognitions, I argue, also shaped the Soviet-Mexican popular entanglements, as exemplified by *Yesenia*.

Such foregrounding of the common good over individual self-interest presented an alternative to the "Western" worldview: this notion of the commons could be shared precisely by all those who have been historically excluded from and exploited by the privileges and rewards of Western liberalism—the very liberalism that has been inseparable from the capitalism and colonialism in which it flourished. This notion of the commons found its manifestation in postrevolutionary anti-imperialist economic and cultural policies in both Mexico and the Soviet Union—such as nationalization of resources (in particular, the nationalization of the oil industry, which took place in Mexico in the 1930s under the presidency of Lázaro Cárdenas, a development that would play an increasingly key role in Mexico's positioning in global economic flows, especially in the 1970s). The same emphasis on shared resources and collective ownership shaped mass educational projects in both Mexico and the Soviet Union, from the eradication of illiteracy to the accessibility of the canon of world literature to popular readership—developments that shaped telenovelas and other melodramatic forms, further allowing for the transnational familiarity of their iconic figures.[78]

Beyond such organized, state-sponsored efforts, the figure of the commons reactivated earlier precapitalist forms of community that continued shaping informal social organization and its imaginaries, including those that increasingly departed from the hegemonic nationalist state projects. This could manifest in everyday practices, where notions of collective ownership and shared resources (the commons) intersected with communal values (*communitas*), while at the same time frequently overlapping with the traditional (bazaar) market forms.[79] The imaginary of the Roma community, shared by the Mexican and Soviet cultures and at the center of *Yesenia,* with its distinctive codes of redistribution of wealth within the community, projects just such a fantasy. And the melodramatic conflict between individual desires that necessitate breaking away from this traditional community (Yesenia falls in love with an "outsider," which sets the film's narrative in motion) further underscores not only its ultimate subordination to modern liberal forms (via marriage and reconstitution of a bourgeois family) but also, paradoxically, the impossibility of containment of the values of *communitas* to one social group—or nation.

At the same time, this shared symbolic emphasis on the collective is also what made it easier for the hegemonic Western discourses to treat all the socialist world through the same Orientalist epistemes with which they have long approached Asia, Africa, and Latin America. This extended to essentialist assumptions that their inherently unruly collectivism made them unfit for civilized liberal democracy, their commons-oriented life choices threatening the spirit of competition inherent to capitalist modernity. In this way, the Cold War episteme inherited the colonialist world view—which continues to manifest itself to this day. Such projections and their continuous reinforcement by Western liberal discourses and representations have furthered the sense of affinities that shaped popular culture. In both, there was an ambiguity at work: a desire for global modernity (as represented, among others, by the tech and glamour of the Western culture industry) and, simultaneously, a mourning and a celebration of being rejected from it—an ambiguity that became even more pronounced as the conditions for real socialism (or a real commons) visibly decayed.

These shared affective structures become visible, among other ways, through melodramatic figurations offering different scenarios of configurations of the individual and the community. It is not surprising, then, that while critical discussions of Hollywood melodrama have emphasized its politicization of the private space of the home (as evident in the title—which quotes, incidentally, an Elvis Presley song—of the canonical edited volume *Home Is Where the Heart Is: Studies in Melodrama and the Woman's Film*), critical traditions outside of the Global North have most frequently discussed melodrama as operating on the interstices of the public and the private. Centering on the very notion of the popular as in some ways a crucial mediation among various social spheres (as well as changing political ideologies), melodrama thus understood also follows a somewhat distinct intellectual and cultural trajectory in its Soviet–Latin American transnational iteration. Whether directly or symptomatically, its discussions in these contexts have been inseparable from continuous attempts to demarcate the relationships between folklore, popular culture, and mass-produced culture, including its vernacular "low" manifestations such as B movies, telenovelas, and other media productions deemed to be in bad taste even by the local intelligentsia. In other words, the crisis of "the people" vs. "the multitudes" and the political agency and potential of these polities found its expression and mediation in the polemics about what constitutes "the popular"—with melodrama frequently posing a problem or, alternatively, a rich space for contestation.

GLOBAL-POPULAR AND MELODRAMA

Melodrama has traditionally been dismissed by cinephiles as an expression of poor aesthetic taste and as cheap entertainment for feminized audiences, and denounced by Marxist critics and Leftist activists as the ultimate enemy of revolutionary media. Scholarly and critical perspectives on it began to shift around the same time that male heteronormative elitist dominance began to erode and as cultural institutions began to change demographically, in tandem with feminism and other civil rights movements. By the 1980s, not only did melodrama become a subject worthy of serious scholarly attention, but many scholars in the Global North began to reclaim it as an inherently transgressive, liberatory popular form. In other words, critical discussions of melodrama have always keenly reflected the larger political stakes of its time. Rather than contributing to these polemics, I am more interested in how, from a comparative and transnational perspective, the critical and popular discourses on melodrama refract some of the same developments and problems that form the core of this book. Periodization thus becomes particularly important here, as do the regional and national points of origin for these debates.

The study of melodrama as a film genre has been central to much of the scholarship on Latin American cinema, especially that on Golden Age commercial filmmaking of the 1940s and 1950s, in which it has come to serve as an avatar of nationalist ideology. The established consensus, however, is that while critical to that era, melodrama waned significantly in the 1960s, as it came under ideological attack by the more politically minded New Cinema practitioners.[80] Until recently, melodrama and popular cinemas of the 1970s and 1980s more generally were presumed to be unworthy of scholarly attention due to their low artistic quality and minimal international impact.[81] Despite some foundational essays on melodrama across film, television, and music spheres of the period (several of which were included in the foundational 1995 volume *To Be Continued* edited by Robert Allen), Lauren Berlant's work, and the theoretical arguments put forth by Agustín Zarzosa, surprisingly little scholarship within the US or North American academy has taken up transmedial approaches to melodrama as a mode. And it has been largely the critical writings on melodrama outside of the Global North (exemplified by Martín-Barbero and Monsiváis in Latin America, and Ravi Vasudevan and Madhava Prasad in India) that have offered a reconsideration of enduring romantic and sentimental modalities in cultural production and spectatorship at large.[82]

Ana López's insistence on the importance of intermediality for broader reconstructions of Latin American media histories at large therefore proves to be even more pertinent to a transnational approach, in which each respective site offers a distinct cluster of intermedial entanglements.[83] While the nineteenth century's sentimental novel, serialized graphic romances, and radio plays were crucial to the development of film and TV melodramas in Mexico, literature (which enjoyed a privileged cultural status under socialism) formed a particularly important aspect of their reception field in the Soviet Bloc. Thus, in the Soviet Union during the 1960s and 1970s, the reception of all Latin American popular culture was shaped through the translation of major works of "magical realism" that emerged from the "Latin American Boom." The works of such authors as Miguel Ángel Asturias, Julio Cortázar, Carlos Fuentes, Jorge Amado, and especially Gabriel García Márquez were read by millions in the Soviet Union, thus becoming an almost immediate point of reference for all things Latin American.[84] Such literary associations awarded additional cultural and political legitimacy to the "lower" forms of entertainment—especially since melodrama as a genre had been consistently decried by the official Soviet culture. Links with literary sources, however tenuous, provided Latin American melodrama with new interpretative and affective frames, at least for critics, if not for the majority of viewers.[85] By the 1980s, this dynamic extended to television, allowing for more successful localization of telenovelas, many of which were, indeed, adapted from literary sources (as alluded to by the term *telenovela*, in reference to the genre's origins in short radio plays and graphic novels, including those reworking classical literature). Understood by critics and audiences as a form of simultaneously ideological and sentimental education, Brazilian and Mexican soap operas in late socialism served an additional geopolitical goal of providing an acceptable alternative to the increasing flow of Western/US cultural products—just as Indian and Turkish ones do in many postsocialist contexts today.[86]

In fact, in the history of Soviet film criticism, discourses on melodrama began to (re)appear—triggered, at least in part, by the evident popularity of Indian, Egyptian, and Latin American cinemas in the early 1970s (even if the category of melodrama was imposed on these films by the Soviet critics and audiences themselves, frequently not coinciding with the films' original designations in their countries of origin).[87] From the late 1920s into the 1950s, unlike many other popular film genres, melodrama was considered irreconcilable with socialist cinema—reflecting the increasingly rigid cultural discourses that posited normative differentiations between folk and popular, socialist and capitalist, progressive and regressive, Soviet and Western. This lacuna was, however, largely discursive: as an aesthetic mode and an affective modality, sentimentalism and melodrama infused much of Soviet culture, including, perhaps most prominently, socialist realism.[88] And yet, in broader cultural and aesthetic terms, the notion of excess—which structures sentimental and melodramatic sensibility—stood in stark contrast to the emphasis on good taste that became crucial for Soviet discourse from the post-Stalinist period on. Good taste implied, above all, moderation in all things. As such, it was a deliberately devised mechanism for creating a socialist version of a rational consumer culture built on the earlier notion of "culturedness" (*kul'turnost'*) associated with the cultural revolution: a vision of the Soviet lifestyle as an alternative to a bourgeois or capitalist one.[89]

Changes within the Soviet media apparatus and its dramatic embrace of entertainment genres in the course of the 1970s virtually forced the Soviet film critical establishment into a frenzied discussion of the question of audiences' preferences and the role of the popular within Soviet cinema, debates that only further intensified in the subsequent decades leading up to the collapse of the Soviet Union. These debates forced critics to acknowledge the increasingly privileged affective charge of the family space outside of the "heroic master narrative" of socialist realism, a position that resonated with the unique pathos of late socialism.[90] At the same time, not only did acceptance of melodrama as a serious scholarly topic trigger a critical reevaluation of the relationship between the public and the private spheres, but by acknowledging a distinct regime of popular aesthetic taste, evidently impervious to either socialist cultural norms or intelligentsia's response to (and against) them, critical exploration of melodrama inevitably introduced the thorny subject of "the popular." The latter formation, according to the official Soviet discourse, was meant to be one with the (Communist) Party and the (socialist) state. Such discussions on the part of Soviet film critics and cultural workers were therefore, at least to a degree, a concession to finding a logic that would reconcile the increasingly commercial orientation of the state film organization with conventional Soviet ideological positions.

What also comes through in local critics' genuine puzzlement over how to make sense of the enduring power of vernacular popular culture (and specifically the role of gender within it) in the Soviet context is the determination to do so on terms that did not coincide with either Marxist or Western feminist positions on the subject, and yet were clearly shaped by the Cold War discourses. Two essays on *Yesenia* written by women critics Neia Zorkaia and Maia Turovskaia, to which we will return throughout this book's narrative, formed part of those efforts. Although both began writing on this topic in the 1970s, Zorkaia and Turovskaia continued their explorations of Soviet popular culture after the country's collapse. Both of them position *Yesenia*'s phenomenal success in the Soviet Union as a trigger for their scholarship on this topic. The public reception of Latin American melodrama confronted these late Soviet cultural critics with the collapse of official categories, together with the whole Soviet way of life. It also exposed the challenges of the intelligentsia's coming to terms with the experiences and desires of "the viewing publics"—or just ordinary people—that were inseparable from this collapse. Connecting and juxtaposing various cultural forms across decades and continents, the Soviet encounter with Latin American melodramatic media proves to have been aesthetic, political, and theoretical: generating new structures of feeling, but also new ways of thinking about the relationship between aesthetic forms, history, and the people.

Although framed by very different cultural and political contexts, critical writing on melodrama and popular culture acquires particular force in film scholarship outside of the Soviet Union in approximately the same time. And just like cultural studies in Britain and postcolonial and subaltern studies in Asia, Latin American critical thought of the last decades of the twentieth century has generated an important body of work that offers crucial conceptualizations of the popular through the writings of Canclini, Monsiváis, Claudio Lomnitz-Adler, and others. In contrast to earlier (Marxist-inflected) perceptions of cultural industry as a monolith, in different ways, they all argue for a reconsideration of the rigid divisions between the categories of high, mass, and folk culture on the one hand, and "top-down" and "bottom-up" approaches on the other. Insisting on the notion of the cultural sphere as formed by complex negotiations between the nation-state, institutional formations, capitalist market forces, and intimate everyday experiences, these Latin American critics offer a corresponding notion of "the popular": it is both a highly heterogeneous body of cultural production and an expression of the mediations of the conflicting forces shaping the social body and its cultural registers. Popular culture, and cinema and media in particular, in Monsiváis's and Martín-Barbero's writing are understood as a crucial site for the democratization and internationalization of Latin American publics, offering, as Sánchez Prado has recently argued in relation to Golden Age cinema, "an expansion of cultural repertoires available to Mexican spectators in relation to the process of modernization."[91]

Here we are confronted with a significant difference in film scholarship's approaches to melodrama. Scholars focused on Hollywood and British cinema have succeeded in foregrounding aspects of feminist and gender studies, whereas both Asian and Latin American scholarship have been centered, above all, on the intertwined relationship between the national and the popular, while late Soviet and post-Soviet critical discourses are predictably concerned with the impact of communist ideology. Questions of gender and sexuality necessarily emerge as inseparable from these latter frameworks—rather than determined by an explicitly feminist theoretical apparatus. This distinction is significant and bears additional reflection. In my discussion of Mexican and Soviet melodrama, I therefore find it productive to resort to conceptual categories developed outside of those national contexts—but without taking Hollywood as an indisputable reference point. Such methodology builds on what inter-Asian cultural critic Kuan-Hsing Chen refers to as *inter-referencing*: multiplying the geographic frames of conceptual reference points to produce a transnational epistemology based on distinct sets of cultural affinities.[92] As the trajectories of gender politics in much of the world followed paths distinct from those of European or North American feminism (and this was perhaps most pronounced in the Soviet case), inter-referencing provides a broader range of conceptual coordinates to help us understand the varied configurations of melodrama beyond Hollywood. Thus, in my study, using South Asian and Latin American conceptual categories of the shifting aesthetic registers of the popular—and, in particular, melodrama's configurations of the private and the public—has proved more relevant for understanding both *Yesenia*'s Mexican production and its Soviet reception.

One example of this approach is how we understand the construction of social spaces in a film like *Yesenia*. Vasudevan's work on melodrama in India offers one of the most conceptually developed models for such analysis, and it is worth quoting him here at length. He argues that at stake in Indian melodramatic modality is "the continued recognizability of many of the features of an apparently archaic narrative, performative, and expressive design in the cinema of the modern and even contemporary post-colonial world" and its "articulation of personalized contexts of home, family, and other fields of primary attachment, with public registers." The public field in Indian cinema, Vasudevan famously claims, "is constituted both by formal and informal structures of power, justice, social identity, and social mobility. As the integument of the social and political realm, the family form does not simply personalize social and political issues. Rather, it renders the personal and political as nondistinguishable registers of fictional organization. However, the family may itself be displaced or drawn into other registers of attachment [that] . . . reside in the register of the popular, and even in the personification of nationhood as a new register of melodramatic belonging."[93]

Within this formation, the family and domestic sphere is not equal to the liberal private realm, nor does the latter occupy the hegemonic position in the way it does for Hollywood melodrama. As both Vasudevan and Mitsuhiro

Yoshimoto demonstrate, this different configuration is part of what propelled the twentieth-century associations of melodrama with "backwardness," understood as generating an intersection between modern and premodern forms and firmly positioned against the progress and modernity associated with realism.[94] This association was especially pronounced within the discourses of the postcolonial Left, where melodrama figures simultaneously as a "backward" form locally and a reactionary form globally—as associated with Hollywood and Western colonial and neocolonial power and the dominant film industry. Melodrama originating outside these locations acquired particularly derogatory connotations within both art and political film discourses, which did not elude the Latin American— and, even more specifically, Mexican—filmmakers themselves. Elena Lahr-Vivaz, in her discussion of Mexican melodrama, quotes Emilio Fernández's reaction to the French critics describing his films as melodramatic: "For you the lives of Mexicans are melodramatic; for us they're a drama. What would you have me do to have it considered a drama? Shall I cut off my mother's head? Or my father's balls? When you say we make melodramas, you are ridiculing us. When you say my movies are melodramatic, it's as if you were saying that they are shit."[95]

The very style of Fernández's comments embodies the melodramatic excess he simultaneously rejects and celebrates. After all, as Lahr-Vivaz rightfully notes, this distinction did not seem to bother his films' audiences—as such rigid markers of taste categories and cultural registers were pertinent only outside (geographically and culturally) the sphere of the popular.[96]

Behind this consistent association between so-called "non-Western" melodrama and underdevelopment is precisely the distinctiveness of its configurations of the private and public spheres. What is absent here is not only the autonomous, liberal, private sphere of the couple, but also the conventionally understood "civil society" as the location of the popular. Recognizing this, as Ghosh observes, scholars like Arjun Appadurai and Carol Breckenridge propose an alternative concept of a *public culture* that could be used in its place: "a flexible rubric, allowing the inclusion of popular practices produced by those with little or no access to the modern associational forms of civil society; public culture was that vibrant zone of contestation where mass-produced commodities could be reassembled to articulate a local modernity."[97] Melodrama can therefore be understood as both projecting and activating such a process. This "articulation of a local modernity" is also what Martín-Barbero, in more triumphalist terms, argues for melodrama in Latin America (understood in its broadest transmedial configuration): "In Latin America, whether it be the form of tango or bolero, Mexican cinema, or soap opera, the melodrama speaks of a primordial sociality, whose metaphor continues to be the thick, censored plot of the tightly woven fabric of family relationships. In spite of its devaluation by the economy and politics, this sociality lives on culturally, and from its locus, the people, by 'melo-dramatizing' everything, take their own form of revenge on the abstraction imposed by cultural dispossession and the commercialization of life."[98]

The "primordial sociality" taking its revenge is, indeed, very close to the understanding of the emergent forms within the subaltern that is articulated in Ghosh and Sarkar's engagement with the global-popular as addressing "the inchoate desires and instrumental aspirations that are afforded in the global-popular: a 'quality' life, a planetary reach, a global influence."[99] Underscoring the political ambivalence and heterogeneity/multidirectionality of such desires, however, Ghosh proposes a different understanding of the political process embedded in such popular expressions: "If we forsake the lure of the organic community, we can posit the potentialities of the popular in a different way: as gradual alterations in lifestyles, tastes, and everyday habit in heterogeneous locales that move toward social transformation—but not in unison. The vanguard motivates, but the directions of change remain highly differentiated."[100]

As this book demonstrates, such differentiated alterations and transformations—both in their potentialities and their subsequent historical realizations—can be glimpsed in the history of Mexican melodrama's reception in the Soviet Union, exemplified by *Yesenia*'s transnational circulation, positing this history as an antecedent of the more contemporary manifestations of the global-popular as conceptualized by Ghosh and Sarkar.

But the story of *Yesenia*—with its negotiations of the shifting figure of the stranger disturbing and interrupting the primal sociality—points to a politics that cannot so comfortably escape into the universals of liberation, however indeterminate. The *now* of my writing comes out of a vantage point that has been constituted by the collapse of the socialist world and the neoliberal regime that has come to dominate the Americas and the former Socialist Bloc alike, as well its accompanying femicide, sex trafficking, and various other manifestations of increased exploitation and commodification of sex and sexuality in both Mexico and the former Soviet Union. On the horizon are new forms of nationalist populism that have a decidedly sinister look—and that very term, *populism*, is increasingly used exclusively in relation to authoritarian and/or right-wing politics. At the same time, we are looking back at *Yesenia*'s intermediality from within a very different media ecosystem, one that has undergone a radical transformation of global entertainment media circulation. From the new rise of Latin popular music, now for the first time integrated into the mainstream global music industry, to new, highly participatory forms of fandom and media piracy, the global media circuit looks nothing like it did in the 1970s, when *Yesenia* first conquered Soviet audiences. And yet, the complex modalities of transcultural popular affinities it speaks to cannot be reduced to the question of new technologies. Nor can it be subsumed by the supposedly all-encompassing power of global capitalism. Fickle and unstable, fraught with political ambivalences and ambiguities, sometimes beautiful, at other times ugly, the force of the global-popular cannot be dismissed or underestimated, just as it cannot be condescended to or fully disciplined. Thus, the power of *Yesenia*—which so puzzled the Soviet critics—remains an open question.

Prelude

The Soviet Stardom of Lolita Torres

The Socialist Bloc's passionate reception of Latin American musical and cinematic melodramas goes back to the Soviet Thaw of the 1950s. During that period of cultural and political opening toward both the West and the post-colonial world, the old Stalinist interdiction of foreign movie imports was dismantled, and Soviet film exhibition became significantly reoriented toward international cinema. In part, this was due to a sheer deficit, as Soviet film production dropped to just six feature fiction films a year in the early 1950s.[1] At the same time, however, this orientation reflected a radical change in Soviet foreign and cultural policies, which happened to be in alignment with the popular tastes of audiences.[2]

In the effort to rebuild the Soviet film apparatus, which, like other divisions of industry, had been severely injured by the war, ticket sales to popular foreign films proved to be a reliable source of revenue. Soviet audiences had already exhibited their enthusiasm for Hollywood cinema in the late 1940s when, in addition to films purchased during the war from the Allies, some of the so-called "trophy films" taken from Germany were also screened commercially.[3] However, as the war alliance fell apart, giving way to the Cold War regime, Hollywood films in the 1950s became not only ideologically problematic but much too expensive to import (although some would be purchased and screened in the late 1960s, and again in the 1980s). Thus, alongside the very popular—but also extremely costly—European films, Indian, Chinese (at least until 1965), Mexican, and Argentinian popular movies came flooding in. Not only did they add up to a fairly large percentage of overall film exhibition and an even larger share of gross revenue, but many became enduring favorites with Soviet audiences.[4]

Latin American cinema was first presented to the socialist mass audience by several of Emilio Fernández's Mexican Golden Age classics, which were screened not only in the Soviet Union but all over the Soviet Bloc in the 1950s and early 1960s. But the peasant-indigenist nationalist vision of these films proved to be considerably less appealing to Soviet moviegoers than the more urban, cosmopolitan stylings of Argentinian musicals directed by Julio Saraceni and Lucas Demare.[5] The star of these films, Lolita Torres, became such a celebrity in the Soviet Union in the 1950s that she spawned many imitators among local singers and actresses, and the name Lolita was given to many girls born in the population boom of the decade. Torres enjoyed comparatively modest success in her native Argentina in the late 1940s and early 1950s, never coming close to the popularity of such stars as Libertad Lamarque, Zully Moreno, or Niní Marshall—but for generations of Soviet audiences she became the embodiment of Latin American glamour. In many ways, Torres's success offers a template for the subsequent Soviet reception of Latin American popular media, especially in relation to the construction of a certain kind of femininity through music, performance, and fashion.

LOLITA TORRES IN ARGENTINA

By the mid-1950s, Argentinian popular cinema had moved past its Golden Age of the 1930s and 1940s, yet its international reach actually expanded, due in part to the burgeoning global network of film festivals. This period coincided with the nationalist-capitalist, worker-supported populist presidency of General Juan Perón (1946–55), which paid considerable attention to cinema, not least through the involvement of First Lady Eva Perón, a former movie star herself. Although the Soviet Union's relationship to Perón's anticommunist government was quite ambiguous (and Perón even instituted a short-lived ban on Soviet films in 1950–51), the two shared a geopolitical antagonism toward liberal democracies and a commitment to rapid industrialization,[6] which created additional motivation for economic and cultural exchanges. As a result, Buenos Aires had been one of the first places in Latin America to have official ties with the Soviet film industry—enabled, however, not through direct government exchanges but through Artkino Pictures, a company founded by Isaak Argentino Vanikoff, a socialist-leaning son of Russian immigrants who had imported and distributed Soviet films there since World War II. In the 1950s, the Argentine film industry was on the hunt for new film markets that were not monopolized by rivals from Hollywood or Western Europe. The 1954 Mar del Plata International Film Festival was organized with that objective in mind, welcoming participants from the Socialist Bloc.[7] The Soviet participants were put under the charge of Vanikoff, who served as an intermediary for potential commercial exchanges between them and the Argentinian film industry.[8]

According to Torres's recollections, the Soviet delegation to Argentina for the first Mar del Plata festival in 1954 was also tasked with the mission of finding films for popular consumption in the Soviet Union with "social content," but no violence and no sex. Those with a lot of music were preferred.[9] Thus the Soviets selected the critically successful *Dark Rivers* (*Las aguas bajan turbias*, Hugo del Carril, 1952), a film that reflected Perón's populist message, filling the slot for a film with an explicit social critique. Their other choice was a musical comedy, *The Age of Love* (*La edad del amor*, Julio Saraceni, 1954), featuring Torres, which was respectably free of sex and violence, thus adhering to Soviet standards. While director Hugo del Carril would go on to become a regular of the Soviet festivals, his works exemplifying the kind of socially engaged cinema the socialist film circuits promoted well into the 1970s, it was Saraceni's *The Age of Love* that went on to considerable box office success.[10] After the three-year dictatorship following Perón's ouster (during which del Carril spent two months in jail for his collaboration with Perón's government), in 1958 the Soviet organization in charge of import and export of cinema (Sovexportfilm) established itself in Argentina.[11] It promptly grabbed up another musical starring Torres, *Un novio para Laura* (Saraceni, 1955). This movie followed the success of *The Age of Love* and solidified Torres's celebrity with Soviet viewers. From the late 1950s onward, these films were continuously screened in the Soviet Union—both in theaters and, eventually, on television. Even twenty years later, during Torres's tours in the 1970s and early 1980s, she had star power enough to easily fill ten-thousand-seat theaters for her musical performances all over the Soviet Union.[12]

TORRES'S ON-SCREEN PERSONA:
THE INGENUE AS THE MODERN GIRL

Torres's on-screen image was a variation on "the ingenue" (*la ingenua*) and the "modern girl" (*la chica moderna*), marked as much by her childish naïveté as by her daring. Her films characteristically followed story elements from the Italian "white telephones" romances and Argentinian and Hollywood screwball comedies, with a heavy dose of Spanish folkloric *españoladas*—all film genres unfamiliar to Soviet audiences.[13] She was usually cast as a spunky ingenue with a comic touch—young, vivacious, dynamic, active, eager to take charge of her own life. Her body was nimble (Soviet commentators were particularly obsessed by her impossibly narrow waist), her movements and gestures quick and agile, communicating youth and impatience—but with decorum and a certain constraint. This combination was similarly conveyed by her voice, with its considerable range and depth and its warm timbre. Both her body and her voice were put fully into play in the musical performances that formed an important part of these films. Always the "good girl," Torres's characters never kissed her romantic partners on screen—but left that to the audience's imagination, which corresponded to the representational norms of Soviet postwar film. In this and other aspects of her movie persona— sincere, passionate, idealistic, with just the right amount of fascinating glamour and exoticism—Torres combined official Soviet norms of sexual morality with the fresher spirit and the cult of youth of the Thaw.

Youth and internationalism became, in many ways, code words for the Soviet culture of that period, and Moscow's Sixth World Festival of Youth and Students in 1957 can be seen, in retrospect, as "the culmination of the conceptual shift towards cultural universalism and coexistence."[14] The focus on youth was likewise reflected in the ages of filmmakers and actors who entered the cinematic institutions and industries after the war. In 1955–56, in an unprecedented shift, more than fifty Soviet films were directorial debuts. These included films that would come to be seen as iconic of the Thaw, such as *The Carnival Night* (*Karnaval'naia noch'*, El'dar Riazanov, 1956), *The Forty-First* (*Sorok pervyi*, Grigorii Chukhrai, 1956), *Spring on Zarechnaia Street* (*Vesna na Zarechnoi ulitse*, Feliks Mironer and Marlen Khutsiev, 1956), and others. Casting reflected this shift as well, further emphasizing the youth of characters portrayed in the Soviet films emblematic of this period, from *Cranes Are Flying* (*Letiat zhuravli*, Mikhail Kalatozov, 1957) to *Walking the Streets of Moscow* (*Ia shagaiu po Moskve*, Georgii Daneliia, 1964). The young actors' physical appearance was characterized not the least by, in Oksana Bulgakova's words, "their alternative body language . . . further accentuated by the contrast between their thin, flexible, fragile bodies and the corpulent, athletic bodies of the older generation."[15] The political significance of youth was further manifested in the cinematic trope of seeing the world through the eyes of a child, in order to convey an ideologically uncontaminated freshness of perception in implicit opposition to the ossification of Stalinist socialist realism—as seen in *Ivan's Childhood* (*Ivanovo detstvo*, Andrei Tarkovsky, 1962) or *Welcome, or No Trespassing* (*Dobro pozhalovat', ili postoronnim vkhod vosprishchen*, Elem Klimov, 1964).[16]

With the emphasis on youth, however, came the first vestiges of a distinctive youth culture, and that culture expressed itself, among other things, through clothes and other consumer objects. As with the other nations that had been devastated in World War II, postwar Soviet reconstruction entailed a much-needed increase in the quality of life. War austerity was left behind and Soviet economic policy began to embrace certain forms of consumerism. Even the notion of luxury was reevaluated—it was declared that the proletariat, which ruled society, now had an ideological right to those luxuries it could afford. And yet, importantly, this had to take place within the parameters that differentiated socialist consumer culture from its capitalist, bourgeois forms.[17] Women played a crucial role in this process: as wives and mothers they were also, by default, both homemakers and educators, as well as builders of socialism. They were thus called upon to be the guarantors of good socialist consumer taste—for it was, above all, the cultivation of taste and moderation that coded consumer culture as Soviet.[18] Consistent with Soviet pro-nativist policies instituted under Stalin, as well as the implicit gender conservatism of the petit bourgeois origins of the notion of *kul'turnost'*—the master discourse governing the prescriptive behavior of Soviet citizens—this "good Soviet taste" included well-defined evaluative norms of women's appearances.

In the 1950s, as elsewhere in the postwar period, these norms in the Soviet Union turned toward decidedly more feminine fashions—emphasizing skirts over pants, for example, but also tailored skirt-suits and dresses.[19] In the absence of other media outlets explicitly devoted to these issues, for which a separate media genre developed only in the course of the 1960s, cinema—and foreign film and music performers in particular—provided powerful models for the complex self-fashioning of the early Thaw's Soviet Woman.[20] Lolita Torres's stardom was part of that project.

The combination of childlike vivaciousness with conservative sexual heteronormativity as constitutive of her image was crucial. For, in spite of the changes in gender norms in relation to legal rights and professional employment that took place under socialism, the Soviet ideology maintained patriarchal notions of the importance of preserving "women's honor" (albeit, unlike in Latin America, divorced from any religious connotations).[21] Not only did sexual morality have to conform to traditional norms that made the stability of family and procreation a non-negotiable priority for every Soviet woman, sexual promiscuity by the 1950s had persistent political connotations—associated with the decadent West and, in the context of World War II in particular, with the betrayal of the Motherland, evident in such iconic female on-screen villains as Pusya, the mistress of the Nazi officer, in Mark Donskoi's *Rainbow* (*Raduga*, 1943). In this context, the sexual restraint scripted into Torres's roles—manifested in the rejection of an on-screen kiss—was, indeed, fully consistent with the Soviet public morality of the 1950s.

And yet, especially after the war, these official gender ideologies were also highly contradictory: privileging public over private, and civic over subjective realms, while also insisting on the sanctity of motherhood and filial obligations (grounded in a very traditional bourgeois notion of the private sphere) as well as on the cult of romantic love, which was manifested, for example, in persistent courting rituals and corresponding expectations of gender roles performed through them.[22] To negotiate these seemingly conflicting ideologies, within the Soviet representational regime—in melodramas or even popular music—romantic love, while unchallenged, was consistently presented as constitutive of public/collective demands—not as an independent goal of personal fulfillment. Romantic couples' dedication to each other was inseparable from their shared duty to the Motherland, larger contributions to the building of the socialist society, and the fulfillment of family obligations. This allowed plenty of room for family romance, and by the 1950s, war (specifically, home-front) melodrama—even though not labeled as such by critics, who continued to use the term *melodrama* to connote a bourgeois aesthetic not suitable for socialism—was in fact a dominant cultural genre.[23] The same was true of Stalinist musicals and musical comedies made in the 1930s, whose popularity with Soviet audiences extended into the 1950s and 1960s—in them, romance was central even as it was narratively subordinated to other, collectively or socially minded, concerns. Even in lyrical popular music during the 1930s and 1940s, subjective sentiment was framed as a necessary counterpart to the "civic" ethos.[24]

During the brief period of the Thaw, however, the contours of public and private, like many other aspects of culture, were being renegotiated—entering the phase that Mikhail Epshtein famously called "socialist sentimentalism."[25] Against the hegemony of state-mandated patriotic sentiment, Indian and Latin American musical melodramas during that period represented alternative models for the representation of gender and romance, undetermined by either experiences of World War II or explicit political prerogatives of building socialism.[26] Certain Soviet films of the late 1950s and early 1960s, too, began to openly foreground both ambivalences and conflicts between social expectations and "private feelings." This triggered a series of debates on the compatibility of the latter with the socialist ethos, especially within cinema.[27] Films that were at the center of these polemics—such as *Cranes Are Flying; Gals* (*Devchata*, Iurii Chuliukhin, 1961); and, most notoriously, *But What If It's Love?* (*A esli eto liubov'?*, Iulii Raizman, 1962)—still framed love and romance explicitly in relation to the country's political, industrial, and cultural transformations. And yet, they also clearly opened a space for the exploration of subjective desires, in particular those of their female protagonists, showing them as being irreducible to ideological goals. What Soviet audiences of that generation saw in iconic female protagonists such as Veronika in *Cranes* (Tatiana Samoilova—impulsive and sensual but always sincere and devoted to her romantic ideals) or, in a more populist vein, Tosia in *Gals* (Nadezhda Rumiantseva, imitating Giulietta Masina—childish and unrefined but vivacious and passionate), was at least in part a refraction of Lolita Torres's persona that they fell in love with in July 1955, when *The Age of Love* was screened in Moscow.[28]

THE AGE OF LOVE IN CONTEXT

To fully explore the intersections between Argentinian and Soviet cinematic forms and their receptions, it is worth giving a brief summary of the film. Its story starts in 1928, when the celebrated stage performer of Spanish music and dance Soledad Reales "La Chispera" (played by Torres) is about to marry Dr. Alberto Méndez Tejada, a young man of considerable fortune. But unbeknownst to him, the engagement is broken off by his father, who considers marriage to a stage performer a social disgrace. Alberto is led to believe that Soledad betrayed him. Twenty-five years later, his son, a failed lawyer and aspiring popular music composer, meets the daughter of the deceased Soledad, Ana María Rosales (Torres, again). Ana María is promoted from being a chorus girl to replacing an arrogant and temperamental stage diva in the production of a musical, for which Alberto Jr. is writing the music—much to the delight of the other chorus girls and the whole stage crew, who see her as their champion, as well as a talented star. Unaware of the family history, Alberto and Ana María fall in love—and this time, it's the grandfather who convinces his outraged son to allow the two to marry by revealing his role in what happened twenty-five years prior and his regrets about it. Not only are the two lovers reunited, but Alberto Jr. joins Ana María on stage, announcing to his family his decision to quit law and permanently dedicate his life to musical theater.

Combining the conventions of both melodrama and musical genres, the plot of *The Age of Love* privileges romance over social norms and family obligations—but, by using the device of intertwining romance and the heroine's successful ambitions as a stage performer, it also affirms women's entry into the public sphere, avoiding the usual melodramatic retreat into total domesticity, thus conjoining the audience's taste for popular genres with progressive social values. In its two-part structure, with the present-day part and the new couple demonstrating progress in the country, the film perfectly illustrates Clara Kriger's argument that Argentinian films of the Perón era could focus on depicting social injustices, as long as they were in the past.[29]

In this, Argentinian films of the era particularly comfortably matched the Soviet representational norms of the Thaw, when implicit critique of the earlier (i.e., Stalinist) period—from within the socialist position—informed most of the arts. The Soviet audiences also shared with their Argentinian counterparts a long-standing love of musicals (or musical romantic comedies). In the Soviet case, it was rooted in the success of the 1930s domestic films directed by Alexandrov and Pyr'ev as well as Hollywood movies that were among the cache of "trophy" films and dated mainly from the 1930s and 1940s. Among the favorites of Soviet audiences were Franciska Gaal, who was particularly famous for her 1930s versions of the tango, which she first performed in the Austrian-Hungarian comedy *Peter* (*Peter, das Mädchen von der Tankstelle*, Henry Koster, 1934), and Deanna Durbin, who starred in many of Henry Koster's Hollywood musical comedies. Both Durbin and Koster's films were equally popular in Argentina in the 1940s, thus laying the foundation for a shared cinematic culture, reflected in *The Age of Love*.[30]

As European exiles in Hollywood in the 1930s and 1940s—including directors like Koster and musicians like Russian-born Nicholas Brodsky—infused the Hollywood musical with the traditions of Viennese operetta, Argentinian musicals further "Europeanized" the form by infusing their versions of it with Spanish and French musical vaudeville performance traditions, albeit in their Argentinian iteration—all while retaining the Hollywood musical's classic narrative format. This combination was particularly resonant in the Soviet Union, for while the lowbrow European musical stage genres—operetta, vaudeville, revue—were long gone from the US cultural repertoire by the 1950s, they still formed a vital part of Soviet entertainment culture. These latent generic elements within Argentinian musicals (whose own cultural genesis was likewise hybridized and retained closer ties to such older performance forms) were therefore more easily legible to and fully appreciated by their Soviet audiences.[31]

Also among the foreign musical melodramas that became popular with Soviet Thaw audiences were Indian films brought to the Soviet Union in 1954 as part of the first Indian film festival in Moscow. In fact, Raj Kapoor's *The Vagabond* (*Awara*, 1951) became the highest-grossing film of that decade, seen by 63.7 million viewers in 1954.[32] Categorized by the Soviet film establishment as "Indian melodramas," and dependent on their popularity not least for their unforgettable song-and-dance numbers, Indian films modeled yet another alternative for negotiating the public, the private, and the contours of masculinity and femininity. To discuss the reception history of *The Age of Love* necessarily entails some reflection on the continuities and differences between it and *Vagabond* and between their respective stars, Lolita Torres and Raj Kapoor, for these two films together occupied an important space within the Soviet movie culture of the late 1950s and early 1960s, advancing a certain new style of foreign film celebrity.

RAJ KAPOOR vs. LOLITA TORRES

Both films' success in the Soviet Union depended, in many ways, on their representation of their protagonists as outsiders, forming a crucial aspect of their respective star images. Torres's heroine is marginalized by her status as a performer (disreputable in the eyes of high society), while Kapoor's Vagabond is a petty criminal, rejected at birth by his father, a wealthy judge. While affirming humanistic values and drawing attention to social inequalities and the plight of the poor, the Chaplinesque figure of Kapoor's Vagabond stands in highly ambiguous and unstable relation to class structure and politics, and in an even more problematic position with regard to the ideology of socialist productivity, which was as strongly valued in the Soviet 1950s as it was in the earlier era. His opposition to social and political injustice takes a form more akin to the kind of popular revolt analyzed by Hobsbawm in his classic study of bandits—his outlawry is founded not on a class consciousness that interprets the organization of the economic system, but rather on a revolt against all forms of coercive power, especially physical coercion, claimed by the state or by government-like establishments. This notion was quite far removed from the kind of Marxist class consciousness and celebration of the proletariat promoted by the Soviet state.

The Soviet film critical establishment, usually highly attentive to precisely these kinds of ideological complexities in both Soviet and Western cinema (leading to its subsequent rejection of much of European leftist cinema of the 1960s), was certainly willing to overlook them in Indian and other "non-Western" films.[33] And one could speculate that it is precisely this image of an "undisciplined" positive hero who shared all the basic values of socialist society and yet longed to operate outside of its prescribed structures that appealed to the Soviet society coming out of the militaristic urgency and rigidity of life under Stalinism and during World War II. Its appeal is therefore not rooted in mere escapism, but in its alluding to a different utopian image, effectively communicating an alternative structure of liberation in marked difference from its culturally hegemonic socialist context. And while Kapoor's lovably boyish character, embodying Nehru's "sunny post-independence optimism"[34] in the 1950s, certainly sounded the same notes in the Soviet Union's de-Stalinization period, the film itself is surprisingly dark. In *Awara*, Kapoor's cheerful independence is in contrast to—and has to be negotiated with—the law, both in its traditional and its "modern" (state juridical) forms, visually depicted with almost grotesque brutality.

If, as Manishita Dass has argued, in the cinematic universe of *Awara* the city streets—especially in the setting of the song-and-dance numbers—subtend a *cinetopia*, originating in the leftist utopian imaginary of the Indian Proletarian Theatre Association,[35] in *The Age of Love* it's the literal, diegetic stage that, as in the tradition of the Hollywood musical, plays a similar functional role. It is a space of liberation—not only in the sense of Richard Dyer's famous discussion of the utopian function of non-narrative symbolic aspects of musicals in his "Entertainment and Utopia," but also as a space for broader social and labor reorganization, which enters into the plot of the film as stage politics.[36] Torres's Ana María Rosales represents a new kind of a leading lady: in contrast to her rival, the arrogant diva, she remains "one of the people," joining the chorus girls in their revolt against the tyrannical manager—clearly referencing Eva Perón's trajectory.[37] And it is on stage that the final reconciliation between her and Alberto occurs, as he joyfully takes his place next to her—not as an admirer or patron but as a stage partner. This new unity serves as an implicit affirmation of the egalitarian status of all artists, mirroring the contemporary notion promoted by the Union of the Argentinian Cinematography Industry of all participants in the cinematic process as "film workers."[38] It also affirms the ideals of social progress and the advancement of women brought about by modernity and a vision of a more egalitarian society, where class antagonisms have been minimized if not suspended—a perfect Perónist "state of harmony between capital and labor."[39]

If the first part of *The Age of Love* is a Castilian-infused rendition of *The Lady of the Camellias* and, thus, a nod toward the sentimentality of late eighteenth- and nineteenth-century Europe (which had enormous impact in creating melodramatic cultures in both Argentina and Russia), the second part breaks new melodramatic ground as a triumphant celebration of cosmopolitan modernity, modeled on Hollywood but with a populist Perónist slant. Yet, without the final kiss to take the diegetic couple into the private sphere of the liberal nuclear family and intimacy, the diegetic world of this romance stays within the social realm, here embodied in theater (and, implicitly, cinema itself). In this, it allows for further harmony with Soviet representational rules—as well as those of Indian popular cinema with its traditional prohibition of on-screen kissing.[40]

Despite certain similarities between formal ideologies and representational strategies, the gender difference between the Soviet reception of Indian and of Argentinian stars here is noteworthy. In the case of Indian cinema, foreshadowing similar status of other male Indian movie stars in subsequent decades, from Amitabh Bachchan to Mithun Chakraborty, it was Raj Kapoor who became a global icon in the Soviet Union (as well as in China and many other places). Against his on-screen (and off-screen) love interest Nargis, voluptuous and statuesque—all slow grace and expressive, soulful eyes—Kapoor's Chaplinesque vagabond role is all movement, with quick gestures and facial expressions, very much at odds with the monumentality of Stalinist, socialist realist male heroes, and therefore much more in line, in many ways, with the Thaw's changes to the physiognomy of Soviet cinema as described by Bulgakova.[41] But Kapoor came to embody more than his on-screen persona: he was a star-director-producer cum political figure in his own right, playing an active role in Soviet-Indian cultural diplomacy for decades.

Torres's stardom within Soviet culture was of a different kind, resting exclusively on her physical appearance, her musical repertoire, and her fashion sense. Hers was a politics of the celebrity lifestyle, combining the liberated plasticity of postwar bodies and the ultimate image of postwar feminine glamour: the French couture dress. Even as her roles were located historically in the neverland of show business, and abundantly supplied with both period and folkloric musical stage costumes, Torres consistently embodied Dior's "New Look" with its ample A-line skirts and narrow waistline emphasizing the new hyper-femininity of European high fashion. This was, indeed, highly deliberate: early in her career, she asked to make a change in her wardrobe on and off screen. She moved away from the more old-fashioned dresses, selected by her aunt, in which she appears in her earlier films, to more up-to-date fashion in Saraceni's films. This change was decisive in creating her image as "elegant and modern"—and this association with high fashion also shaped her Soviet reception.[42]

DIOR LUXURY IN THE SOVIET 1950s

Just as foregrounding the romance plot revalorized subjective experiences against social and collective demands, couture luxury implicitly contrasted with Soviet fashion's emphasis on practicality and functionality, which was rooted in the 1920s avant-garde conventions of industrial arts. The new postwar acceptance of such notions of luxury was, as Larisa Zakharova argues, part of "an attempt to maintain social consensus in a society where the material conditions of ordinary people were defined by shortage," during a time when the new privileged social stratum of Soviet bureaucratic nomenclature began to enjoy its expanded lifestyle opportunities.[43] As one expression of this change, starting from the late 1950s, the Dior New Look began to dominate women's fashion in the Soviet Union, its hyper-femininity fully in line with Stalinist-era nativist policies and monumentalist aesthetics—and yet with a fresher, younger, more

FIGURE 1. Lolita Torres in *Un novio para Laura*, 1954. DVD screen grab.

romantic touch.[44] And the Argentinian cinematic celebration of such romance and luxury held undeniable appeal to Soviet audiences' fantasies, perfectly mediating such conflicting cultural models.

Torres very quickly became a fashion icon—she is mentioned with striking regularity in memoirs and interviews as a point of reference for glamour

FIGURE 2. Liudmila Gurchenko in *Karnaval'naia noch'*, 1956. DVD screen grab.

among Soviet men and women of the generation of the 1950s and 1960s.[45] Soviet magazines furthered this: in a departure from the usual emphasis on progressive political stances or the working-class background of its profiled foreign stars, the women's magazine *Rabotnitsa* (The Worker Woman), in its coverage of Torres aboard a Soviet ship in Buenos Aires to meet her fans, the sailors, gives a detailed description of her attire and all her fashion accessories.[46] Unsurprisingly, she became a frequent object of emulation for women throughout the country—and because Dior attire was certainly unavailable in Soviet stores, the memoirs of the era are full of accounts of women sewing their own clothes and styling their hair to look like their favorite Argentine star, especially since *Rabotnitsa* conveniently offered patterns and cutting-and-sewing guides.[47] As Kaganovsky rightfully notes, "this also contributed to the retrenchment of gender norms in the 1950s and the 60s, when women were once again saddled with domestic chores, which were now declared not burdensome, but 'pleasant.'"[48]

Attention to style—both visual and musical—was similarly taken up by Torres's many official Soviet mediators. Gelena Velikanova and Aleksandra Kovalenko, popular singers in the Thaw period, performed her songs with Russian lyrics; Maia Kristalinskaia sang them in a mix of Spanish and Russian. Edita P'ekha visually styled herself after Torres (as is particularly evident from her 1960s album covers). But the most famous Soviet embodiment of Torres is Liudmila Gurchenko in her iconic performance in the highly popular musical comedy *The Carnival Night*, which not only signaled the return of this genre within Soviet film production, but fascinated audiences with Gurchenko's own Dior New Look clothing in the final song of the film. The story of the young actress auditioning for *The Carnival Night* with a performance of Torres's songs from *The Age of Life*, dressed the part (only, as Gurchenko claimed, with an even narrower waistline and fuller skirts!), became part of the actresses' and the film's public mythology.[49]

TORRES'S SOVIET MUSICAL RENDITIONS

It wasn't, however, just Torres's look that ensured her popularity in the Soviet Union—it was also her musical performances that won over audiences' hearts. The dissemination of her songs was fully supported and promoted by the Soviet state: record-producing factory Aprelevsky zavod released two of her singles in 1956 almost in tandem with Torres's first appearance on the big screen in Moscow, while by 1959 there were at least three other records, issued in Moscow, Leningrad, and Riga. In 1959, Music Publishing House (Muzgiz) issued a book of musical notations to her songs with Russian translations of their lyrics.[50] Issued repeatedly and with relatively large print runs, these editions allowed Soviet fans to perform Torres's music themselves, thus literally "domesticating" a foreign import, bringing it inside people's homes and making it their own. While, in the postwar era of transistor radios and vinyl albums, the Western music-publishing industry "had to reinvent itself as a licensing or copyright industry, collecting royalties from radio, film, and recording,"[51] the state-owned Soviet copyright regime operated differently. Not only did it encourage DIY "musicking" through continuing music publishing, but it also treated music covers as fair use. And, in fact, Soviet renditions of Torres's songs entered the mediasphere even earlier: the year of the release of *The Age of Love*, a Russian version of "Coimbra Divina"—retitled "The Student Song"—was released by three record companies (in Moscow, Leningrad, and Riga). It was performed by Aleksandra Kovalenko, the lead singer of the State Popular Music Orchestra of the Russian Federation, directed by the famous Soviet jazzman Leonid Utesov; it was this version that frequently went out on the radio, and Kovalenko was followed quickly by Velikanova and Kristalinskaia—both major stars of 1950s Soviet popular music (*estrada*).[52]

The popularity of Torres's songs both eased and advanced the acceptability—and desirability for audiences (if not necessarily for the Soviet cultural establishment)—of other "accented" performances: Soviet versions of foreign songs (with or without acknowledging their original source) or, literally, singers who performed in Russian with an accent.[53] Both were common practices since at least the 1920s, furthered in the 1930s by the official advancement of musical traditions hailing from non-Russian Soviet republics and from ethnic minorities. Many popular musicians included Moldovan, Georgian, Yiddish, and Romani songs or musical motifs in their portfolios. This was also often used as a reflection on political events, such as when music from the Spanish Civil War entered the Soviet cultural sphere. During the 1940s, in the atmosphere of Stalinist xenophobic suspicion and wartime patriotism, most musicians switched their official repertoire to Soviet lyrical patriotic songs, but by the early 1950s the popular foreign favorites came back. Thus, when

Kovalenko recorded Torres's song, her music selection—in addition to many Soviet movie songs from the period (including, eventually, the songs from *The Carnival Night*, performed in the film by Gurchenko)—featured several jazz standards and Spanish, Mexican, Cuban, and Uruguayan folksongs. These recordings were widely played on the radio between 1953 and 1958 (when she left Utesov's orchestra).

However, such an enthusiastic embrace of foreign popular music was not without consequences: thus, in 1955, just a few months before Torres became such a sensation in the Soviet Union, another popular singer, Ruzhena Sikora (Russian-born, of Czech and Polish origins), who was one of the first to perform foreign songs in other languages, was harshly attacked on the pages of the major Soviet newspaper *Sovetskaia kul'tura*. The article denounced her performances of the Mexican bolero-cum-international standard "Bésame Mucho" (under the Russian title "Song of the Heart"), a Spanish antifascist song called "¡Ay Carmela!," and a song from the film *Rome, 11 o'Clock* (*Roma, ore 11, 1952*) by communist Italian neo-realist filmmaker Giuseppe De Santis, a well-known friend of the Soviet Union.[54] The author claimed that all three songs originated in "fascist jazz and American pornographic gangster movies" and that their "primitive harmonies have nothing to do with genuine music of Italian, Spanish, or Mexican people," accusing Sikora of pandering to the tastes of *stiliagi*—the Soviet countercultural followers of Western fashions.[55] This rhetoric promoted the differentiation between commercial versus folk music, further mapping these divisions along geopolitical lines (American vs. Italian, Spanish, or Mexican). Continuing much earlier Soviet polemics, jazz was therefore associated with Western (US) capitalist mass culture as opposed to the "authentic" folkloric musical cultures.[56]

And, in their endless vigilance, the Soviet critics were not entirely wrong—the song from *Rome, 11 o'Clock* had, indeed, come to Italy via Charles Vidor's 1946 Hollywood film *Gilda*. And by the 1950s, much of the "Latin sound" was mediated internationally through the "mondo exotica" film music circuit, originating in the Hollywood of the 1940s, whose Latinomania is best exemplified by Xavier Cugat and Carmen Miranda. It was subsequently appropriated by the Italian postwar *dolce vita* culture (evoked, first critically, then more ironically, by Italian neorealists—finding its culmination in Fellini's 1959 film *La Dolce Vita*).[57] The worldwide circulation of "Bésame Mucho" was, indeed, triggered by Jimmy Dorsey and His Orchestra's hit recording in 1944, which reached number one on the US music charts and was also featured in an all-star vaudeville show produced to boost US troops' morale, *Follow the Boys* (Eddie Sutherland, 1944).

Given these associations, Latin popular music—just like Soviet *estrada*—needed the ideological cloaking of folklore to restore its status as "people's" music and therefore acceptable to the official communist culture. And, like Soviet *estrada*, it could be appreciated for its lyric and romantic aspects (seen as intrinsically linked to its folk origins), as long as they were clearly separated from sexuality and, preferably, framed in generally progressive "civic" rhetoric.[58] Thus, Soviet renditions of these songs—usually with toned-down Russian translations of lyrics or, when performed in another language, unfamiliar to most listeners—aided in domesticating these foreign cultural products, assimilating them to ideological and cultural Soviet norms, while never submerging entirely the "foreignness" that made them appealing both to musicians and to the listening audience. If, from the contemporary perspective, this historical phenomenon may appear to be both a flagrant violation of intellectual property rights and a wholesale cultural appropriation, such an evaluation has to take into account the distinctiveness of socialist theories and practices of intellectual property, as well as of the power relations at play (where assigning a "dominant" or "minority" cultural role to either side is not entirely obvious). It is further complicated by the political role this process played in the Soviet Union of the time.

CULTURAL POLITICS OF MUSICAL TRANSLATION

The official shift to a more vigorous and committed internationalism in the late 1950s, led by Khrushchev, created space for the broader acceptability of markers of non-Russianness in Soviet popular culture. This extended to the complex multiethnic and multinational composition of the Soviet Union itself—and, especially in the immediate postwar period, to its new Soviet (Baltic republics) and Socialist Bloc acquisitions. Thus, Velikanova, another popular performer of the Soviet version of "Coimbra Divina," was Polish-Lithuanian; and P'ekha was a French-born Polish Jew who made her debut in Moscow at the 1957 World Festival of Youth and Students, where her group (aptly named Druzhba, or "Friendship," referring to "the Friendship of the People," the Soviet lingo for internationalism) performed songs in several languages, including Spanish. For the duration of her long singing career, P'ekha had a strong Polish accent, which itself became an object of imitation by numerous singers—while barely tolerated by the authorities, resulting in frequent mentions in the press of her working hard on perfecting her Russian.[59] On the other hand, Gurchenko, who was Ukrainian, was told in no uncertain terms that she could continue at the Moscow Film Institute (VGIK) only if she "fixed" the way she spoke, because her accent marked her as "uncultured."[60] She was also denounced by Victor Shukshin (future writer, filmmaker, and actor—and the head of the VGIK's Communist Youth unit), for being an imitator of foreigner stars—namely, Torres—at one of the official meetings. Gurchenko, well known for her temper, just stormed out of the room, and the denunciation remained a pure exercise in political demagogy—after all, most of the country was imitating Torres.[61]

Similar ambivalence extended to the facial features of the stars: Soviet admirers of Torres, for example, repeatedly described her exotic, "wild slanting eyes."[62] Thus, Torres's Latin American ethnic identity was perceived as white and European and yet also, somehow in excess, visibly manifesting a subtle racial transculturation (in this case, presumably, suggesting traces of indigenous heritage).

This resonated with the complex negotiations of the racialization of beauty standards for Soviet (female) stars, which emerged during the Thaw. Thus, in contrast to the female movie stars of the 1930s—Liubov' Orlova and Marina Ladynina, both of whom were blond and stereotypically Slavic-looking—in the postwar era, Tatiana Samoilova, the star of *Cranes Are Flying*, was widely seen as somehow not quite Russian, with an "Asian slant" of her eyes; similar descriptions followed the sisters Marianna and Anastasiia Vertinskaia (the latter making her debut in *The Amphibian Man*, a sci-fi underwater romance with Latin American themes, to which we'll soon turn), even as they were simultaneously presented in the press as the undisputed beauties of 1960s Soviet cinema, frequently compared to Vivien Leigh and Audrey Hepburn.

These markers of national and racial belonging/non-belonging—such as an accent or perceived physiognomic features—played an ambivalent role in the circulation of global cultural icons, setting in motion a dialectic between exotic foreignness on the one hand and a feeling of familiarity or affinity on the other. The fandom this engendered engaged various informal modes of circulation, from homemade posters and magazine cut-outs to sing-alongs and DIY fashions and hairstyles in imitation of the stars. Such modes inevitably bypass capitalist conceptions of intellectual property, pointing instead to a certain shared understanding of the cultural commons, whose internationalist universalism had particular purchase in the exuberant atmosphere of the post-Stalinist Soviet Union.[63] The political effects of such appropriations and transculturation via informal means of circulation are necessarily contradictory and often ambivalent, enabling the expression of popular desires that do not fold neatly into progressive ideologies or dominant cultural and political hegemonies.

The complexity of this process was similarly reflected in Torres's music. Her overall musical identity was decidedly more "Spanish" than Argentinian. While in the late 1940s, when she began her stage career, the Perón regime was supporting the revival and popularization of Argentinian folklore, Torres chose instead to specialize in Spain's regional folkloric and popular repertoire. In fact, she was noted for accurate reproduction of various regional Spanish accents.[64] Many of her subsequent film performances—including *The Age of Love*—reflect this polyvocal identity. Thus, despite the intentional contrast between the musical repertoires of the characters of the mother and daughter (the former as traditional Spanish, the latter as modern Argentinian) in that film, its most popular songs belong to the "Spanish" part (and "Coimbra Divina," which became the biggest hit in the Soviet Union, extended that geography further into Portugal).

Based on its musical style, *The Age of Love* is influenced by the genre of *españoladas*.[65] These quasi-folkloristic films were developed in the 1920s and became a staple of Franco's Spain, especially in the 1940s. Reflecting the alliance between Perón and Franco, many of them were successfully imported to Argentina, where they had considerable commercial success.[66] Yet there were ideological differences between the *españoladas* and Torres's Argentinian star vehicles like *The Age of Love*: the former typically celebrated the rural idyll as the expression of the national(ist) spirit, with women as absolute guarantors of tradition, whereas Saraceni's films presented a very different, markedly Perónist progressive view of women's social and class roles. While borrowing some of the markers of *costumbrismo*—from traditional dress to music—*The Age of Love*'s genre as a self-reflexive stage musical instead highlights the performativity (as opposed to any presumed authenticity) of the Spanish identity of its characters.[67]

In the Soviet context, *españoladas* and their associations with Franco—which would have raised inevitable political conflict, given the centrality of the Spanish Civil War to the mythology of Soviet internationalism—were largely unknown. As a result, Torres's on-screen persona's generic associations with Spain and Spanish culture, somewhat paradoxically, were filtered through the cult of the Spanish Republic that was familiar to Soviet audiences, whose knowledge of Argentinian culture at the time was limited, at best, to European and Russian renditions of tango. For them, Torres's pan-Latin repertoire therefore served as a vector for (Luso-)Hispanic popular musical culture, simultaneously introducing audiences to the basic genres of Latin American music: not only the ever-popular (but associated with the prewar and even the prerevolutionary period) tango but also the rumba, samba, and bolero. Torres's version of "Bésame Mucho"—which, notwithstanding its associations with US jazz standards, was a bolero originally written in 1940 by the Mexican composer and pianist Consuelo Velázquez, who started her career in a 1938 Argentinian musical, *Noches de Carnaval*, directed by none other than Saraceni—was also one of its most popular renditions in the Soviet Union. The association between Torres and this popular song further added to its enduring status as the musical embodiment of Latin American sensuality, as well as to the confusion regarding the song's origins—as we'll see in the concluding chapter.

Latin American musical and dance culture in all its many forms provided, in the Soviet Union as elsewhere, a viable alternative to white European, middle-class aspirational cultural forms and practices, as tango and other global vernaculars of the 1920s functioned vis-à-vis, say, the Viennese waltz or the Parisian operetta.[68] Increasingly, it also offered an alternative to the "standard bearers of musical modernity as defined by North American taste"—which, by the 1950s, meant American (and, by the late 1960s, increasingly British) rock and roll, totemically represented by Elvis Presley and the Beatles.[69] In the Cold War context this was increasingly important, and the Soviet cultural establishment was indeed eager to delineate and amplify these distinctions despite—or because of—the difficulties of keeping them entirely apart, given the hybridizing realities of both global music circulation and local consumption habits; the dynamic we can see already in the presence of earlier European popular formats in Torres's own cinematic repertoire—and their resonances in Soviet stage and, later, TV culture. But while virtually all of Latin American popular music from the 1920s through the Stalinist era arrived via its double US-European mediation, this trajectory changed in the late 1950s, in sync with the growing nationalism and international reach of Latin American cultural industries. Combined with the shift in Soviet cultural policies, these developments placed Soviet audiences in more immediate contact with Latin performers, whether on stage or on the big screen.[70] Lolita Torres became the first—and, perhaps, the best-remembered—Latin American performer disseminating this alternative musical culture, in which the hazards of domestic and international politics produced unexpected results.

LATIN BALLROOM DANCE AND MUSIC CRAZE
IN THE SOVIET UNION

At the same time, its reception is also indissolubly associated with the rehabilitation and evolution of ballroom dance in 1950s and 1960s Soviet culture. Couple dancing was a fundamental, albeit informal, aspect of Soviet (youth) culture of the 1940s, with "Western" dances such as the fox-trot, waltz, and tango dominating the floor. After decades of official denunciation of such practices as anti-Soviet, in the 1950s, Soviet cultural authorities reluctantly institutionalized ballroom dance by setting up clubs and classes, publishing textbooks, preparing instructors, and, eventually, forming professional associations. As with fashion and popular music, the challenge was to strip dance of Western bourgeois associations—vulgarity, excessive sexuality, and the disconnect from national folkloric roots. Initially, the newly created official repertoire of ballroom dances consisted of earlier, prerevolutionary dances and fusions with Slavic folkloric forms, but after 1956 the inclusion of the more contemporary (and informally much more popular) "Western" dances became the norm.[71] As ballroom dance became institutionalized internationally in the 1950s with the formation of such organizations as the International Council of Ballroom Dancing (1950) and the International Council of Amateur Dancers (1956), it was marked specifically as the channel through which Afro-Latin dances—rumba, samba, jive, paso doble, cha-cha-cha—could be accepted into the official program. In the Soviet Union (as elsewhere in Europe and the US), these dances were perceived as especially risqué and were most popular among young people, but by appropriating them to state-supported ballroom dance, the official culture hoped to neutralize their subversive impact.[72] But even so moderated, the official and supervised dance halls in the 1950s and 1960s were intrinsically linked to the organization of intimacy and sexuality: based on sociological surveys of the time, it was at such dances that the majority of first encounters leading to marriages took place.[73] Even though, in the course of the 1960s, the twist became probably the most popular informal dance, ballroom dance, which began to evolve into a more professional form—thus requiring more extensive training, elaborate costumes, makeup, hair, and so on—continued the associations of Afro-Latin dances in the Soviet Union with a more refined and glamorous sensuality, in contrast to more subversive (and informal) "Western" dancing, in spite of the latter's appropriation of African American dance and music styles. As such, the Afro-Caribbean rhythms were stripped of their well-established, racialized Western associations with dangerous deviancy and anarchic sexuality (which, in the Soviet context, were articulated most vehemently in the critiques of jazz of previous decades).

Lolita Torres's persona fit with this cluster of associations: her on-screen dance performances were minimal but highly staged and set to the very combination of musical rhythms that would form the core of Latin American ballroom dance programs (in the Soviet Union and elsewhere), equally "sanitized" via earlier European stage traditions and specifically sentimentalist legacies—overlapping and yet distinct from, for example, the "mambo craze" of the global 1950s–1960s. Jesús Martín-Barbero's insights into the dynamics of the standardization of the *sentimental culture* of Latin America (within which he includes both music and audiovisual forms such as film and telenovela) are particularly apropos here, albeit in a different transnational context. He claims that "the long process of massive, popular identification that was put into motion in the 1940s and 1950s by the Mexican and Argentinean cinema, and by the tango, the ranchera, and the bolero," produced "the mass standardization of ways of feeling and expressing, of gestures and sounds, dance rhythms, and narrative cadences made possible by the cultural industries of radio and cinema."[74] The popularity of Torres's music and movies, crystallized within this new Soviet sensibility and structure of feeling, associated itself with the dense cluster of cultural identifications with Latin American melodramatic culture.

She wasn't the only one, of course. Especially during the youth festival in 1957, the range of Latin performers in the Soviet Union expanded considerably. As a result, as Tobias Rupprecht documents, even visitors from Latin America were surprised by the Latin music craze in the Soviet Union:

> The Peruvian philosopher Francisco Miró Quesada, touring the Soviet Union in the summer of 1959, was surprised to see that 'everyone preferred Latin American music . . . to European music' and that 'many girls were able to sing tunes in Spanish'. The visiting Colombian politician Alberto Dangond remembered that his young guide Ljudmila was very 'aficionada a los ritmos latinoamericanos'. The Brazilian communist Eneida de Moraes was pleasantly surprised that the band in her Moscow hotel played Brazilian music. And her compatriot journalist Nestor de Holanda was overwhelmed to hear rumba and samba in a restaurant in the Black Sea resort town of Sochi.[75]

Most of these performances were very much on par with the kind of music propelled by the 1950s Latin craze in the US—despite the considerable geographic distance and absence of diasporic communities—and their enormous popularity in the Soviet Union demonstrates the irony of the US impression that "the Soviets openly expressed their disdain for Latin American music," which evidently fueled the Cold War logic behind the inclusion of Latin performers on US television.[76] Indeed, the US-sponsored *Trio Los Panchos* was one of the first Latino music groups to tour the Soviet Union.[77] Rupprecht lists *Los Mexicanos*, a Mexican folkloric band that had played concerts in Leningrad and Moscow in the mid-1950s; the *Trio Los Caballeros* from Paraguay, who played multiple shows in the late 1950s and early 1960s; the Argentine group *Los Trovadores del Norte*; and Brazilian singers Silvio Caldas and Victor Simón.[78] Another group that had similar success in the Soviet Union was *Los Paraguayos*, who performed a similar mix of assorted folkloric songs and Latin American romantic songs (boleros in particular).[79]

Rupprecht's acerbic description of the enthusiasm surrounding such performances highlights primarily their indiscriminate mixing of national and regional markers to create a generic spectacle of pan–Latin American folklore, attuned to their audiences' undiscerning taste. Indeed, Soviet cultural critics were also quick to decry these performances as excessively emotional, inauthentic, and lacking in technique. As a way to educate the audiences, music scholars—led by Pavel Pichugin, one of the editors of the journal *Soviet Music* (*Sovetskaia muzyka*)— began publishing academic work popularizing the "correct" folkloric traditions of Latin America. Between the 1960s and 1980s, Pichugin published four major books and numerous articles dedicated to Argentinian, Mexican, and Cuban music, becoming the leading Soviet scholar and propagandist of Latin American musical folklore—without, however, making any significant impact on the enduring love of the Soviet people for the mass-produced bastardized versions.[80]

At the same time, the somewhat indiscriminate mix of folkloric music and international trends that Rupprecht describes in the Soviet context were, in fact, fully continuous with the contemporary pan–Latin American dynamics of both state-supported and commercial articulations of folkloric national heritage and its use in the global music market of the time. On the one hand, Perón's promotion of Argentinian folkloric music in the 1940s; Amalia Hernández's Folkloric Ballet of Mexico, which was founded in the early 1950s; and the Cuban National Folkloric Ballet, founded in the early 1960s, were all part of a complex and contradictory process of "the nationalization of vernacular musics," spearheaded by left-leaning and/or populist governments as well as by grassroots movements (in Latin America and elsewhere in the postcolonial world) seeking to ground themselves in a space independent of US domination, and manifested, among other ways, in the importing of consumer culture.[81] On the other hand, the "invention" (to use Pablo Palomino's term) of Latin American popular music's global commercial circulation was deliberately engaged in various forms of both homogenization and hybridization of distinct local sounds.[82] The leftist nationalist political projects in fact intersected with the marketing strategies of selling tango, son, bolero, salsa, and other forms as authentically national and yet as belonging to the hemispheric Latin American imaginary.

What is important in the Soviet context is that these national-popular and commercial articulations formed a distinct transnational Latin American musical (as well as cinematic and cultural) circuit, whose Soviet nodes were strongly shaped by Torres's popularity. Like the Chinese-language musicals in Hong Kong and Taiwan in the 1960s analyzed by Andrew F. Jones, these Soviet versions of the Latin craze furthered the process of the global circulation of popular musical cultures by engaging with a range of Latin American and Afro-Caribbean genres.[83] While they were increasingly globally standardized, in their socialist circulation they formed a distinctive circuit with its own geography and symbolic points of reference (the Spanish Civil War, Perón's Argentina, the Mexican and Cuban revolutions), at once internationally recognizable as bearing not only aural and visual signatures of its era (such as the mambo sound of the global 1960s), but also unmistakable traces of the local vernacular.

THE AMPHIBIAN MAN

Cinema and television were crucial parts of these circuits. Thus, a combination of Torres's stardom, the enthusiasm for the Cuban Revolution in the early 1960s, and the longer, more familiar markers of Mexicanness (going as far back as the 1920s), account for the setting and music in the Soviet blockbuster *The Amphibian Man* (*Chelovek-amfibiia*, Gennadii Kazanskii and Vladimir Chebotarev, 1962), a sci-fi musical romance about a sea monster taking place in an unidentified Latin American country, which became the highest-grossing film of the entire Thaw period, surpassing the previously uncontested *Awara*'s box office success when it came out in 1962. The film's original director, Chebatorev, was going for "an average Latin American style,"[84] which was achieved by mixing Mexican sombreros, colonial architecture reminiscent of Havana, and Cuban revolutionary-style hair and beards (in addition to elements of the nineteenth-century adventure-novel "pirate" imaginary).

The film announces this cluster of associations sonically through the predominance of bongos—audible already in the opening sequence—on its soundtrack, the generic signifier of "the rhythmic pulse assumed to be the fundamental syntax of the genre."[85] Less than halfway through the film, the ideological conflict at its core is set up musically by two diegetic songs within one fifteen-minute sequence, both written by the celebrated composer Andrei Petrov (who scored both diegetic and nondiegetic music for the film), both referencing Latin traditions. One is a jazzy number performed in a nightclub and, in an original version of the film, accompanied by a striptease (subsequently edited out by censors),[86] with, in the words of its composer, "convulsing pulsation of the ecstatic rhythms of 'mambo mambo, samba samba'"—mirrored in the repetitive Russian lyrics: "Nam by, nam by, nam by, nam by . . ."—which became known as "The Song of the Sea Devil."[87] The other, a lyrical and mournful "Fisherman's Song" ("If the fisherman doesn't return, he must have found peace on the bottom of the sea . . ."), was clearly intended to be reminiscent of a bolero, with sparse guitar accompaniment sung by a poor street musician in a heartfelt, sentimental manner.

These two songs bookmark the two different sounds of the era in the Soviet Union—the first an offspring of the debauched global 1960s, an American/jazz-style mambo, the second an extension of the long-standing folk/vernacular idiom. The former, "The Song of the Sea Devil," became a much-loved hit, continually performed informally at parties and dances, but strongly criticized officially; while "The Fisherman's Song" was continuously singled out by critics as the film's big success, its notations repeatedly reprinted by the musical publishing house and versions performed by stage and television stars.[88] In retrospect, the latter turned out to be the very first in a string of extremely popular romantic ballads, or *romansy*, by Petrov—written both for movie soundtracks and for *estrada* performers such as P'ekha in the course of the 1960s, 1970s, and 1980s, connecting the bolero tradition to Russian "gypsy" sentimentalist music (a link that will become particularly relevant in our analysis of the reception of the Mexican *Yesenia* in the 1970s later in the book).

But while both songs are meant to be representative of the same "average Latin American style" the director attempted for the film as a whole, the link to Lolita Torres becomes most visible in the performance of *The Amphibian Man*'s female lead, Anastasiia Vertinskaia. Not only does she incorporate Torres-like mannerisms, her dancing a vague but unmistakable imitation of flamenco moves (as depicted on the poster for the film), but her very character is yet another echo of the Torres type, marked by the same combination of childlike naïveté (and Vertinskaia was, in fact, seventeen at the time of the film's production), spirited willfulness, and decorous femininity.

Torres's stardom, then, participated in (re)legitimizing the melodramatic impulses in the music and cinema beloved by the Thaw generation, as much as it set the standards for Soviet femininity in the postwar era. But it was also the perception of Torres's spatial accessibility and therefore proximity that created a particular experience of affective intimacy so constitutive of her stardom, in contrast to other Western stars. This different affective regime, I argue, set the foundation for the later (1970s–1980s) embrace of Latin American melodramatic heroines, perceived by Soviet audiences as somehow "one of us" even as they retained the signifiers of exoticism. Such cultural and affective translation was crucial for ideological reasons, being a way to officially justify Torres's stardom despite her largely apolitical, nonsocialist credentials. But they also gave audiences reason to sustain a decades-long dedication to the star and a sense of her importance to their personal lives. This intimacy was dependent upon the media circuit itself as it emerged in the postwar Soviet Union. Radio, film, and eventually television played key roles in this process, aided by the structure of programming: by 1960, more than half of radio airtime, and almost 20 percent of television airtime, in the Soviet Union was given over to music.[89] The film exhibition network exploded during the same

FIGURE 3. Poster for *The Amphibian Man.*
Personal collection.

decade, by the mid-1960s reaching the highest level of moviegoing per capita in the world.[90] However, the phantasmal media presence of Torres was reinforced by her well-publicized personal visits to the Soviet Union, beginning with her appearance at the Third Moscow International Film Festival in 1963.

CREATING INTIMACY THROUGH FANDOM

The sense of geographic distance between Soviet audiences and their foreign idols was rendered unbridgeable geopolitically, given the infrequency of international travel more generally, and across the Iron Curtain in particular. Foreign stars belonged to that other imaginary world, "abroad" (*zagranitsa*), rendering the sense of remove from them even greater.[91] Stars visited Moscow during the International Film Festival, but their interactions were limited to the Soviet officials. They were not allowed contact with the local audiences—the only exception being at the Tashkent Film Festival, albeit, again, only for non-Western stars like Kapoor. Among the idols of Soviet music lovers in the 1950s and 1960s, only Yves Montand visited the country with concerts.[92] Unlike Montand, however, Torres had no prior connection to the Soviet Union, antifascism, the working class, peace activism, or the shared cultural hegemony of France—thus making the process of cultural translation of the star into "one of us" potentially more challenging.[93] More pragmatically, the costs of travel and the underdeveloped travel infrastructure between Argentina and the Soviet Union meant that compared to visits from France or Italy, the logistics of Torres coming to Moscow were infinitely more complicated.

In the years immediately following the first screenings of her films in the Soviet Union, it was athletes and sailors stationed in Buenos Aires who seemed to function as the connection between the star and the Soviet people: they came looking for Lolita Torres to present her with presents and ask for signed autographs. The resulting visit and an impromptu a cappella performance by Torres in 1957 on board a Soviet ship were much publicized, both in the Soviet Union and in Argentina. While Soviet newspapers were delighted to give accounts of the star's elegance, including details of her dress and her impeccable manners, at home the kindness she showed to such undignified audiences gave rise to speculation. *Mundo Radial*, one of the leading popular magazines of the 1940s and 1950s dedicated to radio, film, and theater that enthusiastically propagated Perón's ideological program (and was subsequently shut down soon after Perón fell), in its coverage of Torres performing for the Soviet sailors reported that "Lolita Torres surprised everyone with her kindness towards the crew of the Soviet ship," and, referring to the political instability and ideological conflicts in Argentina in the post-Perónist period, wondered: "The ways things are right now, one has to choose sides. Will Lolita go with the communists?"[94]

As with the original establishment of the distribution network between Argentina and the Soviet Union, the film festival network came in handy once again, and after a series of failed attempts (due to Torres's personal circumstances), in 1963 Torres finally joined the Argentinian delegation to the Moscow Film Festival. Upon arrival she was greeted by hundreds of journalists, photographers, and screaming fans. Her film screenings and performances filled multi-thousand-seat theaters. Torres's recollections make it clear that she had never experienced such fame. As she waved to her fans from the balcony of the Kremlin theater, she told her husband, "Look, I look just like Perón greeting people on Plaza de Mayo."[95] But if the scale and format of such events were anything but intimate—indeed, they were reminiscent of political showmanship and the "cult of personality" (equally resonant in Argentina and the Soviet Union)—the physical presence and proximity to their foreign idol was a rare event for Soviet fans.

The personalization and domestication of Torres's image was particularly marked in her TV appearances: she took part in a recently launched variety show, *The Little Blue Flame* (Goluboi Ogonek). The show was staged as a "café" with its own stage for performances and little round tables for guests, who included a mix of celebrities (movie stars, singers, circus performers, poets, writers, and cosmonauts) and distinguished workers. The format promoted the experience of intimacy: stars were presented as "regular people" sitting around the table, enjoying chatting with guests, and audiences were interpellated into the imaginary space, whether as hosts or guests.[96] It was extremely rare to have a foreigner on the program (just as it would have been unthinkable to have one in one's living room, or at a café for that matter), and Torres's appearance on the show was remembered as a meaningful bonding experience with her larger audience, underscoring how much she was unlike those other bourgeois stars, who, however popular with Soviet audiences, would have been impossible to imagine within such a familiar (symbolic) space.

If Torres herself had not quite imagined the level of popularity she had in the Soviet Union before her first visit, the Argentinian press seemed to be quite aware of it. Popular magazines quickly took it up as an opportunity to reflect on the Soviet reception of *The Age of Love* as evidence of the superiority of local commercial filmmaking over its competitors, to differentiate its national (and, more broadly, Latin American) cinema from that of Hollywood and Europe, and to reaffirm the superiority of its melodramatic codes as the best and most accurate reflection of reality. Thus, *Mundo Radial* claimed that Torres's Soviet popularity was evidence that Soviets both recognized and rejected "the violence and delinquency" at the core of Hollywood cinema, and European cinema's "distortion and disfiguration of reality under the disguise of modernist realism" in their representation of "the eternal sentimental conflict between the sexes as if man and woman were irreconcilable, wild beasts in a tremendously hostile jungle" (an argument we will see repeated in 1970s Mexico in subsequent chapters).[97] *Radiolandia*, meanwhile, claimed Torres's success as one of the main events signaling "the Soviet Thaw" after the death of Stalin—a return to love stories "after many years of having to conform to the issues of collective farming, work problems and the construction of socialism."[98] Thus, both articles aligned the Soviet taste for the melodramatic imaginary with the Latin American (and specifically Argentinian) mode of commercial filmmaking as participating in a shared alternative to both socialist or European realism and Hollywood, positing its normative understanding of gender relations as crucial to this new shared aesthetic and geopolitical model.

As surprising and exciting as her appearance on *The Little Blue Flame* was, Torres's media self-presentation fit in perfectly with Soviet cultural expectations—even in Argentina she was known for being a "real lady" (*una dama*) who "made good manners a way of life."[99] Her persona was strongly identified with her character in *The Age of Love*, a perfect alternative to an image of the spoiled diva: she was always polite, well spoken, composed, and well behaved (in fact, much of her early artistic career was fully controlled by her father, who concentrated on maintaining an image of decency and morality for her, within the limits entailed by box office success).[100] Even the choice for her fado in *The Age of Love*, which was so beloved in the Soviet Union—"Coimbra Divina"—wasn't arbitrary: the Coimbra fado is unlike its Lisbon equivalent. While the latter is associated with the working-class quarters and popular cafés, the Coimbra fado was more refined and cultured, linked to university students (it is because of this connection that in Russian the song's title is "The Student Song"—which conveniently also disguised the associations between Coimbra and the Portuguese fascist dictator Antonio Salazar, who taught there).[101] As such, Torres's demeanor was in perfect harmony with the Soviet norms of *kul'turnost'* (culturedness), imposing essentially bourgeois/middle-class behavioral standards and emphasizing propriety and good education (the note struck by *The Little Blue Flame*). Torres was, indeed, always gracious with her hosts, even if she had reason, in private, for her outrage in discovering that without her knowledge or consent, she was to be paid for her performances in Russian rubles, which could not be converted to "hard currency"—forcing her to spend all of it in the Moscow stores. Her financial distress was all the worse for her having been assured, by various Argentinian friends who had visited Moscow, of her popularity there and that she would surely be paid "any amount of US dollars, deposited directly to a Swiss account."[102] Always a lady, Torres never complained or betrayed her disappointment to her Soviet hosts. Nor did it discourage her from undertaking future tours—and, in the course of the 1970s and 1980s, she gave a series of concerts throughout the Soviet Union, always to full auditoriums, ensuring her ongoing popularity decades after the original screenings of her films. While her biographer gives the total number of her tours as seven, present-day Russian-language internet blogs and fan sites continue to reference up to twelve visits—evidencing the popular (Russian) perception of the Argentinian star's close and continuous relationship with the Soviet Union, an impression of presence that signaled a particular kind of emotional intimacy.

This intersection of intimacy and a universal—more precisely, cosmic—transnational affinity finds an emblematic form in the anecdotes about Torres's "number one fan," the first man in space, Soviet cosmonaut Yuri Gagarin. The twenty-one-year-old Gagarin was apparently in the audience for the first screening of *The Age of Love* in Moscow in 1955, becoming one of her great fans. In 1962, via the Soviet Embassy in Buenos Aires, the actress received a letter from the cosmonaut, who had orbited the Earth just a year prior. The letter confessed his adoration and asked for a signed autograph, which Torres was happy to provide. In return, she received Gagarin's autographed photo and another letter, which told the singer that he had always listened to her music during the hard years of training, so that when he went into space her songs "exploded in his heart, and he couldn't but hum them"—making them "the first music to arrive into space, the one I carried in my mind and my heart—that is, your voice!"[103] The story is entirely plausible, as Gagarin was in fact well known for his love of popular music and his interest in singers (rumors of his "close friendship" with Edita P'ekha, who was, indeed, one of those many Soviet stars fashioning themselves after the style of Lolita Torres, were said to have ruined her marriage).[104] But its rehearsal in both Russia and Argentina (which continues to this day on the internet) signals a desire for Torres's affair with the Soviet public to be not merely a transnational phenomenon, signaling affinities between Argentina and the Soviet Union, but something more transcendent: a love story projected on the planetary and even the cosmic level: the story of Latin American melodramatic sentimentality—romantic and pure—embodied in music and cinema, conquering the world via its Soviet fans.[105]

In the subsequent decades, as we'll see in the next chapter, it would be specifically the ethos of melodramatic suffering—already embedded in Torres's films and performances but given an optimistic Thaw/Perónist gloss—that would come to dominate the reception of Latin American culture in the Soviet Union, tapping into older traditions of Russian vernacular expression. This was no longer an expression of the national-popular, but rather a sign of complete disenchantment with the project of the state culture, as much as it was inseparable from it. We'll see how the changing models for femininity and sexuality were tied to this reception, as were fashion and other forms of ordinary cultural consumption and appropriation, with their embedded reliance on alternative notions of intellectual property and informal circulation, and their movement toward melodramatic media as a conduit for neoliberal modes of gender and sexuality. The first contours of these developments are already visible in the story of Torres's fame in the Soviet Union in the 1950s, whose transnational affective community tells us as much about Khrushchev's socialism as about Perónist populism. Matthew Karush's conclusion that Perónist social transformation and the binary moralism of its discourses were rooted in the melodramatic tendencies of its preceding mass culture, movies, and music is particularly pertinent here. He observes how

> Perónism appropriated mass cultural discourses that expressed both the popular resentment over social inequality and the popular desire for the trappings of wealth. This discursive framework imposed limits on the utopias Perónism might imagine. Thus, Perónism often endorsed bourgeois standards of propriety and conventional models of beauty. It also reproduced the contradiction between working-class pride and envy, a contradiction that resurfaced whenever economic conditions prevented the state from delivering on its economic promises to workers. In a sense, these limits were the consequence of Perón having built his movement out of melodrama rather than Marxism.[106]

In the following chapters, we will trace the further development of a different version of such "melodramatic" populism as it found its manifestation in the reception of the Mexican "gypsy" melodrama *Yesenia* in the 1970s. The rest of the book therefore jumps some twenty years forward in time, focusing on the distinctly Soviet-Mexican circuit of sentimental media, its aesthetic regimes, and its political contexts. By that time, however—while the ideology behind the Mexican presidency of Luis Echeverría Álvarez that enabled Soviet-Mexican exchanges was, indeed, in many ways strikingly similar to Perón's—state- and nation-centered forms of cultural populism were no longer viable in either country. And yet, despite the crucial historical and geopolitical differences, the contours of this new transnational sentimental community are already visible in the cultural and social dynamics of Lolita Torres's Soviet stardom of the 1950s. As the following chapters demonstrate, many of the major themes and problems emerging from this earlier Soviet-Argentinian encounter reemerged with a vengeance within the changed, considerably less buoyant environment of the 1970s.

1

Yesenia in Mexico and the Soviet Union

It would take twenty years from the release of *The Age of Love* for another Latin American movie to achieve comparable cultural impact in the Soviet Union. By that time, the country was in the midst of what subsequently came to be known as the period of Stagnation.[1] Nikita Khrushchev was deposed in 1964, and his successor Leonid Brezhnev instituted a more rigid order to stabilize the cadre. The expanded official ideologies of the Thaw narrowed considerably, while the policy of developed socialism, in tandem with détente, produced lifestyle benefits for many members of the Thaw generation. Their children were better educated and wealthier than any generation in Russian history. And yet it also became evident that the solemn promise made by the Communist Party in 1961, that within twenty years the Soviet Union's production and consumption would outpace those of the developed capitalist countries, was a pipe dream—as the consumerist revolution and youth culture of the Swinging Sixties transformed the West, making all comparisons of lifestyle between the two simply untenable.[2] Soviet consumerism of a controlled kind eroded the vestiges of the spirit of war-communism while failing to replace it with any overriding ideological goal. "Socialism with a human face," the slogan of the Prague Spring, which in many ways embodied the aspiration of the 1960s generation across the Socialist Bloc, was crushed in 1968—and the consequences of that fateful year continued to reverberate among the Soviet intelligentsia.

At the same time, in the second half of the 1970s, international cultural and scientific exchanges between the Soviet Union and the rest of the world were at their peak.[3] Cinemagoing was at its all-time high, and television viewing was increasingly becoming the norm as well: if there were only ten thousand TV sets in the whole of the Soviet Union in 1950, by 1976 Soviet factories were producing seven million sets annually.[4] The children of Lolita Torres's fans, at least those living in big cities, were increasingly more curious about the world of British and American rock and roll, giving rise to several countercultural currents. Within just a few years, the Euro-Caribbean disco sensation Boney M would break through the Iron Curtain, giving multiple concerts in Moscow in 1978 and, alongside ABBA, entering the pantheon of most popular musical performers in the Soviet Union (with the record company Melodiia promptly releasing both bands' albums, albeit in entirely idiosyncratic versions). French, Italian, and even Hollywood movies were becoming considerably more common on Soviet big screens, and Soviet cinema and television, too, had shifted production toward entertainment genres, including musicals and melodramas.

And yet, it was a Mexican melodrama set during the Second Franco-Mexican War—*Yesenia* (Alfredo B. Crevenna, 1971)—that, in 1975, went on to become the highest-grossest film in the history of the Soviet Union. Based on ticket sales, an astounding 91.4 million viewers saw the film in the first year of its release, and it was shown in movie theaters for years to come, eventually migrating to TV screens, and still later was sold on videotapes and then on DVDs, through both official and informal markets.[5]

In 2019, a Russian-dubbed version of the film was uploaded to YouTube, generating enthusiastic user comments, many of them reminiscing about how they watched the film repeatedly and shed tears over it, usually mentioning also their mothers and grandmothers.[6] Another YouTube video, uploaded in 2015, featuring the theme song from *Yesenia*, similarly drew nostalgic user comments in Spanish, Russian, and Chinese, praising the emotional power of both the music and the film's romance.[7] Several mention naming their daughters Yesenia—or having that name themselves. A brief glimpse into these recollections establishes some discursive continuities with the earlier reception of Lolita Torres: the emphasis on the affective impact of the music, the beauty of the performer (although, significantly, very few Soviet viewers remember the name of the actress who played Yesenia, Jacqueline Andere—simply referring to her by her protagonist's name), the memorable costumes, and the sense of gendered multigenerational community created by the film, underscored by the passing of the name to newborn girls.

But the differences were significant as well. Torres's success in the Soviet Union as it emerged from World War II and the deep wounds of Stalinism was, as we have seen, at least partly the result of a cinema-starved domestic market in the heady atmosphere of the Thaw's internationalism. And unlike many other foreign films of that era screened in the Soviet Union, which typically enjoyed success in their home countries as well as abroad, *Yesenia*—even though it was based on a popular telenovela and even more popular comics—was only a moderate success with Mexican film audiences. Its main cultural impact was most visible in the local fashion and personal care industry's mimicking of the protagonist's iconic hair and dress styles.[8] The film's international circulation was limited to the Soviet

Union and, later, China, and it remained largely unnoticed by scholars and critics outside of those two countries. Indeed, *Yesenia*'s reception and quick fandom were not entirely supported by the Soviet film and cultural apparatuses, which seemed at times perplexed by, outraged by, or willfully ignorant of its enormous success.

And if Torres's Argentinian musicals arrived in the Soviet Union just a few years after its own film industry's prime, *Yesenia* was a product of a considerably longer period of decline in Mexican cinema, decades past its Golden Age of the 1940s. Many critics and scholars have considered the Mexican cinema of the 1970s and 1980s—recently evocatively referred to as "the Lost Cinema of Mexico"—the lowest point in the national industry's history.[9] This "loss" refers not to the low number of movies made—in fact, Mexican film production was at its height in the 1970s—but to the critical consensus over the decline of their artistic quality. After decades of wide circulation of the Golden Age classics both commercially (if largely within Latin America) and at international film festivals, by the 1970s, Mexican cinema's international prestige was fully exhausted. Most historians and critics seem to be completely unaware, however, of the one part of the world where Mexican cinema of that period found a wide and enthusiastic viewership: the Socialist Bloc. It was seen by audiences during "weeks of Mexican cinema" in Moscow and Beijing and in international programs at the Moscow, Karlovy Vary, and Tashkent film festivals, achieving broad commercial exhibition and considerable success all across the socialist sphere.[10]

While the promotion of Soviet-Mexican cinematic contacts throughout the decade (as we'll see shortly) was part of concerted state efforts, the enormous popularity of *Yesenia* nonetheless caught Soviet film institutions by surprise. Its box office numbers were in sharp contrast to the number of reviews in the press or, in fact, promotion of any kind. Unlike Torres's films and songs, *Yesenia* became a hit without the crucial element of the construction of stardom through publications and other news coverage to create additional intimacy with the viewing public. It is evident that its success was not entirely anticipated by the Soviet film distributors either—even though, reflecting the changes that had taken place in Goskino (the central state apparatus in charge of cinema in the Soviet Union), newly reformed in 1972, the film was distributed in an unprecedentedly high print run of almost two thousand copies. This, it turned out, proved entirely insufficient, leading to record use of those printed copies—49,500 uses per copy in 1975 alone.[11] Nor was this success shared with the Mexican media and state. Far from deliberately created or orchestrated as a form of cultural diplomacy, *Yesenia*'s enduring popularity was a "bottom-up" process within an otherwise highly formal and state-controlled cinematic culture—a phenomenon that has puzzled critics for generations.

Maia Turovskaia was one of the few Russian scholars who addressed the film's popularity head-on.[12] Writing retrospectively, in the 1990s, Turovskaia admits that neither she nor her fellow film critics had seen the film or even heard about it at the time when the box office numbers were announced, making *Yesenia*

FIGURE 4. Poster for *Yesenia*. Personal collection.

the highest-grossest film in Soviet exhibition history. The previous box office leaders—the Soviet comedy *The Diamond Arm* (*Brilliantovaia ruka*, Leonid Gaidai, 1969), the Hollywood Western *The Magnificent Seven* (John Sturges, 1960), and the Indian *The Vagabond* (*Awara*, Raj Kapoor, 1951)—fell behind it by some fifteen million viewers.[13] But unlike Turovskaia's colleagues who merely ignored this remarkable fact, she decided to watch *Yesenia* to confront the mystery of its success.[14] Describing this experience in detail in her later writings, Turovskaia offers a brief and acerbic summary of the film's plot: "An officer from a hacienda falls in love with a gypsy and marries her. Also in love with him is a rich heiress who, alas, is dying of tuberculosis. After various adventures it turns out that the gypsy is her illegitimate sister, given away by the mother, who had sinned. Therefore, no misalliance. *Happy end* [*sic*] for the healthy."[15]

After watching the film in a theater, the critic, appalled by what she sees as the film's abysmally primitive artistic qualities, asks a woman sitting next to her, who was crying throughout the movie, what moved her so much. The woman responds categorically that the film is "about her." Turovskaia persists, pointing to the ludicrous disconnect between the film's diegesis and this Soviet woman's reality: "Which part is about you: the mother's sin, the gypsy camp, the hacienda, the officer, the tuberculosis, which?"—to which the woman resolutely responds, "All of it!"[16]

The scene played out here—the confusion mixed with disdain on the part of the critic, a true member of the intelligentsia, and the intense emotional identification and reaction of the audience, one of "the masses" (Turovskaia mentions that the woman had a bag of groceries with her, as if to highlight her status as a commoner)—mirrors the reception of the film, and that of many other "*churros*"[17] like it, in Mexico. And it would be repeated regularly in the late Soviet era following *Yesenia*—in the reception of the Indian megahit *Disco Dancer* (1982, released in the Soviet Union in 1984) and several other Indian and Egyptian films, and even more intensely with the Brazilian TV series *The Slave Isaura* (*A Escrava Isaura*, Globo, 1976, screened in the Soviet Union in 1988; hereon *Isaura*). The mass reaction to this kind of melodrama reached fever pitch with the Mexican telenovela *Los ricos también lloran* (1979–80, broadcast in Russia in 1991).[18] *Yesenia* fits comfortably within this larger sentimentalist media corpus—all produced by major film/TV industries of the Global South, explicitly intended for popular consumption by "naïve" or "earnest" audiences (that is to say, lower-class viewers, presumed to be largely uneducated, at least when it comes to film aesthetic criteria), all heavily engaging the melodramatic mode.[19]

Yesenia's triumph in the Soviet Union seems to form an exception to the assumption within global film history that, by the 1970s and 1980s, film melodrama became emptied of its impact, increasingly an object of, at best, camp following. Furthermore, the popularity of *Yesenia* and of other genre films from the Global South appears to contradict the well-established Russo-Soviet cultural orientation toward the West, as viewed by both the Soviet cinema policymakers at the time and cultural historians since.[20] And yet, it appears that the antics of a Mexican "gypsy" appealed more to the Soviet audiences than the sophisticated cool of Audrey Hepburn (who starred in *How to Steal a Million*, 1966, which was screened the same year but was largely unnoticed by most moviegoers).[21] The earnestness of late Soviet *Yesenia* fans is striking, too: while authenticity and sincerity were the catchwords of the Soviet Thaw culture of the late 1950s and early 1960s, the period of the 1970s and 1980s, often referred to as Stagnation, is usually associated with the culture of ironic distanciation.[22] Such an affective regime seems at odds with the intensity of emotional identification that was witnessed by Turovskaia and expressed in fan letters sent to film magazines of the time, and repeated in present-day YouTube user comments.[23]

This question that so troubled the Soviet critic—why *Yesenia* found such powerful resonance among late Soviet audiences—would be raised by the film establishment over and over again throughout the late 1970s and 1980s. It is one that animates this inquiry as well. What did Soviet audiences cry over when they watched *Yesenia*—what were they responding to, and why? And, beyond the experience of the Soviet viewers, how can we understand the distribution flow between the Soviet Union and Mexico (and Latin American film and television industries more broadly, soon extending to Brazil and elsewhere)? Its shared affective space reveals, I argue, common underlying cultural mechanisms of responses to the global post-1968 crisis in Mexico and the Soviet Union. At the same time, I see it as activating a profound, if politically highly ambivalent, set of cultural intimacies set in motion through these networks.

Of course, *Yesenia*'s popularity was not merely a question of preferences on the part of the audience. First of all, it was determined by the choice of film imports by Soviet state organizations, which had already realized that the increased presence of melodramas from Asia (India and Egypt) could sell more tickets without undermining any fundamental ideological principles. *Yesenia* was bought for $20,000 with no percentages or royalties, and its box office success demonstrated a clear commercial gain from this film import policy. Hollywood films, even the old ones, were considerably more expensive and their distribution agreements were reciprocal, requiring exporting an equal number of Soviet films, which most Western distributors were not commercially motivated to accept. Moreover, many films from "developing countries" (such as India and Egypt—albeit not Mexico) were frequently imported into the Soviet Union through barter exchanges, which were favorable to both sides.[24] Ideologically, it was also considerably easier for the Soviet agencies to justify such frivolous (if extremely profitable) cinematic choices by alluding to their anti-imperialist elements, which were easy to find in most postcolonial narratives, including Mexico's abundant revolutionary iconography.

In other words, to some extent the popularity of Latin American, Indian, and Egyptian melodramas over their Hollywood or European counterparts in the Soviet Union was simply due to the latter's predominance on Soviet screens.[25] And yet, when it came to genres, which heavily rely on emotional identification, films from the Global South consistently proved to be more accessible to Soviet audiences than their Western counterparts, their affective translatability more powerful, their "structure of feeling" more successful in mediating the conflicts and changes people were experiencing—some of which were apparent at the time, others of which we may see more clearly now.

In what follows, this chapter begins my analysis of the film by first sketching out the broader context for its production and its subsequent distribution in the Soviet Union in the midst of the intensification of Soviet-Mexican political and cultural relations in the 1970s. In order to understand *Yesenia*'s production history as reflecting broader Mexican cultural and political dynamics, I further draw on its intermedial genealogy within women's literary and graphic culture and the rise of the telenovela.

MEXICAN BACKGROUND

Virtually every account of Mexico in the 1970s describes it as being in a state of crisis, undergoing a series of dramatic transformations in response to the aftermath of the political turmoil of the global 1960s and the start of economic decline, after decades of growth and stability. The decade was marked by loss of state legitimacy exacerbated by the repercussions of the Tlatelolco student massacre of 1968 and the subsequent dirty war fought by the state against Mexican leftists, the failure of the leading party (PRI) to produce the policy of social and economic cohesion promised by revolutionary nationalism, and the increasing cultural and political segmentation that emerged in tandem with that failure. The rise of counterculture and women's movements gained increasing importance—both offering an alternative to the mainstream culture and being reluctantly incorporated into it.[26]

The figures of failure and crisis permeating historical discourses on (and of) the 1970s likewise pertain to Mexican cinema.[27] If the Golden Age of the 1940s and 1950s offered a powerful projection of a unified and triumphalist nationalist mythology, 1970s film culture in Mexico visualized the country's increasing political fragmentation and "the rupture of the social contract."[28] For one thing, the period saw the significant emergence of the cinema of "independents"—such as Jorge Fons, José Estrada, and Felipe Cazals—which emphasized the sense of social alienation and ultimately demonstrated the "impossibility of the construction of a collective subject of Mexican politics."[29] At the other end of the spectrum, the predominance of the "low" cinematic genres decried by critics and the intelligentsia resonated with the local audiences, symptomatically addressing and at times subverting the normative system of representation, in particular when it came to racial and gender norms.

The presidency of Luis Echeverría Álvarez (1970–76), who placed his brother Rodolfo in charge of the state film institutions, was characterized by a significant increase in state support of the industry: out of the 437 films produced during that period, 116 were financed with state resources.[30] This meant that after decades of impenetrability of the film industry, dominated by the same figures, the younger, more creative and politically minded filmmakers were given opportunities, with a relative lack of censorship. This support was part of the larger political project: Echeverría was eager to project an image of someone who, unlike his predecessor, was capable of connecting equally with the young, educated, leftist elites (de facto diverting attention from his responsibility for the Tlatelolco massacre), the working class, and the peasantry. His support for the young political filmmakers was part of demonstrating his "ability to speak the language of the intelligentsia's Marxist critique of global capitalism and structural inequalities," as his populist appeal relied on embracing Third-Worldist rhetoric and reorienting his international policy toward greater multipolarity within the Cold War order.[31]

Eager to establish or reinforce Mexico's relations with countries across Latin America, Africa, Asia, and the Soviet Bloc, Echeverría was the first Mexican president to make official visits to Cuba, China, and the Soviet Union. This brought about a dramatic increase in Mexico's political, economic, and cultural ties with the Soviet Union over the course of his presidency, with a new favorable trade agreement and a mixed trade commission set up in 1973, as part of the president's visit.[32] The Soviet-Mexican Cultural Association, set up in 1966, also drastically increased its activities in the next decade, and there were more overall contacts between the two countries between 1973 and 1978 than in the whole postwar period, including those between the state-supported film institutions.[33]

The cinematic exchanges continued even when Echeverría's successor, José López Portillo, in 1976 placed his sister Margarita in control of the newly unified Dirección General de Radio, Televisión y Cinematografía, marking a significant reversal of Echeverría's policies more generally, and of film policies in particular (notably without breaking with the fine tradition of nepotism). Singularly hated by the film community for her ill-informed bureaucratic and authoritarian style of management, lack of interest in art cinema, and resulting defunding of the state film apparatus, Margarita López Portillo aggressively pursued commercial contacts with other national industries, especially those with potential for coproductions. The Soviet Union's film industry was one of the few that eagerly responded, thus furthering cinematic commerce between the two nations.[34] Despite President López Portillo's fervent anti-communism—aggravated by the infamous attempted kidnapping of Margarita by radical guerrilla group Liga Comunista 23 de Septiembre (or September 23rd Communist League) in 1976, whose repercussions included severe governmental repressions leading to the total annihilation of the Liga—the mutual commercial interests between the Mexican and Soviet film industries trumped all ideological considerations.[35] In 1978, Margarita even participated in the Moscow International Film Festival and took part in celebrating the jubilee of both the Russian and Mexican revolutions and the release of Sergei Eisenstein's (newly reedited) *¡Qué viva México!* as iconic of both. She used this as an opportunity to negotiate for a new Soviet-Mexican film coproduction (it would end up including Italy as well), which resulted in a large-budget, two-part epic flop based on John Reed's Mexican revolution reportage, released as *Las Campanas Rojas* (*The Red Bells*, Sergei Bondarchuk, 1981–83).

SOVIET-MEXICAN EXCHANGES
AND CULTURAL DIPLOMACY

In short, with the US-Soviet détente and the simultaneous reorientation of Echeverría's geopolitics, and due to mutual commercial interests within their respective film industries, the 1970s were a period of unprecedented expansion of cinematic exchanges between the two countries. As in so many other aspects of both countries' cultural establishments, they tended to rely on informal networks and existing personal and familial relationships that overlapped with the institutional structures.

On the Soviet side, the Soviet-Mexican Cultural Association was headed by Lev Kulidzhanov, a celebrated filmmaker and one of the leading figures in the Union of Soviet Filmmakers. His role in the association both underscored and enhanced the importance of cinema as one of the privileged venues for Soviet-Mexican exchanges. The Filmmakers' Union (unlike the umbrella organization for Soviet cinema, Goskino) was a progressive group, genuinely dedicated to the development of Soviet cinema and to its internationalization, as well as to improving conditions for its members' creative work—and Kulidzhanov, despite his numerous official Party-affiliated positions, was well liked within the cinematic intelligentsia.[36] A regular lecturer at the Moscow Film Institute (VGIK), he cultivated relationships in particular with the older generation of Mexican muralist artists with ties to the Soviet Bloc, such as David Alfaro Siqueiros and Guillermo Chávez Vega.

Another important mediator between the Mexican and Soviet cinematic spheres was the director Sergio Olhovich, who studied cinema at the VGIK between 1961 and 1969. After graduating and moving back to Mexico in 1969, he became increasingly involved in film production politics, tirelessly advocating an easier entry into the industry and support for the new generation of filmmakers. Olhovich also founded Cinematográfica Marco Polo, a production company that promoted the work of the new politically minded directors, and in 1975, along with Paul Leduc, Felipe Cazals, Miguel Littin, and several others, he founded the group National Front of Cinematographers, whose manifesto was closely aligned with the political and aesthetic spirit of the New Latin American Cinema. In the course of the decade, Olhovich remained in close contact with the Soviet film institutions, promoting his vision of politically conscious Mexican cinema and supporting Rodolfo Echeverría's initiatives.[37]

And indeed, in both 1972 and 1976, the "weeks of Mexican cinema" in the Soviet Union featured almost exclusively New Mexican Cinema's films of social critique, including Olhovich's own, which were consistently praised by Soviet critics.[38] Many of the same directors were simultaneously featured in the Moscow International Film Festival and the Tashkent Festival of Cinemas of Asia and Africa—contributing to the official inclusion (in 1976) of Latin America in that festival's purview. Olhovich's 1974 film *El encuentro de un hombre solo* was enthusiastically received at Tashkent, and the following year his next film, *La casa del Sur* (1975), was entered in the Moscow Film Festival, where Lev Kulidzhanov handed him one of the awards. Virtually unknown anywhere else, Olhovich's films were frequently reviewed in the Soviet press, hailed as evidence of the increasing social and political engagement of Mexican cinema and the success of public-sector filmmaking.

A very different, but equally active, cultural ambassador of Mexico to the Socialist Bloc was Sonia Amelio, who found fame as an internationally celebrated dancer (of both classical and folkloric traditions), pianist, and actress. Her father,

Salvador Amelio García, was the director of the state film distribution company Peliculas Nacionales, which, among other things, worked with the Soviet film export agency bringing Soviet films to Mexican screens.[39] Amelio García was also one of the founders of the pro-communist Partido Popular in the 1940s, and it was through his friends in the Soviet film export agency that arrangements were made for Sonia to tour the Soviet Union in the 1960s and put her in close contact with the Soviet artistic elite.[40] In 1967 she participated in the Moscow Film Festival, where she presented her cinematic debut in Emilio Fernández's *Un dorado de Pancho Villa* (1967).

Parallel to her ballet and music career, from 1972 to 1974 Amelio also acted in the telenovela *Los Hermanos Coraje*, costarring Jorge Lavat, the lead male protagonist of *Yesenia*.[41] But in 1972 she took time off from her shooting schedule to accompany Rodolfo Echeverría as part of an official visit for the opening of the "weeks of Mexican cinema" in Moscow, Leningrad, and Tbilisi. She also attended the Tashkent festival that year, where she was keen to solidify plans for a Soviet-Mexican coproduction, in which she intended to star. The project was to be directed by the celebrated Soviet filmmaker Sergei Gerasimov, filmed in both countries, and produced in cooperation with Peliculas Nacionales.[42] While this large-scale project never came to fruition, Amelio made cameo appearances in Soviet films produced at the time and continued to participate in Soviet-Mexican exchanges for the duration of the decade. She thus perfectly embodied all the prevalent aspects of cultural diplomacy, combining high-level state and commercial connections as well as classical, folkloric, and popular genres focused on music, dance, film, and eventually television.

These Soviet-Mexican cultural mediators, however, presented very different cultural and political positions. Sonia Amelio's folklorically inflected vision of Mexican culture was at direct odds with that of Olhovich. As part of his participation in the subsequent 1974 edition of the Tashkent festival, he pleaded with the Soviet organizers to only support "serious" Mexican cinema made by the independents, instead of buying and exhibiting the products of the commercial studios, "banal movies with guitars, songs, dances, and horse riding."[43] And yet, at the same festival, the most visible Mexican guests, appearing in numerous photos as part of the festival coverage and fondly remembered by the Soviet participants, were Amelio's friends: Susana Dosamantes, who was best known for acting in telenovelas and film adaptations of another famous historieta, *Kalimán*; and Alicia Encinas, the star of several telenovelas, whose career was advanced by the newly founded Televisa producer Valentín Pimstein.[44] Both Dosamantes and Encinas were there to promote their films for Soviet commercial distribution. The following year, Mexico was represented at Tashkent by actress and singer Isela Vega, another sex symbol of the period, best known for posing in *Playboy* and being an activist for nudity (celebrated now as a symbol of libertarianism and transgression of the Mexican film scene of the time). While their performance histories were

FIGURE 5. Embodying *lo Mexicano*: Susana Dosamantes and Alicia Encinas at Tashkent, 1974. Personal collection.

largely unknown to the Soviet festival organizers, the actresses' much-documented participation at the festival was always memorable and certainly contributed to associations of Mexican cinema not only with horse riding but with striking—and strikingly liberated, especially by Soviet standards—female leads.

However, in choosing Mexican films for wide exhibition, Soviet distributors faced particular challenges. Not only was politically driven cinema considerably less popular with audiences, but when it came to depictions of nudity and sexuality, much of Mexican cinema in the 1970s—whether the socially conscious or the popular—was much too risqué for the highly rigid Soviet norms. Virtually the only genres that could be counted on for popularity without presenting problems to the Soviet censors were children's films and historical musicals and melodramas. And, of course, these were especially likely to include "guitars, songs, dances, and horse riding" (and, as importantly, attractive but fully dressed female actresses as protagonists). To justify the inclusion of such genre films at festivals, Soviet reviewers' faint praise emphasized their connection to the Mexican cinema of the Golden Age and their "unique connection to genuine folklore: . . . deeply nationalist, exciting and touching . . . attracting viewers not by their logical analysis but their capacity to evoke emotions."[45] As a result, already in the 1970s, virtually all the Mexican films purchased for commercial distribution in the Soviet Union were exactly the kind of popular films that Olhovich campaigned against.[46]

It is easy to see how *Yesenia* fit the bill for what the Soviet distributors were looking for in a Mexican movie: in addition to its evident "capacity to evoke emotions," the film was undoubtably "deeply nationalist" as well—with its setting during the Maximilian period of Mexico's nineteenth century celebrating Benito Juarez's antimonarchist liberal ideology. In fact, the setting of films in this earlier, proto-revolutionary moment in Mexican history appeared to offer a perfect compromise endowed with ironclad nationalist revolutionary credentials. Thus, the winner of a Special Prize at the Moscow Film Festival in 1973, Felipe Cazals's historical drama *Those Years* (*Aquellos años*, 1972)—while diametrically opposed to *Yesenia* in its stark cinematic and narrative style, as well as its political poignancy—takes place during the same historical moment. This is also the case with another high-grossing Mexican import, *The Mushroom Man* (*El hombre de los hongos*, Roberto Gavaldón, 1976), which earned 27.3 million Soviet viewers in the first year of its exhibition.[47]

These three films—*Those Years, The Mushroom Man*, and *Yesenia*—set in the same iconic period of Mexican history give a comprehensive glimpse of the diverse cinematic formations at play in 1970s Mexico. Cazals was the best-known auteur of independent political cinema, and his film was a denunciation of the reified iconography of the Mexican Revolution. Gavaldón, one of the last remaining filmmakers of the Golden Age era, was experimenting with countercultural influences, and his film's antiracist, anticolonialist message is filtered through an unmistakably psychedelic aesthetics. And Alfredo B. Crevenna, despite having started making films in the 1950s and directing a number of popular melodramas, by the 1970s was associated with low commercial genres (having directed two other films— *La satanica* and *Santo y el Aguila real*—the same year he made *Yesenia*).[48] Yet all three are ostensibly historical films rooted in one of the foundational moments for Mexican nationalist discourse—demonstrating the same kind of continuous engagement with the historical revolutionary iconography that resonated with both Soviet audiences' expectations of the exoticism of Mexican culture and their intimate familiarity with their own Soviet "historical-revolutionary" film genre.

Evidently, the commercial interests that bound together the Soviet and Mexican sides carried more weight than the aesthetic ideology or Marxist economic critiques voiced by Olhovich. As Echeverría's presidency came to an end in 1976 and Margarita López Portillo assumed the reins of the Mexican film apparatus, positions like Olhovich's became further marginalized, and commercial cinema came back to center stage, making *Yesenia* the paradigmatic winner not only of the Soviet market, but of the Mexican media industry.[49] Only when the Chinese delegation visiting Mexico in 1976 approached Jorge Lavat requesting copies of the film to be screened in China did the Mexican film establishment find out about *Yesenia*'s popularity abroad—but without coming to terms with its true scale.[50] While the immense success of *Yesenia* in the Soviet Union and its considerable revenues were never made public in Mexico, that success led to the film's subsequent distribution in China, and to the subsequent arrival of telenovelas on socialist screens, securing the international positions of the same commercial industries that filmmakers like Olhovich dedicated their lives to fighting.

SOVIET BACKGROUND

To understand this seeming contradiction between the political demands of a socialist state and its choice of film imports, we need to turn to the changes within the Soviet cinematic institutions. Just as Echeverría's policies were an attempt to placate the political crisis of 1968 in Mexico, the intensification of official political rhetoric and artistic censorship around the 1968 Soviet/Warsaw Pact invasion of Czechoslovakia created a sense of deep crisis within the Soviet film industry and culture at large. In 1972, when Filipp Ermash became the new head of Goskino, the state organization in charge of cinema, his policy was to look for a compromise between the Party and the filmmakers, who were particularly concerned with their films being rejected due to censorship, before or after they were made. Ermash's solution was to favor "lighter" fare in both film production and exports: such films raised fewer objections "from above," giving more opportunities to filmmakers, and thus minimizing conflicts.[51]

This ideological compromise perfectly suited Sovexportfilm, as by then the commercial advantages of exhibiting foreign entertainment-driven cinema—especially if it could be purchased inexpensively—had become obvious. Since "serious" films, whether Soviet or foreign, came under closer political scrutiny, in the course of the 1970s the exhibition of foreign films came to be dominated by Italian and French comedies supported by their respective communist parties, a handful of older US and British genre films (prohibitive costs prevented importing the more recent ones), and an even greater mix of Indian, Egyptian, and Mexican movies, in addition to a considerable number of Soviet comedies, musicals, and, increasingly, melodramas.[52] As ticket sales for domestic production consistently fell behind what was planned by the state (which always set unrealistic goals), this further encouraged turning to the commercially popular imports. This even led to the informal practice, among local theater administrators, of switching the screenings, showing foreign films instead of the less popular Soviet or Eastern European ones that were scheduled, as the only sure way for local theaters to increase revenues.[53] With foreign commercial cinema in high demand, mid-1970s Mexico, whose film exports were at their all-time low, was a natural business partner.

The exhibition of foreign cinema was thus divided into the screening of more "serious" cinema as part of festivals, retrospectives, and "weeks of foreign cinema," with wide commercial film exhibition increasingly relying on genre films, furthering the audience segmentation between the urban intelligentsia and the rest.[54] This emerging fragmentation into "high" and "low" cinematic forms signaled the end of the relative cultural cohesion of the Stalinist and Thaw periods, when cinema served as a space for working through shared national preoccupations, projecting a space of common belonging. This shift signaled one of the facets of the crisis of the official culture as an extension of nation-state ideology and the increasing appeal of impinging forms of commercial mass culture. The history of *Yesenia*'s production will further articulate the Mexican specificities of this dynamic.

YESENIA

Although Turovskaia's summary of the plot, which opens this chapter, captures the gist of *Yesenia*, it is worth outlining it in slightly greater detail here.

Yesenia is a beautiful, spirited Roma who lives in a caravan with her mother and grandmother. She falls in love with an officer named Oswaldo, who has just sworn allegiance to Benito Juarez. Oswaldo asks the patriarch of her community for permission to marry Yesenia. At that point, the grandmother reveals to the patriarch that Yesenia was adopted from a noble family, whose daughter eloped and gave birth to a child, who wasn't accepted by her family. As the only proof of her parentage, she was given a Virgin of Guadalupe locket. Yesenia and Oswaldo get married under Romani law—but the society doesn't accept them. When Oswaldo is recalled to army action and is captured by the enemy, Yesenia is left alone and is led to believe that Oswaldo abandoned her. Brokenhearted, she returns to her caravan. Oswaldo comes back and finds out that Yesenia left him—in despair, he proposes marriage to the granddaughter of his godfather, Luisa. Yesenia and Oswaldo meet again, and at the same time Yesenia discovers her true family—and that Luisa is her half-sister. Yesenia is accepted into her ancestral home and renounces Oswaldo, sacrificing her love for the sake of her newly found sister. But Luisa, who has an incurable heart condition, finds out about Oswaldo and Yesenia's love and leaves for Europe—and the two lovers get married before the altar of the Virgin of Guadalupe, to the outrage of bigots, while outside the church, Yesenia's Romani family throws a celebration.

Filmed in just over a month and released five months later, in November 1971, *Yesenia* had its pre-premiere in Cine Rex. It was part of the celebration of that movie theater's much-lauded restoration, intended as a demonstration of the new administration's commitment to the modernization of the film apparatus, including its exhibition sector.[55] The film's official opening was in Olimpia, the oldest movie theater in Mexico City, associated with the splendor of the early days of cinema, where it played for four weeks to decent box office success.[56] This success was, without a doubt, due to the fact that Yesenia was already well known in Mexico, as the heroine of immensely popular romance graphic novels and the eponymous telenovela, which was screened on Mexican TV just the previous year. In fact, the speed of the movie's production was no doubt geared toward capitalizing on this connection. The film's cast was initially meant to be the same as that of the telenovela, but at the last moment Fanny Cano, who played Yesenia on TV, became unavailable due to undergoing a "surgical intervention" in the US. She had to be replaced by relative newcomer Jacqueline Andere, which generated much gossip as to the true reasons for this switch.[57] Yolanda Vargas Dulché, the author of the *Yesenia* franchise, including the script for both the telenovela and the film, blamed the comparative lack of success of the latter on this replacement: the audiences, she claimed, "fall in love with a character and do not admit any changes."[58]

At the same time, as noted by Emilio García Riera, the speed with which the film was made was also characteristic of the industry's general attempt to increase production at minimal costs regardless of the results.[59] Such an accelerated schedule was itself a reflection of the emerging dominance of industrial practices associated with the production of telenovelas. As such, it signaled a broader shift within the Mexican commercial cinema of the 1960s and 1970s—and the Mexican cultural industry at large—in its orientation toward private television, as embodied in the establishment of Televisa in 1973.[60]

Yesenia embodied this shift on every level. The original 1970 TV version was produced by Valentín Pimstein, whose career in Mexico began in the 1950s with the second-ever telenovela made in Mexico, *Gutierritos* (1958). Pimstein would become the leading figure in the fiction branch of Televisa throughout the 1970s, 1980s, and 1990s. It was he who set the standard for industrial telenovela production in Mexico, responsible for Televisa's status as one of the two leading producers (alongside the Brazilian Globo) of serialized television shows in the world during those decades. Crevenna had been part of that history as well, as he had been involved in the very first adaptations of telenovelas to cinema: *Gutierritos* (1959); *Teresa* (1961), based on the 1959 telenovela, also produced by Pimstein; and *Senda prohibida* (1961), the film version of the very first telenovela ever produced in Mexico.[61]

Pimstein was a close friend of Emilio Azcárraga Milmo, a member of one of Mexico's most powerful media clans, the owner of Churubusco Studios (where *Yesenia* was filmed), and, eventually, founder and owner of Televisa. Azcárraga, better known as "El Tigre," in the 1970s would become one of Mexico's most influential businessmen, directly responsible for the massive integration of Mexican cultural industries—cinema, music, news, magazine and book publishing, talent agencies, and so on—under the Televisa umbrella, making it the most powerful media conglomerate and a major expression of cultural and political hegemony in Mexico.[62] Pimstein came to Mexico from Chile with ambitions of becoming a cinema producer and was initially resistant to the lure of the television market. As recounted by Claudia Fernandez and Andrew Paxman in Azcárraga's biography, El Tigre finally convinced Pimstein to work with him by not only lending him money for paying off the gambling debts but also putting a down payment on his house. This evidently convinced Pimstein to produce the

FIGURE 6. The garish colors of *Yesenia*.

first telenovela for Azcárraga's TV company TSM, *Murallas blancas* (1960), successfully finding sponsorship by Colgate-Palmolive, and to stay by Azcárraga's side for the duration of his career.[63]

Yesenia's relationship to the increasing dominance of the telenovela aesthetics did not escape the attention of Mexican film critics.[64] Indeed, the summary of the film given by García Riera in his *Historia documental del cine mexicano* (which remains virtually its only review in Mexico) perfectly reflects attitudes apparently shared on both sides of the Atlantic: "Filmed as part of an overproduction plan, with its ugly colors, uneven mise-en-scene, apathetic actors and an even more apathetic and clumsy director . . . *Yesenia*, a long soap opera (*culebrón*) with infinite dialogues clarifying conflicting relationships, is worthy of reproaches that are more boring than indignant."[65]

Curiously, the color scheme of the film—indeed very gaudy, especially by the standards of 1970s independent cinema—was likely one of the reasons for its attractiveness to Soviet audiences. It was in sharp contrast to the "unforgettable greenish palette" of most domestic films of the same period, which resulted from the quality of color film stock produced by the Soviet factory Svema, which made even the most vibrant mise-en-scène appear drab.[66] As we will see later in this book, the film's colorful costumes, in particular, contribute to its success with both Soviet and Chinese audiences.

Both the telenovela's and the film's appeal in Mexico, on the other hand, rested on audiences' familiarity with the character of Yesenia from the women's graphic romances (historietas) written by the most prolific and celebrated author of this genre, Yolanda Vargas Dulché. In its graphic novel form, *Yesenia* was part of one of the most popular series in the country, *Lágrimas, risas y amor*, which in the 1970s was still selling over six million copies monthly.[67] And Vargas Dulché was involved in writing the script (or libretto) for both the telenovela and the film. Her relationship with Pimstein and telenovelas went back to 1966, when her other popular historieta, *María Isabel*, was first adapted for Azcárraga's company TSM, lauded for "introducing the new social custom of integrating señoras and their female servants" as part of the same TV viewership.[68] Pimstein was well known for cultivating relationships with successful writers to integrate literature into television scripts. This was equally true for the popular genres as it was for classics, and intended to provide additional cultural cachet for productions while enabling a tighter synergy among the different parts of cultural industries—and historietas were a particularly commercially successful sphere.[69]

Reflecting on the announcement in 1971 that *Yesenia*, which had just finished its run as a telenovela, was being made into a film, one critic sarcastically reflected on the prevalence of Vargas Dulché's and other women writers' romantic creations in the mediasphere: "There should be a law preventing the public from such abuses, otherwise some historian of the twenty-third century without a doubt will be led to enlist in its discussion of the greatest problems of our epoch 'Simplemente María' and 'Yesenia.'"[70] The critic's prediction, however, came true considerably earlier than in the twenty-third century. *Yesenia* would have yet another incarnation as a Televisa telenovela in 1982. And *Simplemente María*—here referring to a highly popular Peruvian 1969 telenovela version, popular in Mexico at the time, based on the romantic novel by an Argentinian woman writer Celia Alcántara—would be remade by Televisa in 1989 (and again in 2015). Alongside *Los ricos también lloran*, the 1989 Mexican version of *Simplemente María* would prove to be such a resounding success with post-Soviet audiences in the 1990s that Belarusian biologists would name a new pear variety after it, and Victoria Ruffo's telenovela heroine would be transformed into one of the main (male) characters of the notorious 1996 postmodernist novel *Chapaev i Pustota* (*Chapaev and the Void*) by Victor Pelevin.

Given that the author of the sarcastic comments, Tomás Perrín, was in charge of advertising and marketing publicity, his mocking of "low women's genres"—historically so closely connected to the very trade he belonged to—appears at best hypocritical. And yet, to understand the persistent impact of women's romantic writings and the historietas, telenovelas, and films associated with them on cultural life in Mexico and elsewhere—an impact evidenced by

Yesenia's enormous success in the Soviet Union—we need to undertake a brief historical detour into their origins in the earlier part of the twentieth century, the ideological functions they served, and the cultural niche they occupied for many subsequent decades.

HISTORIETAS

The origins of historietas—comics generally, and serialized, weekly, pocketbook-size graphic romances in particular—are rooted in the period of literacy campaigns and "socialist" (public) education of 1930s Mexico. Those efforts were accompanied by an explosion of illustrated magazines, various kinds of comic books, and other hybrid written and visual forms, all of which contributed to enhancing literacy and the formation of a shared, modern, mass national-popular culture.[71] Revolutionary modernity, state progress, and the creation of reading publics were thus linked, and, as Anne Rubenstein explores, for women, reading historietas in the postrevolutionary decades was both a public form of participation in this revolutionary culture and an alternative to its more institutionalized didactic narratives. This was especially important in that the inclusion of women as both major targets and disseminators of public education in all its forms was one of the campaigns' big goals. But it was met with a unified conservative resistance, a push-back that took different forms, "from mild satire to burning of rural schoolhouses and the murder of teachers."[72] As such, historietas formed a major sphere of mediation between the state ideology and vernacular cultural norms with their more traditional conception of gender norms. They were an important interface between audiences and the public sphere, with readers, especially female readers, frequently writing letters to the publishers to share their reactions and opinions.[73] And they were also an early and remarkably tenacious product of a distinctly women's cultural sphere—partaking in *estéticas cursis*, or "corny aesthetics"—a notion to which we will return at greater length in chapter 3.[74] Associated with feminine and lowbrow to middlebrow taste formations, this aesthetic extended to various genres of "women's culture"— from novels to women's magazines, telenovelas, and historietas. These were also the areas of cultural production where women could be authors within an entirely male-dominated literary field, as demonstrated by the careers of both Fernanda Villeli, the author of *Senda prohibida* (the historieta that was made into the first Mexican telenovela in 1958, as well as a film, directed by Crevenna ten years before *Yesenia*, in 1961), and Vargas Dulché, the author of *Yesenia*.

Vargas Dulché came from a lineage of women writers: her mother was a journalist and her aunt, Catalina D'Erzell, was a famous author of radio novels (one of the generic prototypes of telenovelas). Vargas Dulché was highly educated and spoke French and English. She began her career working for Emilio Azcárraga Vidaurreta, the father of Emilio Azcárraga Milmo, on the radio station he owned, XEW-AM, first singing popular romantic songs (boleros) by iconic performers like Agustín Lara, Pedro Vargas, and Toña la Negra and then forming a duo with her sister and even perhaps performing with Lara himself.

Eventually, she started supplementing her income from singing by writing radio plays, movie scripts, and historietas—all sharing the same romantic melodramatic sensibility, recognizable as much in the boleros she sang as in the stories she wrote and illustrated. As her writing achieved increasing popularity, Vargas Dulché became not only fully financially independent, but together with her husband (and coauthor) she founded what would become one of the four major industrial groups producing comic books: Editorial Argumentos (later Grupo Editorial Vid), which captured 23 percent of the comic book market. Despite working closely with Televisa in the course of the 1970s and 1980s, Vargas Dulché exercised a great deal of creative control over the many transformations of her historietas into telenovelas and even managed to keep her publishing house independent (unlike the other two major publishers, Publicaciones Herrerias and Editorial Novaro, which were absorbed by the Televisa Novedades group).[75]

It is hard to overestimate the importance of historietas within the Mexican media environment of the early 1970s. According to some estimates, they were the second most popular mass medium after the radio, with television coming in a distant third.[76] Their production process led to an easy integration into television: Mexican historietas, before they are illustrated, resemble movie scripts, including full dialogue and detailed instructions for their visualization—making their adaptation to either film or television a rather seamless process.[77] Even as television became increasingly dominant over the course of the 1970s, production of historietas (and the derivative form called *photoroman*) tripled, reaching seventy million a month by the end of the decade.[78] And, despite the assumption that romantic historietas like the Vargas Dulché series *Lágrimas, risas y amor* were directed only at women, surveys conducted in the late 1970s suggest that although lower- and middle-class women readers were indeed in the majority, that series was read by literally everyone.[79]

In their negotiations of culturally dominant constructions of femininity, crucial for the *cursi* aesthetic and the historieta narrative mode has been the archetype of *la chica moderna*. As explored by Rubenstein and Joanne Hirschfeld, this culturally specific iteration of the "modern girl" was a figuration of the compromise between hegemonic, culturally conservative gender norms and the pressures of modernity that demanded a great deal of individual agency. *La chica moderna* was thus independent, especially in the choice of her romantic objects and in her willingness to stand up against certain social and communal norms of feminine behavior when following her passions. At the same time, she displayed traditional standards of sexual attractiveness and absolute compliance with heteronormative, monogamous romantic notions of love and the importance of family/motherhood.[80] And while this figure is particularly well known from Mexican and other Latin American cinemas of the Golden Age, the stakes of redefining the image of the modern woman "for the masses" were equally high in the 1970s, with the advent of the feminist movement in Mexico.

When asked in 1978 whether feminism left a mark in the telenovela genre that she helped define, Vargas Dulché unequivocally claimed that her heroines from the very beginning, well before the feminist movement of the 1970s, were liberated women. "My female characters who want to 'make it' do so!" she claimed, citing both Yesenia and María Isabel as examples.[81] "I have always tried to teach a lesson," she added, with a characteristic reference to literacy: "And I take honor in saying that *historietas* have taught the people to read better."[82] These claims of didactic intent were similarly furthered by her husband and coauthor, Guillermo de la Parra, who asserted that in their historietas (many of which traded in exoticized images of other cultures and included now-infamous racial representations bordering on caricature), they always attempted both to entertain and "to provide information on history, traditions and customs of other countries."[83]

However disingenuous such claims may seem, the impact of historieta-based telenovelas on literacy has repeatedly been affirmed in both personal accounts and the press—their popularity purportedly led to many women learning to read so that they could follow the stories in the original publications, should they ever miss an episode or want to revisit the intricacies of the plot.[84] Such attempts to endow historietas and telenovelas with a didactic mission and additional cultural capital were, indeed, not uncommon throughout the 1970s, when the government even issued an historieta advocating family planning as a way to improve the quality of life, appropriately titled *Una mejor vida* (A Better Life).[85] And connections to high literary culture were not uncommon either—thus, Televisa's first telenovela, *Cartas sin destino* (1973), also starring *Yesenia*'s Jacqueline Andere, was loosely based on Edmond Rostand's classic late-nineteenth-century romance *Cyrano de Bergerac*.

The next chapter will take a closer look at the various cultural institutions in Mexico and the Soviet Union that played the role of providing this kind of gendered sentimental education—and at the women who were usually framed as the recipients of such lessons—to understand the function of Yesenia as a global icon in this dual context.

Mexican and Soviet Womanhood, circa 1970

Having considered the context of *Yesenia*'s production in Mexico and its exhibition in the Soviet Union in chapter 1, the goal of this chapter is to locate the film against the background of political, social, and cultural changes for women in both countries. This chapter argues that in the context of the 1970s, the ideas of women's liberation mediated by mainstream and conservative cultural spheres—such as women's journals—played a key role in shaping Yesenia's image as a transnational icon. It explores the impact of sexual revolution in both Mexico and the Soviet Union as it intersected with the reemergence of the melodramatic regime and sentimental culture at large, albeit in a remediated form, reinforcing the essentialist notions of gender and female sexuality. Sentimental media, Lauren Berlant famously argued, creates a "culture of 'true feeling' . . . that sanctifies suffering as a relay to universality in a way that includes women in the universal while attaching the universal more fully to a generally lived experience."[1] To see how *Yesenia*'s transnational reception formed part of such a process, it is worth attending both to the realities of the lived experiences of women in Mexico and the Soviet Union and to how the notions of universalism or cosmopolitanism inflected gender discourses in both cases.

At first glance, women's lives in 1970s Mexico and the Soviet Union couldn't be more different. Statistical data provides an instructive glimpse here. Based on the 1970 census, the average Mexican woman had 7.3 kids, and at least half of women dedicated approximately twenty-five years of their lives to taking care of children. The divorce and separation rates were just above 2 percent, and abortion was illegal.[2] Twenty-one percent of women were illiterate, and 17.6 percent were part of the labor force. Fifteen percent of the students in secondary education were women.[3] The Catholic Church exercised a great deal of cultural and social control, especially in women's lives.

In the Soviet Union, by contrast, full participation in the labor force was mandated by the state, and almost 90 percent of able-bodied adult women were either employed or engaged in full-time study by the mid-1970s, which constituted 51 percent of the overall labor force.[4] Literacy rates were at 99.7 percent and the female-to-male ratio in higher education was at almost exact parity.[5] Women constituted three-fifths of the white-collar labor force.[6] The average length of a woman's employment in her lifetime was 33.5 years.[7] Abortion was legalized in the 1920s, and briefly prohibited during Stalin's regime. The divorce rate, at least in the European part of the country, was nearly 50 percent, and most divorces were initiated by women.[8] Not incidentally, women outnumbered men in the general population, as they had since the end of World War II. In 1950, there were 76 men for every 100 women, while by 1979 there were 122 men for every 144 women.[9]

Birth rates and population control were seen as matters of official priority in the 1970s in both countries, as part of the regime, which Michelle Murphy refers to as the "economization of life"—where, in the interest of the developmentalist paradigms of economic growth, the state's objective was to "designate and manage surplus aggregate life."[10] This was a crucial decade for decreases in birth rates and numbers of children for both Mexican and Soviet women. Yet this development was approached from opposite perspectives. In Mexico, it was the direct result of public policy concerned with overpopulation, the introduction of birth control, and legal changes introduced in 1974 that reformed article 4 of the Mexican Constitution. This new law provided equal rights to men and women, which included the rights of women to protect their family and decide on the number of children.[11] In the Soviet Union, on the other hand, increasingly low birth rates (in its European republics) were framed as a major "demographic crisis" that necessitated pronatalist measures, and increasingly more conservative gender policies and attitudes, which were largely embraced by the women themselves. Abortion was used as virtually the only form of birth control.[12]

The practices and attitudes toward women's participation in public life were similarly contrasting. In Mexico, the 1970s witnessed the institutionalization of women's movements and their impact on state policies, explicitly aimed at challenging the hegemonic gender norms. For the Soviet Union, it was an era of increased public awareness of persistent sexual discrimination despite legal (and, with some caveats, economic) equality between men and women, and further disillusionment with Soviet ideals of women's social and political agency. These developments, however, impacted social life in both countries in ways that were far from homogeneous, finding different manifestations within different classes and social groups and through different cultural forms.

At the same time, this period was marked by some shared cultural and social dynamics, of which the technocratic metrics reflecting the status of women within the broader political economy can give no indication. The rising public awareness of the "women's question" in both countries forced closer attention to subjective and personal experiences. This legitimized questions that were otherwise relegated to the private sphere and, thus, ignored or undermined within male-dominated official discourses. At the same time, this attention to women's private lives had the effect of reactivating gender essentialism, framed as a celebration of "authentic" and highly romanticized and sexualized femininity. Set out to challenge their respective hegemonic patriarchies, these representational models entered popular culture in a way that frequently led to reaffirmation of many crucial aspects of that same patriarchal order. Infused with the increasing appeal of international consumer culture, these changes set the stage for a distinctly neoliberal self-commodification. *Yesenia* as a cultural text positioned at the intersection of these shared dynamics fully embodies their multiple internal contradictions and conflicting cultural forces.

THE 1970s IN MEXICO: GENDER POLITICS

The 1970s in Mexico was undeniably a period of expansion for women's movements.

Women's liberation became a dominant motif of public practices and discourses, equally manifested in such seemingly diverse domains as religion (such as the radical program of the Roman Catholic Diocese of Cuernavaca, inspired by Marxism and liberation theology) and counterculture (with its open celebration of nudity, free love, and the lifting of gendered cultural taboos such as cursing). While their expressions were understood and practiced differently across the political and cultural spectrum, by the 1970s the demands for change in women's status and identity in Mexican culture and society nonetheless reached the mainstream. This was increasingly visible in the media: in 1971, Lolita Ayala became the first woman coanchor of television news (she moved to Televisa when it was founded two years later), a decision based on market research confirming the importance of women viewers and, consequently, women reporters.[13] Between 1970 and 1976, at least six major women's activist groups were formed, including Mujeres en Acción Solidaria in 1971, Movimiento Nacional de Mujeres in 1973, Movimiento de Liberación de la Mujer in 1974, and the latter's splinter group Colectivo la Revuelta y el Movimiento Feminista Mexicano. For the first time in Mexico's history, these groups were able to take an active part in shaping the country's public and political life.[14] By the end of the 1980s, not least through the efforts of small yet vocal activist groups—further enabled by the United Nations World Conference on Women, celebrating the International Women's Year, which took place in Mexico City in 1975—the disconnect between the social and political status of women in Mexico and those in the Soviet Union would not look nearly as stark.

As Eli Bartra notes, in the 1970s, the notion of "the women's condition"—understood as the realization that women's inferior social position was not a matter of individual circumstances but a collective and shared situation—came into focus and reached across the spectrums of class, politics, and culture.[15] At the same time, the 1975 UN World Conference, as Jocelyn Olcott explores at length, also highlighted conflicting notions of what constituted women's liberation, as argued by the various parties involved in the event.[16] State-socialist and Third-Worldist activists largely rejected questions of desire and sexuality as "bourgeois" and at odds with the overarching political goals of economic and political equality on a global scale. Many European and, especially, North American participants took the opposite position, refusing to engage with broader political and economic problems, which they considered beyond the scope of women's activism and pertaining to the male sphere of influence. Only the more radical women's groups, who admittedly constituted a minority within the conference, including those from Mexico, reframed the supposed "private" issues of queer identities, sex work, and family organization as inseparable from the global struggle against various forms of exploitation and violence. These diverse understandings of the goals of various women's movements at the time—and their reflection in the conference itself—led to vocal, highly publicized disagreements and outright conflicts.[17]

On the "bourgeois feminist" side of the conference, Betty Friedan represented the position that was equated with the US. On the other side of the divide was Domitila Barrios de Chúngara, a Bolivian tin miner's wife, known for her participation in one of the key films in New Latin American Cinema, *The Courage of the People* (*El coraje del pueblo*, Jorge Sanjinés, 1971), in which she famously reenacted her role during the 1967 army massacre of the miners. As an organizer of the Housewives' Committee—a women's organization that actively supported miners' unions and dealt with issues that directly affected women within that community—Domitila was an activist for economic justice. Skeptical of alliances with Western feminists and disdainful of their discourse on sexual rights (including those of sexual minorities), she saw them as undermining the economic and political rights for which she was struggling. She rejected the idea that questions of gender were articulated through sexuality, linking women's issues directly to social and economic geopolitical inequality.[18] In that perspective, she was joined by the women representatives of the Socialist Bloc, who together opposed what they perceived as a depoliticized version of women's liberation as sexual liberation, put forth by feminists like Friedan, emphasizing instead the need for socialist transformation, modernization, and progress. Their version of equality of the sexes, though articulated in highly technocratic terms, was based on highly conventional notions of sexual difference, as we'll see shortly.[19]

Mexican women activists occupied a somewhat ambivalent position within this confrontation. Demonstrating Mexico's proximity to its northern neighbor, they were considerably more impacted by the political and intellectual development within US feminism than many of their Latin American and/or Third-Worldist counterparts, and significantly more aligned with countercultural currents, also broadly associated with the US. As such, the rights of sex workers and sexual minorities, domestic violence, and general resistance to the culture of machismo were central to most Mexican women's activist platforms. At the same time, they were highly aware of issues of broader economic and geopolitical inequality as constitutive of patriarchy, making their position one of mediation between the two emergent currents at the Mexico City conference.

Overall, however, the event itself brought additional attention to both sets of issues confronting women in the country. And throughout the 1970s, the question of "women's condition" found an equally visible expression in the cultural sphere—from the reluctant but increasing inclusion of women writers within the literary establishment, preparing the stage for the *boom femenino* of the 1980s, to the interconnected circuit of television, movies, and women's magazines, all of which actively shaped public perceptions of appropriate models of femininity.[20]

WOMEN'S MAGAZINES IN MEXICO

One of the reflections of social and cultural changes and economic transformations in Mexico was the sharp increase in the number and general orientation of women's magazines in the 1970s, pointing to women's increased spending potential. Thus, in addition to the already existent *Claudia, Buenhogar,* and *Kena,* debuting in 1973 were *Nueva Vida, Bienestar, Cosmopolitan,* and *Fascinacion,* joined in 1975 by *Casa, Mujer, Ser Mujer,* and *Activa.* All of these magazines were geared toward women readers—primarily of the middle and upper-middle classes—and included a considerable amount of writing by women about women. They marketed a vision of the modern and increasingly "liberated" woman primarily through cosmopolitan consumer culture in its broadest definition—from fashion, cosmetics, design, food, and domestic products to luxury travel, vacations, and the book and music industries. At the same time, many saw their mandate in educating their readers, which entailed engaging in cultural and social debates on issues affecting women's lives. This didactic role is implicit even in their featured interviews with and articles on Mexican actresses and singers—including all the main protagonists of this book—as well as in their international coverage, which extended as far as the Socialist Bloc. In these magazines, we can decipher ongoing negotiations between notions of romantic love, marriage, sexuality, and femininity refracted in various domains.

The explosion of women's magazines in Mexico during the 1970s also marked the increasing corporate synergy of an integrated cultural industry and, more specifically, the growing power of Televisa as a cultural and media monopoly. Rómulo O'Farrill Sr., one of the owners of the publishing company behind *Claudia* and *Novedades* (the latter serving as a springboard for many aspiring women journalists, who regularly contributed to all the women's magazines at the time) was also one of the leading associates in Televisa (and TSM before it), and thus directly connected to the production of telenovelas.[21] It was O'Farrill who, in 1977, signed the first agreement between Televisa and the Soviet Union facilitating the broadcast of Mexican music programs on Soviet TV.[22] Provenemex, which published *Activa* and *Buena Vida*, also published *TV y Novelas* (since 1978) and *Historietas* (directed by Frank Calderon, the ex-director of *Cosmopolitan*).[23]

This media synergy effectively integrated women's cultural consumption—of magazines, novels, historietas, films, and telenovelas—within one shared field, even if the class and cultural identities of these outlets were very clearly marked and did not allow for as much slippage as one would imagine. For example, during much of the 1970s, *Kena* and *Claudia* included very few mentions of telenovelas (let alone historietas), as these were cultural objects presumably belonging to a different class and social milieu. Yet, much like historietas, melodramas, and telenovelas, despite their different class orientation, magazines such as *Claudia* and *Kena* constructed the image of a modern and "liberated" woman through modes of empowerment that could be contained within—while occasionally exceeding and renegotiating—traditional patriarchal norms. Self-fashioning through consumption offered a perfect outlet for such modes of empowerment.

As has certainly been the case historically throughout the twentieth century, these modes also explicitly engaged in mediations of national belonging and imaginaries of the global. In the coverage of foreign cinema and stars, for example, we see a significant overlap between changing notions of femininity and an orientation toward foreign models of culture: to be a cosmopolitan woman increasingly meant being a liberated woman, and vice versa. And despite the increasing politicization of gender issues (even conservative women's magazines began to frame women's conditions in relation to broader social and political developments), this notion of a liberated cosmopolitan woman was primarily framed through greater sexual agency and mediated through romantic tropes. Both sexual and romantic self-fashioning are ultimately realizable through consumption. The same dynamic is visible in cinema's and television's addresses to women, and even historietas addressed to lower-class readers gave many of their heroines culturally exotic—and yet relatable—identities that could be emulated through fashion and other forms of personal consumption; conversely, narratives of the humble heroine's transformation were also visualized through their increasingly more modern—and international—self-fashioning. But as underscored by Yolanda Vargas Dulché's comments quoted in chapter 1—"I have always tried to teach a lesson," and "*historietas* have taught the people to read better"—this self-fashioning was filtered through a highly didactic narrative of self-improvement.

The range of contributors to *Kena*, by far the most conservative of the women's magazines of the era, reflects both the diversity and the internal contradictions of the available positions on women's liberation. All three main contributors to the magazine in the late 1960s and early 1970s—Emma Godoy, Esperanza Brito de Martí, and Helen Krauze—were established women writers, were highly educated, and belonged to prominent and culturally elite families in Mexico. They were also part of the same sphere of literary production as the authors of romance novels and historietas, occupying the only space available for women writers in the male-dominated Mexican literary establishment during the period. In the 1960s, journalism became an increasingly available option for women writers but many of them still had to find their footing in publications that were associated with female cultural consumption. The three did not, however, share exactly the same political positions, including on women's issues. Brito (who became a major activist for women's reproductive rights in the 1970s) was decidedly more radical in her pronouncements, while the considerably more religiously conservative (and older) Godoy took a cautionary tone, reminding readers that the excesses of sexual freedom were dangerous. Krauze (the mother of Enrique Krauze, one of Mexico's leading liberal cultural brokers, and grandmother of Daniel Krauze, the writer of some of the most popular recent Televisa and Netflix Mexican TV series), on the other hand, limited her discussions of women's roles specifically to the area of arts and culture, steering clear of any direct associations with contemporary feminist positions. Overall, in the early 1970s, these magazines gave an impression of coming to terms with social changes. As *Kena*'s summary of its article "Love and Sex: Liberation or Subjugation?" clarifies, "this article doesn't censor or applaud the so-called 'sexual revolution' but rather confronts its existence."[24] And alongside the difficult topic of sexual liberation, the magazine's cover features two additional, apparently equally pressing queries: "Blond or Dark Hair? Secrets of a Good Hair Dye" and "When Should You Hit a Child?"[25]

But what is perhaps most striking in both *Kena* and *Claudia*—the two most widely read women's lifestyle magazines in the early 1970s—is not the diversity of their contributors' positions or the relentless focus on consumption (through fashion and cosmetics advice and advertisements), domestic arts (food recipes, DIY décor, and crafts), and various forms of "light" occult content (horoscopes, articles on magic, palm reading, Nostradamus's predictions, etc.), perfectly coexisting with occasional appeals to Catholicism. Instead, what consistently comes across is the emphasis on self-perfecting narratives as a way to bring out the social/political/ethical dimensions of women's culture—constructed as distinct and gender-specific. Not only are there regular sections dedicated to women in politics—mostly foreign in *Kena*, from Indira Gandhi to Golda Meir, and markedly more Mexican in *Claudia* (although still frequently featuring wives of politicians)—but even the discussions of fashion models, singers, and actresses often take a decidedly didactic turn.[26] Thus, a 1970 issue of *Kena* contains an article on the "Russian Twiggy," a twenty-two-year-old Muscovite named Galia Milovskaia, presenting her not just as a fashion model but as a model for self-improvement. She is contrasted with the "real" (British) Twiggy, who apparently was unable to adequately answer questions in an interview in the *Saturday Evening Post*. Conversely, in her responses to the same questions, Milovskaia speaks eloquently of her role as a cocreator of fashion,

FIGURE 7. "Russian Twiggy" in *Kena*, 1970. Hemeroteca Nacional de México.

her learning French, her plans to enter the foreign language institute to pursue a career as a translator, and her interest in politics ("How could anyone nowadays not be interested in politics?" she asks), thereby setting the cultural standards for other women's looks and behavior.[27] Similarly, an article about the former teen star, actress, and singer Angélica María (known as La Novia de México, Mexico's Sweetheart) in *Claudia* is titled "Angélica María Became Self-Aware," reflecting on her personal and social growth as a woman and a politically engaged artist.[28] In other words, women's culture and the agency of its protagonists are reclaimed as serious business—albeit via their most traditional cultural spheres.

Over the course of the decade, the articles in *Kena* and *Claudia* became more aligned with Mexican feminism, extending their discussions to topics such as how women can achieve financial independence, the benefits of entering the workforce, improved education for young girls and women to encourage aspirations beyond matrimony, fathers' responsibility not to undermine daughters' self-esteem, and, above all, mothers' responsibility for instilling new progressive values in sons. On the pages of these journals, women were encouraged to find their sexuality (usually within the confines of marriage—although curiosity about extramarital sex appears even in the most conservative articles on the subject) and to direct their husbands to provide pleasure and avoid harm. This is best illustrated by the statement, from an article in *Claudia*, that "in the present day, just as the woman is demanding the right to vote, she is demanding the right to have an orgasm."[29] This extension of the political and consumerist fields—framed as a matter of rights—was paradigmatic of the liberated subject as it emerged from the pages of women's magazines throughout the 1970s.

These various facets of self-realization were presented through a dense apparatus of consumer practices, most of which were highly sexualized. From fashion advice on how to achieve maximum femininity with "the new colors of intimacy" and "modern" styles of underwear[30] to cosmetic beauty tips for breast enlargement and other kinds of plastic surgery (advertisements for which were heavily featured even in *Kena* as early as 1969), advertising discourse was fully interwoven with articles that discussed the self-fashioning of a "real woman." A case in point is an advertisement for the "Institute of Personality: Elegance Paris," which offered classes in "the incredible art of increasing your personal attractiveness," covering topics such as the perfect wardrobe, makeup, hairdos for all occasions, and social comportment (the ad features a demure, silk-clad woman with Yesenia-style hair, elegantly holding a champagne glass).[31]

And if social modes of perfecting oneself, as the name Elegance Paris suggests (complete with an extra accent, just to underscore its "Frenchness"), were culturally and geographically specific, these same discourses on womanhood were underwritten by universalist scientific-medical frameworks like psychology and psychoanalysis (the latter much debated on the pages of these journals) and by references to cutting-edge medical practices, from plastic surgery to "scientific cosmetics." The latter advertised the use of innovative computer technologies to determine one's skin type, making even personal cosmetic preferences appear scientific.

A particularly striking articulation of such a combined approach is evidenced by a special issue of *Kena* in 1970 (the year the telenovela *Yesenia* aired) titled "Super-feminine Edition: Prohibited to Males."[32] The issue features an exposé on the possibilities of human parthenogenesis (reproduction without insemination), presented both as scientific proof of the accuracy of the Bible's notion of immaculate conception and of the seemingly boundless potentiality of womanhood; an interview with an electrical engineer who designs silicone breast implants titled "How to Get Precious Artificial Breasts: An Electrical Engineer Possesses the Secret of Many Beautiful Mexican Women's Beauty"; a fashion photo shoot titled "The Road to Liberty," with a caption claiming that "today's fashion allows women like never before to choose whatever best fits her personality," and, in its literary section, a translation of an excerpt from an essay penned by Margaret Anderson, under the title "Love. Love. Love: The False Woman and the Woman Woman."

The excerpt from Anderson's essay and its framing are a particularly telling illustration of what the editors promoted as "super-femininity" (as referred to in the title of this special issue). In an editorial, a staff writer explains that Anderson's goal in the essay is to define what constitutes the "complete woman" by using the writer George Sand as a cautionary tale illustrating its opposite, the "false woman." Sand, the editor claims, was unable to have fulfilling relationships because she was not sufficiently different from men, thus failing to achieve the complementarity of perfect soul mates. "A true woman is the other in her complete integrity," demanding the same from her lover, daring him "to live in an implacable realm of passion in which a true woman places her love," claims Anderson in this published excerpt.[33] The editor, unsurprisingly, fails to mention anything about Anderson herself. Considered one of the so-called New Women of the American literary establishment and openly a lesbian, she edited, together with her lover Jane Heap Anderson, the notorious radical literary magazine *The Little Review* (which, among other things, was charged with obscenity in 1918). In the 1930s, she became a devotee of the spiritual self-development teachings of the mystic and philosopher George Gurdjieff.[34] The article excerpting her essay, "Love. Love. Love [. . .]," failed to provide the crucial context—both in terms of sexual politics and religious beliefs—that would have conveyed Anderson's actual intent, which was to argue that Sand was "butch" and that therefore, to achieve "true universal unity" through love (one of Gurdjieff's key concepts), she needed a "femme" and not a man. The excerpt published in *Kena* instead serves to underscore the importance of heterosexual passion and femininity as key attributes of the "true woman." And, of course, this call for spiritual self-improvement was appropriately placed alongside an advertisement for breast enhancements.

The specific references to Sand and the inclusion of Anderson, however, served the additional purpose of pointing to a women's literary canon that is rooted in the legacy of the nineteenth-century sentimental social novel. This tradition indeed provides a historical link between different melodramatic modes of representation—from the sentimental novel to the feuilleton to the historieta to the telenovela. In many ways, these traditions culminate in *Yesenia*, with its corresponding structuring conflicts of women's personal freedom and communal obligations.[35] The excerpt's literary references to France and the US further legitimize the message of what constitutes an "authentic woman," which is curiously presented as simultaneously nationally specific and cosmopolitan.

Indeed, the large majority of the material in both *Kena* and *Claudia* appeals to French, Swedish, American, or even Soviet/Russian models of womanhood or feminism—whether used as positive or negative examples, these models were marked by their national origins. Foreign movie stars such as Barbra Streisand, Vanessa Redgrave, and Katherine Hepburn were featured regularly in these magazines, as were cultural and political figures like the French director of the women's magazine *Elle*, Indira Gandhi, leader of the Czech Parliament Soňa Pennigerová, and British writer Agatha Christie—all of whom were presented as women pioneers in their respective fields. They were clearly meant to lend appeal to the ideas of women's liberation not only by their celebrity status but by their belonging to the cosmopolitan class, confirming the idea that being an authentic woman, a liberated woman, and a cosmopolitan woman were intrinsically interconnected. And as much as the phrase "American feminist" was used as shorthand for an "exaggerated" or "unhinged" (both words used frequently in the magazine to describe them) version of the women's movement, virtually all the sources in psychology, sociology, anthropology, and medicine to which the articles in these journals refer are American (or occasionally British), many authored by women—their nationality and institutional affiliation used as rhetorical substantiation for the validity of their claims. This certainly also reflected the practices and cultural orientation of these journals' middle- and upper-class readership.

Overwhelmingly, such cosmopolitan ideals translated into specific consumption practices. These ideals mediated between the desirability of foreign and cultural standards and an insistence on the importance of national identity by rhetorically embracing the eclecticism and apparent contradictions of the positions offered to the readers as markers of freedom. In short, being a liberated woman meant having unlimited choice. These discourses on fashion, similarly to variety shows in the US entertainment industry of the Cold War era conveying the image of racial liberalism, were meant to project the idea of freedom and plenitude of choice.[36] Starting in 1970, women's magazines repeatedly declared that you could wear anything—and thus be anyone. The fashion briefs in *Claudia* and *Kena* declared that the newest trend in fashion is "anything goes": both miniskirts and maxiskirts are in, pants can be just as feminine as ball gowns, and both are absolute "fashion essentials." Mexican fashion was pronounced "both modern and traditional."[37] Mexican fashion was also international fashion, claimed another headline in *Claudia*, and the pages of both *Kena* and *Claudia* offered a virtual fashion tour of the world, both in their coverage of international fashion shows and in the mode of cultural appropriations of various national styles in the Mexico-made apparel they advertised. *Kena* had its own clothing line in Mexico's oldest and most luxurious department store, El Palacio de Hierro, including not only Italian, US, and French but also African, Japanese, and Peruvian themed collections, all

Trajes regionales de la colección de Luis Márquez, que sirvieron de inspiración a la línea "Contraste Mexicano 70", lanzada por Verona Internacional.

FIGURE 8. Regional dresses as inspiration for Verona's clothing line, "Mexican Contrast 70." Advertisement in *Kena*, 1970. Hemeroteca Nacional de México.

of which combined folkloric elements with space-age looks.[38] Needless to say, as is usually the case with fashion in women's magazines, these were purely aspirational choices. As we will see in chapter 4, in the 1970s, even the middle classes increasingly could not afford store-bought retail, let alone the high fashion advertised in the pages of *Kena* and *Claudia*. But the fantasy they constructed was both nationalist (in accordance with President Echeverría's protectionist policies, international brands were not welcome in Mexico in the first half of the 1970s) and cosmopolitan, with a Third-Worldist and indigenous-revival touch (as evident in the Mexican Contrast 70 collection of the Mexican clothing brand Verona that combined folkloric elements directly inspired by "regional costumes" with miniskirts and pantsuits, advertised on the pages of *Kena* throughout the early 1970s).[39]

We will return in chapter 4 to the "ethnic" aspects and specifically "gypsy" fashion in Mexico and the Soviet Union in the 1970s. But for the argument at hand, the magazines' emphasis on polystylistic fashion foregrounded the image of the woman of the future—the true, authentic, fully self-realized woman—as, above all, free and individualistic in her self-fashioning. At the same time, as both the fashion and its discourses equally emphasized, the true woman's full self-realization is possible only through romance. This is expressed directly in a *Kena* article titled "The Woman of Today and the Woman of Tomorrow," featuring Eileen Ford, a former fashion model and the cofounder of Ford Models in New York City, one of the earliest modeling agencies in the world and, in the early 1970s, among the most internationally recognized. In the article, Ford praises the freedom of choice and individualism of contemporary fashion. At the same time, she cautions, while it is certain that tomorrow's woman will be more liberated morally and mentally, one shouldn't forget that "when romanticism dies, love dies."[40] This notion was also continuously affirmed in women's magazines by engaging earlier

FIGURE 9. Advertisements for Verona dresses in the pages of *Kena*, 1970. Hemeroteca Nacional de México.

models of sentimental and melodramatic cultures: from bolero and other genres of romantic music, which dominated the music reviews and advertisements on the pages of *Kena* and *Claudia* throughout the 1970s, to repeated coverage of the stars of the Golden Age Mexican cinema.

This equal focus on sexual liberation and romantic ideals, combined with the ethos of change, is perfectly embodied in a series of advertisements for dresses by the same Mexican brand Verona ("Vestidos Verona"), which were featured in both *Kena* and *Claudia* throughout the early 1970s. One ad outlines the contour of a woman with wild curly hair, wearing a dress onto which a sunset over the beach is projected. The main tagline reads "If today you are feeling romantic, Verona dresses." Another ad by Verona features the silhouette of a naked woman from the waist down, her private parts covered with a leaf in the colors of the brand, with a significantly longer tagline: "What do I put on? There are some women who do not conform to a simple dress, women who feel the desire to look beautiful, to change and renovate continuously. These special women never have anything to wear—until they discover Verona dresses." These advertisements clearly outline the two aspects of their projection of an ideal woman as defined, respectively, through romance and sexuality—in a way that is self-possessed (they are the lone figures in the picture), hyper-feminine, fairly explicit in its references to sexuality, and entirely removed from any references to work or public participation.

Through women's magazines and popular cinema, the 1970s discourse of women's liberation was coded through a greater sexualization of all aspects of a woman's life, from fashion to food to money. The image of the modern woman was prescriptively constructed through a combination of consumption and sexuality, in many ways preparing for the further neoliberalization of Mexican culture in the 1980s. *Cosmopolitan* magazine, introduced to Mexico in 1973, famously embodied this notion, codifying it as the "Cosmo woman." However, this ideal was evident in Mexican media even before the magazine's debut. One aspect of this, as demonstrated in *Kena* and *Claudia*, is that over the 1970s, sexual liberation discourse moved away from the normativity of ethics or religion to the scientific/medical framework. Governmentally, this was combined with an aggressive (and largely successful) campaign against population growth that necessitated an expansion of birth control methods, which formed part of the demands of the sexual revolution.[41] At the same time, the emphasis on sex and sexuality was manifested in new discourses on sexuality in women's magazines aimed at a culturally mainstream and middle-class readership,[42] including the representation of highly sexualized women "without guilt or concealments, capable of desire," in New Mexican Cinema[43] and the *fichera* comedies of the late 1970s, when a more radical form of Mexican feminism found a media foothold (the latter best exemplified by the founding of *Fem* magazine). Counterculture provided an outlet for educated youth, while the pairing of romantic ideals with sexual agency was directed at the conservative stratum of the upper and aspiring middle class. This left historietas and telenovelas to speak to the lower classes, translating these changing notions of femininity for a demographic bereft of the spending power required to realize them, thus fully maintaining class hierarchies.

While mandating sexuality as "natural" for a woman—a big departure, indeed, from the patriarchal family norms of previous generations—within this new ideal the norms of femininity were absorbed into the list of responsibilities any "true" woman should take on. This included openly sexual self-expression as part of maintaining—if not augmenting—conventional desirability as the prerequisite for the ultimate goal of upward mobility, mostly achievable through marriage. This logic of sexualization did not necessarily legitimize representations of explicit sex, which remained taboo in Mexican melodramas and telenovelas alike, just as they did in Soviet cinema (although pornography would remain dialectically inseparable from them, looming large as their Other). Instead, sexuality (including increasing suggestions of female nudity) is most clearly manifested through women's self-presentation, especially in fashion and performance.

Yesenia's image in this respect is exemplary: her sexuality is highly feminized, emphasized by flowing "gypsy" skirts, revealing, low-cut ruffled tops, and dresses in soft silky fabrics and colorful, flowery designs. Her iconic hair is particularly telling in this respect—it's long and wild, unmistakably 1970s, so completely unlike the perfectly controlled beehives or helmet hairdos of the 1960s.

FIGURE 10. Yesenia's hair. DVD screen grab.

It is hyper-feminine (long and abundant), carrying unmistakable sexual connotations ("bedroom hair"), and "natural" (suggesting lack of styling), blending the traditional "gypsy" image with the "hippy/flower-child" one. It is noteworthy that the shift in hair fashion took place in 1971, which marked the arrival in Mexican fashion magazines of the kind of long, wavy hair that would culminate in Farrah Fawcett's famous feathered haircut in the US television show *Charlie's Angels*. The changes in Yesenia's hair and dress mark her transformation from the first to the second half of the film. The increasing refinement—and disciplining— of her look culminates in the wedding in the film's finale, which brings out the most traditional vision of feminine splendor in her moment of ultimate triumph.

In the Soviet context, the contrast between loose hair and the more "contained" hairdos of earlier decades was interpreted in even starker ideological terms, seen by Soviet cultural authorities as an undeniable sign of Western influence, the sexual revolution, and general moral decline. A cartoon from a satirical Soviet Lithuanian magazine illustrates the difference between a "woman" and a "café-goer"— making clear the connection between loose hair and, presumably, loose morals and/or a general state of chaos characterizing the lives of those women who frequented cafés, a common form of leisure and socialization from the 1960s on. Such loose hair became explicitly associated with "Western" sexuality—and, as a result, both extremely popular and publicly criticized—slightly earlier, after the French film *The Blonde Witch* (*La sorcière*, André Michel, 1956), featuring a sexy female lead played by Marina Vlady sporting long, tousled hair, was shown on Soviet screens.[44] Although the censorious attention of Soviet authorities had shifted by the 1970s, primarily toward men, for whom long hair was seen as evidence of their membership in the "informal" hippy culture, the associations evoked by Yesenia's hair were still similarly unmistakable in the Soviet context.

Throughout the film, Yesenia's sexuality is also conveyed by her mannerisms, with her posture and movements drawing attention to her plunging neckline, which is further emphasized by the signature shoulder shake of her Romani

FIGURE 11. "Woman" (left) vs. "café-goer" (right), *Šluota*, 1963. Personal collection.

dancing. She is openly at ease in expressing her feelings, which is coded as an extension of her passionate nature—and, indeed, most of the romantic scenes in the first part of the film take place outdoors, in nature. She "owns" her sexuality in her appearance, dialogue, and actions by pursuing her desires against conventional expectations, whether those placed on her by her Romani community (by marrying an outsider) or by the high society (by refusing, at least for the majority of the film, to accept its bigoted norms). And yet, ultimately, these conflicts are resolved by her incorporation into the aristocratic family, bringing her desires into harmony with the social norm while ensuring her upward mobility.

One interesting example of the complex negotiations between different models of femininity and sexual norms is the way Yesenia stands up to all unsolicited sexual advances, including those of her love interest. She slaps Oswaldo not once, but twice: early in the film, when they first meet and he kisses her against her will, which earns him an immediate slap in the face that sends him flying back into a chair; and later, during their first romantic sojourn, when he makes uninvited sexual advances and she doesn't merely slap him but knocks him out cold with a rock. The scene is constructed for comic effect, with the eruption of violence underscoring our female protagonist's impulsive temper—coding her as a typical "unruly woman."[45] From its contemporary vantage point, however, Yesenia's explosion signals not only her unruliness and disobedience, but specifically her lack of tolerance for nonconsensual sex, even with the man she loves. Only after a conversation about, essentially, the importance of consent does the couple join in a reciprocally passionate embrace.

Such behavior comes across as decidedly empowering, especially given that Mexican women (as well as those of the Soviet Union) routinely experienced intense physical abuse. In fact, prohibition of sexual violence in all its forms and the decriminalization of abortion were the two issues that successfully united various feminist movements in 1970s Mexico. Measures against rape and domestic abuse were the crucial axes along which women's coalitions were formed and upon which they acted, resulting in the establishment of centers of support for rape victims and in other, similar legal and social initiatives.[46] The embedded thematization of sexual violence in *Yesenia* uncannily prefigures the preoccupation in Mexican audiovisual culture with—and the further exacerbation and eventual

FIGURE 12. María Félix in *Enamorada*, 1946. DVD screen grab.

eruption of—gendered violence and femicide, which came to characterize Mexican life from the 1990s onward.[47]

At the same time, these scenes replay—once literally, and a second time in a more comic and exaggerated form—an earlier iconic moment of cinematic violence: the famous *cachetada* that the protagonist played by María Félix in *Enamorada* (Emilio Fernández, 1946) gives her soon-to-be lover, a revolutionary general, when he makes comments about her appearance—a slap, quickly followed by another.

Against the striking visual similarities between these scenes in the two films (down to the shared mannerisms and body language of the two heroines), the differences between them are worth pointing out. The actions of *Enamorada*'s Señorita Beatriz Peñafiel, who is the daughter of the richest man in town, speak to her expectation of the public respect that her class awards her; its violation, especially from an upstart *pelado* like Pedro Armendariz's character, is not tolerated. In the case of *Yesenia*, the class dynamic is reversed: in the first part of the film, our heroine belongs to a social stratum that makes her particularly vulnerable to sexual advances and all forms of violence. Her actions send a clear signal that she is not, contrary to expectations, a "loose woman"—simultaneously affirming her agency and virtue while subtly underscoring the shared logic of class and gendered exploitation.

The threat of sexual violence is palpable in the film, as Yesenia is continually fighting off men's advances. In fact, she is narratively introduced to the viewer through the point of view of a group of men discussing the chances of sexual consort with her and its repercussions—and before we ever hear her speak, she is forced to push one of them back as he tries to embrace her against her will. Yet we soon find out that she can hold her own in a physical confrontation and has no qualms about initiating one. When, already married to Oswaldo but not yet having been accepted into her aristocratic biological family, she is refused service in a restaurant, she knocks the tray from the waiter's hands, pulls the tablecloth from under the table where a particularly bigoted couple is having a meal, and starts a fight that turns into a massive brawl involving the whole restaurant. As pies fly in the diners' faces, Yesenia finally manages to grab a plate and enjoy both her meal and the spectacle of chaos. This scene, clearly reminiscent of the silent cinema's slapstick conventions, positions Yesenia as both initiating the social disruption and eruption of violence and reveling in it. What leads to violence is her spontaneous embodied reaction to injustice and exclusion, and at the same time she manages to remain very much in control—all qualities associated with feminist readings of the figure of an unruly woman as carnivalesque and ultimately empowering.[48]

Yet this kind of representation of passionate immediacy and vitality has its limits, in that it is also a cultural stereotype specifically associated with racialized people and popular classes (one that rings equally true in both Mexico and the Soviet Union). Ironically, in the course of the film, we find out that Yesenia inherited her temper not from her Romani mother—who is meek, loving, and disapproves of stealing—but apparently from her biological father, an aristocrat. This discovery affirms the "power of bloodlines," which forms part of the film's essentialist logic, while paradoxically subverting the stereotype, subtly suggesting that such expression of temper and violence, coming from an aristocratic male, is entirely normalized and likely to find many outlets without drawing attention to itself or constituting a disruption of social order. But despite this knowledge, which undermines the more clearly racialized and gendered assumptions of unruliness, within the narrative of the film it is Yesenia's non-belonging to the social and class order of the dominant society that allows for this fantasy of the reversal of structural violence.

In her vivaciousness, Yesenia's unruly persona serves as an allusion to yet another Mexican cinematic archetype: that of the spirited (albeit equally socially vulnerable) heroine of the *cabaretera* or *rumbera* genre—such as, perhaps most famously, Ninón Sevilla's character in *Aventurera*. As scholars from Joanne Hershfield to Julia Tuñón have repeatedly demonstrated, these spirited *rumberas* offered a disruption of the nationalist hegemony of Golden Age representations embodied in María Félix's and Dolores del Río's iconic heroines.[49] Their temper and expressive sexuality posited a corrective to the tragic passivity of the archetype of the "doomed woman" in Mexican melodrama (the prostitute as a suffering martyr, whose template is *Santa* or *La mujer del Puerto*). Yesenia's identity as "a gypsy," like that of *cabareteras*, is characterized by her sensual dancing and presumptions of sexual transgressions, and is similarly socially and racial marginalized. The racialization is alluded to, in both cases, mainly through stylized "ethnic" dress, hypersexualized dancing style, and music.[50]

As described in detail by Jacqueline Avila and Sergio de la Mora, the integration between the film and music industries in Mexico had particular bearing on melodramas of prostitution. This genre was invested in the theatricalization of "vices"—sexuality and other forms of tainted pleasures. The popular songs that were integral to these films' diegesis already brought with them associations with brothels.[51] This included the sensuous Afro-Cuban *danzón* and rumba, as well as the romantic *bolero*. Boleros' greatest performer, Agustín Lara, authored many of the genre's classics, including "Santa," "Palabras del Mujer," "Pecadora," and "Aventurera"—songs whose lyrics narratively structured their respective films.[52] At the same time, musical and dance performances expressively and affectively structured elements of sexuality and sensuality in these films, as well as their heroines' racial alterity.[53] While marking Yesenia's ethnicity with dark-brown wigs, both Fanny Cano (Yesenia in the 1970 telenovela) and Jacqueline Andere were blondes, which underscores the masquerade of their performances.

By the 1970s, however, both the nationalist melodrama and *cabaretera/rumbera* genres had ceased to be the dominant cinematic expressions in Mexico; the latter was transformed by the end of the decade into the *cinefichera*, while the former found its strongest resonances in telenovela tropes. The porous boundaries between cultural modalities and industrial practices in 1970s Mexican cinema, however, are evident in the career of Isela Vega, the most notorious on-screen *fichera*, whose screen appearances transversed sexploitation films, avant-garde cinema, and independent filmmaking. The latter is, in fact, what allowed for her 1976 participation in the Tashkent Film Festival, despite the notorious puritanism of Soviet film culture, as discussed in chapter 1. While considerably more conservative than Vega, Cano's and Andere's hypersexualized star images (constructed through racy on-screen roles and even racier media publicity) never prevented them from acting as leading ladies in highly conventional telenovelas and large-budget historical melodramas.[54]

If the comedic and even slapstick elements are foregrounded in several scenes of *Yesenia*, the classical melodramatic narrative formula of "sacrificial economy," to use Carlos Monsiváis's famous description of Mexican melodrama, is tempered in *Yesenia*, escaping a tragic "winner takes all" resolution.[55] Yesenia's sacrifice of her love for Oswaldo for the sake of social order (because he is engaged to her half-sister) is short lived. She triumphs even despite her apparent earlier moral transgression (when believing that Oswaldo had abandoned her, Yesenia accepts a Roma lover, who had long been in love with her). And Luisa's final sacrifice of Oswaldo for the sake of her half-sister's happiness, which enables the story's happy ending, is rendered less dramatic by the fact that she does not die (as would be her fate in a nineteenth-century sentimental novel). Instead, she leaves for Europe, where she is more likely to find a cure, both literally and metaphorically. The conflict between individual desires and divergent social obligations is further resolved by not one but two marriages in the film, one Romani and the other Catholic, thus honoring—or, at the very least, acknowledging—both communities in a rare case of such symbolic reconciliation. Any sense of tragedy, in other words, is considerably diluted, even as compared to the moral narrative economy of a "classic" melodrama.

Thus, instead of merely reproducing melodramatic clichés, *Yesenia* references and mediates the longer history of the complex dynamics of the constructions of femininity and sexuality on the Mexican screen and its contemporary context of the global 1960s' conflicting demands of sexual liberation outside the more radical, emancipatory, and class-conscious feminist circles. Much critiqued and despised by the Mexican high bourgeoisie and leftist intelligentsia alike, the telenovela and its cinematic incarnations nonetheless successfully condensed both the cultural legacies of the past and the rapid changes of the present into a form that could appeal to those who remained marginalized by both. At the same time, the actual production and consumption dynamics of such sentimental media speak to the much more porous and dispersed cultural field of the 1970s entertainment industries. This was due in no small part to this genre's gendered nature, as many of its producers—in particular, historieta and telenovela writers and the journalists writing for *Kana* and *Claudia*—were women, largely belonging to the highly educated bourgeois upper classes, despite the association of the genre with the lower classes. Its female stars likewise moved across different media registers and representational modes. As *Yesenia*'s success in the Soviet Union (and subsequently China) demonstrates, such porousness allowed for greater translatability to the gender politics of late socialist culture.

WOMEN'S CULTURE IN THE SOVIET UNION

If, for Mexican viewers, the cinematic version of *Yesenia* was largely an extension of the literary/comic book and telenovela versions, rife with allusions to earlier Mexican melodramas, none of these intertexts were legible to Soviet viewers. While several Mexican Golden Age classics were seen on Soviet screens in the 1950s, this was not the case for the *rumbera/cabaretera* genre, which Soviet authorities would have found too risqué. Serialized television drama was still in its very early stages and tied mostly to historical and detective genres, not to melodrama. There was no historical equivalent of the historieta genre (or graphic novels in general) in Russia or the Soviet Union. After its 1917 revolution, the country underwent a more radical form of state modernization than did Mexico (even if literacy campaigns and state-directed programs for creating classical literature readership among the lower classes played a similarly decisive role in both). The Soviet cultural revolution fully subsumed the more liberal and vernacular forms of expression associated with the prerevolutionary regime, and the genre of women's romance was deemed particularly reactionary by official Soviet culture. Not only was it insufficiently political, but in its associations with lower-class vernacular expressions it clashed with the overall state project of "culturization" (*kul'turnost'*), which was oriented toward middle-class Western behavioral codes on the one hand and high culture on the other. The two major magazines directed at women readers were titled "The Working Woman" and "The Peasant Woman," respectively. And although both titles shared some elements with Mexican women's magazines (such as the domestic arts, advice on proper social conduct or appropriate fashion, and concern with the well-being of family and children), they were couched in a highly politicized socialist rhetoric, which excluded romance and sexuality.[56]

Virtually everything we associate with "women's culture"—its emphasis on private and subjective experiences, its melodramatic excesses, its orientation toward gendered consumption—were as much at odds with the 1920s ethos of postrevolutionary radical transformation as with Stalinist-era political jingoism. Thus, after a vigorous but short-lived cultural debate about the didactic possibilities of melodrama for postrevolutionary society (led by Anatolii Lunacharskii and Maxim Gorkii) within the film industry, it was quickly pronounced incompatible with Soviet cinema.[57] Melodrama's status within Russian and Soviet culture has a complex history. As a literary and theatrical genre in Russia, it deviated from its Western European organic—and arguably progressive—development and function, representing "an imported Western delicacy rather than a theatrical form that gave voice to a new social majority."[58] This was followed by a short-lived period in the early twentieth century, when popular women's romances (such as Anastasiia Verbitskaia's *Keys to Happiness*) became widely read and quickly adapted to the screen by prerevolutionary cinema, thus at least temporarily integrating the melodramatic mode into mainstream Russian culture. This association with prerevolutionary Russian filmmaking was one of the reasons why, despite the otherwise unreserved enthusiasm of the Soviet cinematic avant-gardes for lowbrow cinematic genres (especially those associated with American cinema—from slapstick comedy to Westerns), melodrama in Soviet film culture carried exclusively reactionary connotations. And although a number of popular Soviet 1920s films were clearly perceived as melodramas—and were advertised as such (as film exhibitors were eager to capitalize on the genre's earlier popularity with the audiences)—in criticism and official culture the term was harshly criticized. As a result, some of the same films were reclassified retroactively, and the clearly melodramatic structures and effects within subsequent Soviet films were attributed instead to other genres, whether musical or lyrical comedies or historical epics.[59]

While melodrama continued to be studied and critiqued in various cultural discourses, including Russian formalists' and early Soviet film theorists' writings, it was mainly discoverable in latent and vernacular cultural forms, perhaps most evident in popular music. But as we saw in the preface, the genre's melodramatic and sentimentalist impulses resurfaced again with the liberalization of the Thaw, evidenced by the enormous success of Lolita Torres, and with it came a reconsideration of both gender norms and the discourses on romantic love. After the broad destabilization of cultural norms that characterized the Thaw period during the late 1950s and early 1960s, the polemics on the role of love and gender within Soviet society—and their representation on the screen—intensified in the late 1960s. And finally, in the 1970s, the status of melodramatic culture in the Soviet Union underwent a significant transformation, in the context of a gradual but powerful revaluation of women's position in Soviet society. As part of this process, melodramatic culture, still decried by critics, gradually came to occupy a stable place on 1970s–1980s Soviet screens.[60] This included the emergence of the so-called "woman's film," such as *Stepmother* (*Machekha*, Oleg Bondarev, 1973) or *I Want the Floor* (*Proshu slova*, Gleb Panfilov, 1975). Ideologically compliant with the demands of socialist realism in that they dealt with issues of labor and social conditions in women's lives, these melodramas were decidedly women-centered and ultimately argued for the primacy of the private over the public, most frequently by creating a diegetic contrast between an unhappy public life and a promise—and sometimes the unattainability—of a happy private one (most notoriously in Panfilov's film). They also proved to be some of the highest-grossing films of the decade, serving as "an important harbinger of commercial genre cinema in the Soviet film industry."[61]

As part of this cultural dynamic, such "low" genres as melodrama and the television serial—which emerged in the Soviet Union in the 1970s—became a site of ideological contestation over the status of mass culture under socialism. The goal was to transform popular culture into a form of cultural and political education. For example, in the context of Soviet television production, serials, as Christine Evans argues, were initially not associated with women's culture but instead were understood as "a public, masculine cultural form" charged with politically and culturally elevating tasks on a par with documentary films.[62] Within these early examples of Soviet TV serials, melodrama was the dominant mode—but it was usually linked to the grand themes of revolutionary and war martyrdom, socialist heroism, and collective histories, frequently with a focus on a male protagonist.[63] But the melodramas from Asia and Latin America, along with emerging Soviet women's films during the same period, "posed a formidable challenge to the Soviet rejection of the sentimental and ordinary women's cultures," emerging as "key mediators between the official Soviet norms for gender, sexuality and romantic love, and their vernacular forms, which persisted against the state's 'educational' efforts of the previous forty-some years."[64] Despite all the official attempts to frame these productions through their historical and literary associations, the education they offered to the Soviet—as much as to their domestic—audiences, as Glushneva argues, was first and foremost a sentimental one.[65] And it is evident that the enduring popularity of *Yesenia*—in Mexico through its adaptation from historieta to telenovela to film to telenovela again, and in the Soviet Union through the enormous commercial success of the film and its longevity on cinematic and TV screens—was in no small measure due to the iconic status of its protagonist, as a model of both identification and emulation through fashion and other forms of gendered consumption.

The intensification of the debates on gender during this period, which shaped both the production and reception of these films in both countries, was due to the impact of the sexual revolution, which manifested in the two countries in rather different ways. In official Soviet discussions, the sexual revolution was equated with the "degeneracy" of capitalist culture and was seen as a major threat to the socialist social and moral order, as evidenced in the "demographic crisis" (low numbers of children born to families within the European part of the Soviet Union) of the 1970s.[66] And yet, acknowledgments of the enduring manifestations of patriarchy, unchanged by socialist policies, were becoming increasingly more public. The 1969 publication of Natalya Baranskaia's story "The Week Like Any Other" in the journal *Novy mir* (The New World) famously voiced, in a fictionalized form, the experience of women's exhaustion with their work and family life, which triggered more open conversations over the "double burden" faced by women.[67] The disproportionately high demands on women were even eventually recognized by the state: the head of the government himself, General Secretary of the Communist Party Brezhnev, addressing the Trade Union Congress in 1977, admitted, "We men . . . have thus far done far from all we could to ease the dual burden that [women] bear both at home and in production."[68] In effect, as Mary Buckley argues, the Brezhnev era officially negated the old official line that the Woman Question had been solved—it was now officially unsolved.[69] These official debates, however, were nonetheless couched in the logic of socialist productivist values, positioned within the positivist parameters of political economy.

The state's response to this situation was to further differentiate and demarcate what was appropriately "male" or "female" labor, following their assumed "anatomical-physiological peculiarities" and "moral-ethical temperament."[70] It also became apparent that women occupied a disproportionately high percentage of low-skilled positions and fewer managerial or administrative roles, despite having more educational training in virtually every field of employment, which resulted in poorer working conditions and lower wages.[71] Thus, Soviet discussions of job and pay disparity among men and women—written by both male and female social scientists and policymakers—tended to center on the need to move women "out of unsuitable jobs and into more appropriately feminine positions."[72] This was also often seen as a way to address the high divorce rate and increase the "stability of the family" (which was never questioned as the main goal). Thus, somewhat paradoxically, the resulting official discourses and policies turned considerably more conservative in their gender heteronormativity.

Such positions were, of course, far from monolithic. As Lynne Attwood describes, in a debate between B. Ryabinin and E. Andreeva in the pages of a pedagogical Soviet journal, *Sem'ia i shkola* (Family and School), Andreeva launched a very familiar critique of patriarchy: "In order to believe in his strength, the modern man requires weakness in his female partner, and in order to believe in his intelligence he needs her to be stupid. This need for self-affirmation through the abasement of another person is, in fact, weakness."[73] Her opponent, on the other hand, adhered to the Party line on the need to accommodate the natural limits of women to ensure the most productive outcomes. It was his position that came to dominate public discourses—and find an even greater resonance within popular culture—in the 1970s.

Increasingly departing from a conventional socialist position that more education and better employment for women would lead to greater sexual equality within the family, by the 1970s even official Soviet discussions began to claim the opposite. The documented discrepancy between the division of domestic labor between men and women was largely unquestioned, as these changes further normalized the domestic part of the "double burden" for women as "natural." This nonchalant attitude extended to rampant sexual violence and abuse, which was exacerbated by increasing levels of alcoholism.[74] The relative lack of official Soviet intervention into cases of domestic violence was particularly paradoxical: regulated under the misleading general legal category of "hooliganism," such enforcement was understood as the prevention of violations of public order, therefore seemingly not extending to the private sphere.[75] Police intervention in domestic disputes was largely geared toward reconciliation, even as, by "the 1980s, women in Russia were almost three times more likely to be murdered by their current or former intimate partner than women in the United States, where the rates were also comparatively high."[76] And despite early legal interdiction of sexual harassment of women in the workplace, which took place in the Soviet Union in the 1920s, such cases were never prosecuted. Similarly, marital and acquaintance rape, which remained common throughout the Soviet period, was largely unreported and ignored by the authorities.[77] Lack of contraception and the general taboo regarding official discussions of sex and sexuality remained throughout the Soviet period, even though sex before and outside of marriage was extremely common across social classes for both men and women, despite the image promoted by the official norms.

Yet the coexisting norms of both *kul'turnost'* and romantic chivalry remained dominant, if contested.[78] As anthropologist Anna Rotkirch has shown, the cult of romantic love and courtship (part of unquestionable social rules throughout the Soviet period) and its integration into the collective socialist norms created a latent contradiction with actual sexual practices. The romantic ideal of courtship was based on its prohibition of sexual (or even sensual) expression. This enabled its symbolic integration with the socialist collective, as well as the dominant behavioral code of *kul'turnost'* (which, in turn, was based on middle-class values, which similarly prohibited free expressions of sexuality). Gestures such as flowers or gifts served as its symbolic substitutions. As such, romanticism was linked to the high value placed on tokens of luxury. This was, in fact, the legacy of a romantic courtship model constructed in prerevolutionary Russian culture, which was in other ways precisely what the revolution presumably overthrew and replaced with socialist norms.[79] As we will see in chapter 4, negotiations of feverishly increasing consumerism, which formed an essential part of the Soviet culture of the 1970s and 1980s, partly expressed this paradox as well.

In the face of such stark discrepancy between official norms and the realities of lived experience, over the course of the 1970s and 1980s, popular perceptions of gender relations increasingly departed from both romantic codes and those of *kul'turnost'* and turned to notions of brute physical—and specifically sexual—power as foundational for interactions between the sexes.[80] A good illustration of this thesis is found in *The Princess on a Pea* (*Printsessa na goroshine*, Boris Rytsarev, 1976), a film adaptation of several Hans Christian Andersen fairy tales. In a sequence based on the tale "The Most Incredible Thing," a contest has been proclaimed: half the kingdom and the hand of the princess in marriage will be the rewards of he who can produce "the most incredible thing" to impress her. In the film version, various suitors present themselves to the princess, trying to woo her with their various talents and arts. The one who finally wins her heart, however, is a knight who arrives and ruthlessly destroys all the artful creations presented to her by the other suitors, taking her by force. The episode affirms the masculinist myth that women's interests in culture and learning are merely skin-deep, and what women actually find arousing is sheer brutal power. This notion had long existed in the vernacular figure of the "real man" (*nastoiashchii muzhik*). But until the 1970s, such an aggressive view of male sexuality was deemed unacceptable within official Soviet culture, associated exclusively with the uneducated lower classes, something to be transformed by *kul'turnost'*. The film—with its genre's implicit address to children!—demonstrates instead wholesale cultural acceptance of this notion by the late 1970s. Indeed, this would eventually become the hegemonic model of masculinity in the post-Soviet period.[81] Also remarkable is that this rendition of Andersen's tale directly reverses both the ending and the moral of the original story, in which the princess realizes that "the most incredible thing" referred to in the title is, indeed, art's ultimate ability to withstand both violence and the test of time, and marries the artist. In the film version, the only lesson offered is that of the finale of the title story, revealing the true nature of yet another princess, this one in disguise, celebrating her fine aristocratic sensibilities through her inability to tolerate the pea hidden under her many mattresses (a sentiment that likewise goes against the Soviet emphasis on endurance and asceticism).

Thus, as this example demonstrates, the late Brezhnev period also saw a corrosion of early Soviet principles of proletarian ethics and the gradual disappearance of all celebratory portrayals of the working class, whose symbolic capital was almost absent from 1970s cinema.[82] While serving an important function of de-mythologizing the old Soviet ideology and socialist realist iconographies, this furthered the sense of alienation and antagonism between the urban (largely Moscow- and Leningrad-based) intelligentsia and those outside of its cultural circle, leaving popular entertainment to provide "the masses" with a sense of emotional belonging.

The breakdown of the representation of the heroic proletariat in cinema was inseparable from the cultural discourse on the "crisis of masculinity," which symptomatically signaled the gradual but inescapable bankruptcy of Soviet patriarchy's symbolic power. This crisis was commonly perceived as a direct, albeit belated, result of revolutionary gender politics ("women's emancipation"), which supposedly led to the masculinization of women and their loss of "natural" sexuality—and the corresponding loss of masculinity in men.[83] In the face of this perceived crisis of gender identities, the essentialist notions of what makes "a real woman" and "a real man" were further reinforced—yet in ways that may not be quite obvious.

One common articulation of this "gender panic" within artistic and intellectual circles "advocated a return to a bifurcated gender order in which Russianness . . . [was] represented by rural folk culture that allegedly remained pristine and unaffected by imperial decadence, communist ideology and/or Western excesses."[84] Such rural folk culture offered the space for expressions of emotional authenticity, which was characteristic of the earlier culture of the Thaw in both its "high" and "low" iterations, but which by the 1970s had turned into an unmistakable marker of provinciality and social marginality, reflecting the increasing cultural segmentation. Melodrama—especially historical melodrama set in prerevolutionary times—adopted these idealized imaginary structures and provided a space to code the audiences' vulnerability, powerlessness, and pain as a guarantee of moral superiority and the promise of release.

Mexican melodramatic women's culture—and *Yesenia* in particular—offered a comparable iteration of nostalgic historical temporality with corresponding gender dynamics, as we'll explore at length in chapter 3. Insofar as the period was perceived as a certain crisis of patriarchal authority in both countries—of the state, the party, and the relationship between the intelligentsia and "the people"—it also brought about the need to reconsider the gender norms that undergirded such authority. Yet the more radical political manifestations of the women's movement in the global 1960s were seen by many conservative Mexicans as too threatening to the social order, and for most Soviet women were too reminiscent of earlier postrevolutionary radicalism (which, as we have seen, by the 1970s carried almost exclusively negative connotations). At the same time, decades of full exercise of public agency and cultural and professional participation in social life (as well as, some would argue, longer-standing cultural dynamics) made Soviet women unlikely to accept the notion of women's passivity as a natural or desired state of things. Instead, across the social spectrum these developments translated into an increased emphasis on sexual agency and romantic representation. We can see the repositioning of love and sex(uality) at the center of cultural discourse—as well as the acknowledgment of oppression of women within the domestic sphere—in both Mexico and the Soviet Union as responding not only to local conditions but also to the cultural and political impact of the global 1960s. Demands for change vis-à-vis the status quo, however, were rendered as a return to more traditional models, albeit mediated by some of the more recent socialist transformations as well as by contemporary capitalist forms of sexual commodification.

At the same time, the power of the cultural and affective politics of *Yesenia*, while projecting these modes, also speaks to the overwhelming shared sense of social and political injustices that the progressive position (whether that of the state or of radical intellectual elites) failed to address. Melodramatic culture carved out a socially legitimized space for articulating such sensibilities, which had previously been largely absent from the Soviet cultural sphere. The realm of private feelings, mobilized by melodrama, offered an alternative form of imagined collectivity and shared experiences to those previously prescribed by socialist culture. Melodramatic identification with the suffering of the characters defied the socialist ethos of struggle as the fundamental engine for social and political transformation and solidarity: socialist martyrs, populating Soviet melodramas, suffered a great deal—but always for a greater cause, and they usually died fighting.

In broader terms, the contradiction between the cultural pressures of public participation and performance of agency and the oppressive domestic and private experiences of millions of Soviet women challenged the official ideologies that privileged public over private, and civic over subjective realms. By the 1970s, the contours of public and private were reified once more. The official Soviet discourse simultaneously doubled down on its patriotic and political collective sentiments (with its celebration of the Great Patriotic War and the strengthening of the rhetoric of anticapitalist vigilance) and on the "emotional and spiritual qualities that defined features of the new Soviet person and of Soviet socialist civilization as a whole."[85] Within popular cinema and TV, unlike in the previous decades, the collective emotional life centered increasingly on "private feelings" and a subtle, tacit avoidance of communist ideology. The melodramatic mode, in particular, allowed for the possibility of detaching the representation of love and sexuality from "meaningful" social and political relations, which characterized the official socialist women's movement.[86] As the authors of *Film and Television Genres of the Late Soviet Era* demonstrate, in the 1970s, women's struggle against patriarchy, once a staple of socialist cinema, was depicted almost exclusively in the historical contexts of revolution and war. Elsewhere, in contemporary melodrama, women's professional and economic emancipation was toned down, questioned, or even downright condemned, such that "women's individual self-realization becomes completely separate from the Soviet public sphere, which was usually presented as male-dominated, but simultaneously impotent and corrupt."[87]

Developed explicitly in opposition to official Soviet norms (however much those norms themselves were, indeed, in retreat), this ideological retreat to the private sphere provides the first glimpses of what would prove to be an enduring (neo)liberalization of gender norms and further sexualization of heteronormative femininity characteristic of the postsocialist era.[88] And yet, I would argue, in the 1970s this mode of representation was still in its transitional phase, successfully mediating between the older norms and newer models. As we have seen in the discussion of the film within the context of Mexican women's culture, this kind of transitional gender regime is perfectly embodied in *Yesenia*: foregrounding women's sexuality and individual agency without threatening either the conservative patriarchal order or the importance of communal cultures beyond the hegemonic state-sanctioned norms. As such, *Yesenia* could provide Soviet viewers with the desired qualities they saw as lacking in their contemporary culture (i.e., the emphasis on sensuality and sexuality, along with consumerism associated with femininity). Yet it did so without losing such socialist gains as the ideals of social integration of marginalized groups, or general acceptance of women's agency, both social and personal. This seemingly contradictory position was anything but new for Soviet women, who had been highly accustomed to exercising their agency for several generations. For example, through the Soviet period, women frequently left husbands who didn't satisfy them in marriage and, in the absence of other forms of birth control, resorted to abortion on a massive scale. This was done with or without their partners' consent, and apparently without compromising their strongly held beliefs in the utmost importance of being a mother and a wife, or in the persistent norms of romantic courtship.[89] This effective mediation of deeply seated internal conflicts and contradictions characterized Soviet gender politics for decades.

The intersections between the "feminine" sphere and popular culture, which for much of Soviet history were at best quietly tolerated and at worst actively eradicated by state cultural policies, proved to be crucial for such renegotiations. And unlike in the 1950s, when Lolita Torres's popularity arose against the general context of a relative lack of genre cinema, especially in its musical and melodramatic forms, *Yesenia*'s reception in the 1970s took place precisely in concert with the increasing presence of such genres and modalities on Soviet screens and in the culture at large. Melodrama—with its power to effect catharsis—dealt with the inherent and ongoing social contradictions between what was said, what was felt, and what was done. Such contradictions in many ways characterize sexual and romantic life under patriarchy more generally, but they were perhaps felt most acutely in the late socialist context, when official discourses, everyday practices, and affective experiences were especially incongruous. These contradictions structured both the production and reception of melodramatic media and the kinds of global icons that emerged in the period—finding in *Yesenia* a perfect reflection.

The next chapter investigates more closely the specific aesthetic regimes of bad taste and kitsch that have historically been associated with melodramatic media and the feminine spheres of cultural production and consumption, focusing on their intersecting Mexican (and, more broadly, Latin American) and Russo-Soviet articulations and expressions, both in music and in cinema.

3

———

Between Mexican *Cursilería* and Russian *Poshlost'*

Our *tour d'horizon* of the changing dynamics of women's cultures in Mexico and the Soviet Union provided the context in which to grapple with the aesthetic models that came to define, shape, and characterize them. Despite the significant differences discussed in chapter 2, the significant overlaps between these aesthetic models would, I argue, directly impact *Yesenia*'s transnational history. This chapter places two culturally specific iterations of kitsch—the categories of Mexican *lo cursi* and Russian/Soviet *poshlost'* and *byt*—in relation to each other. It draws out their associations with sentimental vernacular music as well as with melodramatic modes more broadly, as exemplified by *Yesenia*. These intersecting cultural modes, I argue, are crucial to our understanding of both *Yesenia*'s resonance in the Soviet Union and the outrage it caused among the critics and intelligentsia at large. Furthermore, I argue that *lo cursi* in Mexico and *poshlost'* in the Soviet Union found their shared focal point in the figure of "the gypsy"—a cultural appropriation projecting and negotiating the sense of national non-belonging and of exclusion from and marginality to US- and Europe-centered modernity. In my discussion, I therefore zero in on the Mexican and Soviet genealogies of the subgenre of "gypsy melodrama," which impacted both the Mexican production of *Yesenia* and its Soviet reception.

As the previous chapters highlight, in the course of the twentieth century, various forms of popular media—romance novels, historietas, romantic songs, radio plays, women's magazines, movies, and, especially, melodramas and telenovelas—have played the didactic role of providing sentimental education and moral formation for Mexican women. All these cultural forms in Mexico tend to be strongly associated with a specific aesthetic, known in Spanish as *la cursilería*. Variously translated into English as "corny," "tacky," or "tasteless," this category arose in Spain in the nineteenth century to describe the style of the emerging bourgeoisie who were trying to imitate or adopt aristocratic models (in this, the term is directly linked to the etymology of the more familiar *kitsch* in denoting the fake or inauthentic).[1] In Latin America—and especially in Mexico—the notion of *la cursilería* has been integrated into cultural discourses that explicitly set out to define its national and regional specificities. The preeminent cultural critic of Mexico, Carlos Monsiváis, famously linked it to the very institution of Mexican culture, arguing that it constituted crucial elements of both institutional and popular cultural modalities. He famously defined the aesthetic regime of *cursi* as "failed beautiful"—or, in Linda Egan's translation, "failure of elegance"—its form rooted in transgressing the aesthetic norms of good measure and proportion (as the cultural codes of the higher social strata) through "cultural anachronism in style and discourse marked by excessive sentimentality."[2]

This "failed beautiful," Monsiváis argues, needs to be understood as "the elegance historically possible in underdevelopment."[3] *Cursilería*, he suggests, is an anachronistic persistence of a sentimentalist discourse rooted in the nineteenth century, when romantic poetry was perceived by the new bourgeoisie as the ultimate expression of cultivation and erudition, continually re-functionalized in the course of Mexican cultural history. In particular, Monsiváis explored as its foundational moment the emergence of popular twentieth-century Mexican musical forms such as bolero, best embodied in the figure of its most famous performer, Agustín Lara (who has continued to reappear in the pages of this book in multiple contexts). The bolero further reengaged nineteenth-century sentimental discourse through the new media of mass culture—radio, recorded music, cinema—of postrevolutionary Mexico. Throughout the twentieth century, these sentimental modes were never fully in tune with the official state culture, with its vision of revolutionary heroism and progress, although they certainly penetrated its monumentalism, investing it with considerable cursilería. Nor did they ever sit well with the tastes of the Mexican cultural vanguard: notwithstanding considerable changes in the latter's composition over the decades, sentimental modes for them became a source of embarrassment. Thus, the cursi aesthetic found its latent—but enduring—manifestation in the melodramatic language of mass culture, associated with the tastes of the lower classes. As popular music, cinema, and television came to be inseparable from Mexico's national identity, the cursi aesthetic became exemplary of the transculturation that has frequently been discussed as being at the core of Latin American cultural production of the twentieth century.[4]

Yesenia's relationship to the cursi aesthetic is obvious: indeed, the title of the article in the newspaper *Avance* about Chinese interest in the film was "The Chinese Prefer *Cursi* Mexican Movies."[5] In all its historical iterations, *Yesenia* is, indeed, a perfect embodiment of cursilería not only in its heightened sentimentality and ornamentality but in its repeatedly remediated anachronisms. Set in the Maximilian era, *Yesenia* is centered on the travails of conversion into the aristocratic culture. This plays out in terms of the narrative—as Yesenia is domesticated into her biological family's aristocratic lifestyle and behavior. But it is also reflected in the setting—as the period, which ended with the failure of the European aristocracy to impose itself on Mexico, itself reproduced the original scene of cursilería's "failed elegance." This same historical point of reference repeatedly finds its way into the visual style of Mexican telenovelas (and their film adaptations) more generally, regardless of the period in which they are set, as it tends to reproduce, through mis-en-scène and costumes, a consistently anachronistic vision of a past splendor, that very "elegance historically possible in underdevelopment," in Monsiváis's words.[6] This is precisely what emerges from media scholar Florence Toussaint Alcaraz's description of the peculiarity of a typical Televisa telenovela set: "rooms furnished in the Luis XIX style, albeit in a Third-Worldist version: oil lamps, brocade fabrics, luxury curtains, Chippendale desks."[7]

But even more crucially, in the case of *Yesenia*, the most significant anachronism was not just in its nineteenth-century setting, with its gilded surfaces and stock characters, but rather in the film's belatedness vis-à-vis Mexico's own cinematic trajectory. If film melodrama more generally replays aesthetics and ideologies of the eighteenth-century theater and nineteenth-century sentimentalist literary traditions, *Yesenia*'s embrace of the clichés of this genre, some twenty-five years past its Golden Age in Mexico, is particularly jarring—and particularly cursi. Yet it was precisely in this belatedness that the Mexican cursi was able to achieve its transnational legibility beyond its culturally cognate Latin American circuits—prefiguring the later global success of the telenovela format. This translation and the creation of an affective community around it depended on the historical relationship between cursilería and the experience of social, cultural, and geopolitical marginality, which coincided in that moment in both countries. And in both, the gypsy becomes a "safe" figure for a projection of such marginality, rooted in romantic imaginaries far removed from the revolutionary national collectives—while at the same time successfully tapping into intersecting gendered and nationalist anxieties and fantasies.

Indeed, motivating Latin American critics'—including Monsiváis's—ambivalent rather than denunciatory attitude toward cursilería is its inherent belonging to the peripheral or marginalized cultures that characterize the sphere of the popular. Specifically in the case of Mexico, cursilería's vibrancy and resilience in the twentieth century is rooted in its initial response against—and its function as a politically ambivalent alternative to—the hegemonic state of (revolutionary) Mexican culture. Thus, the roots of the bolero are frequently described as reflecting the experiences of the urban lower classes who, in Mark Pedelty's words, could locate "their lives, ambitions, and passions in neither the past genres nor the *indigenista* conceptions of intellectual nationalists . . . and instead saw themselves in the songs of Lara and other boleristas whose music quickly

FIGURE 13. Postcard of Yolanda Vargas Dulché and her sister Elba performing boleros as the duo Rubia y Morena, ca. 1940.

became an ubiquitous part of the postrevolutionary urban experience."[8] And unlike that other quintessential popular musical expression of twentieth-century Mexico, the revolutionary *corridos'* celebration of valiant deeds of heroic men, the subjects of bolero were decidedly more femininized, further gendering this aesthetic mode.[9]

Recently, Alejandra Vela Martínez has brought attention to the female (rather than Monsiváis's male, albeit queered) cultural producers of cursilería—authors and artists of mid-twentieth-century Mexico.[10] Although Vela Martínez focuses on only a couple of exemplary figures, such as writers Rosario Sansores and Rosario Castellanos (as well as the male contributors to the women's magazines, such as Vicente Leñero impersonating Dolores del Río in the pages of *Claudia*), the literary field she describes certainly includes both *Yesenia's* author, Yolanda Vargas Dulché, and women writers for *Kena* such as Emma Godoy and Helen Krauze (discussed in chapter 2). Defining them as "*cursi* feminists," Vela Martínez demonstrates how, in order to carve out their distinctive place in the male-dominated sphere, these authors both adopted and reshaped the cursi aesthetic by recuperating "the feminine" as their operative aesthetic category. Such gender essentialism—demonstrated by flaunting precisely the masquerade of femininity, its man-made attributes, the decorative, the excesses—was central to cursi feminist poetics: as Vela Martínez puts it, "recognizing the value of their femininity and unfolding its prosthesis with singular joy."[11]

In this, it differed from its antecedents in nineteenth-century women's sentimental novels, which shared the preoccupation with the plight of the oppressed, yet treated materialism (and its commodity forms) as the very core of moral conflict between genuine individual desires and the oppressive collective obligations of the society run by money. This extended to sentimentalism's literary formal style that eschewed details of the material world in favor of descriptions of the internal states and excesses of passion.[12] Instead, cursi feminism of the twentieth century—especially in its more overtly melodramatic form—ideologically rejects materialism, yet celebrates the decorative: thus, within it, the feminine excesses in all their forms are constitutive of the woman's virtue rather than designated as part of women's oppression. And the agency that such an aesthetic provides is, therefore, best understood through access to luxury and consumer choices—fashion, in particular—thus lending itself very easily to the popular women's sphere as traditionally associated with consumer culture.

Such affirmations of femininity, however, need to be seen in the national context wherein the status of this cultural production was both defined through and perpetuated by the consistent gender disparity held as fundamental to the construction of literary value in Mexico.[13] This is consistent with the dynamic of the later period of the 1980s, when, as Sánchez Prado notes, the reevaluation of romance as a genre, coinciding with the neoliberalization of Mexico, simultaneously allowed for the recognition of women writers and furthered the notion of "feminine writing" (with its privileging of essentialized assumptions of both gender and genre) as "a commodity that held concrete economic value in the marketplace of cultural goods."[14] Similarly, earlier manifestations of feminist cursi carved the space for female authorship, creating spaces for new (feminine) publics, thus playing an emancipatory role with respect to women's cultural production.

In its investment in profoundly anachronistic signifiers that gesture toward nostalgia for prerevolutionary and provincial ways of life, however, feminist cursi aesthetics as explored by Vela Martínez indisputably presents an inherently conservative cultural mode.[15] Here, too, we see yet another clear connection between the cursi aesthetics and melodramatic modes more broadly. As both Linda Williams and Jane Gaines have famously asserted, a desire to return to the impossible or lost past is at the core of classic Hollywood melodrama, its circular temporality inseparable from its affective, moral, and ultimately political regimes.[16] Mexican melodrama of the Golden Age relied on similar recuperation of the glorious history of the nation's dual indigenous and revolutionary origins constitutive of *lo mexicano*, and it is only in their foregrounding of the disconnect between the promises of that originary past and the realities of the present that those films offer a subtle but crucial current of social commentary and critique.[17]

By the 1970s, however, with the rise of feminist activism in Mexico, such anachronistic temporality came to clash with the movement's decidedly forward-looking, politically radical articulations that mark that decade in Mexican history. But while cursi feminist aesthetics was in many ways challenged by the emergence of these new cultural and political formations, it maintained—and amplified—its presence through the discourses in women's magazines and other articulations of the mass consumer culture (as we saw in chapter 2).[18]

However, the relationship in the 1970s between cursi feminist literary production in its various forms and film and television media was quite complex. Unlike their engagement with literature, music, or the visual arts, cinema criticism in women's magazines like *Kena* and *Claudia* almost entirely eschewed the cursi aesthetic. Their film reviews throughout the 1970s focus almost exclusively on European and American "cinema of quality," occasionally (in *Claudia*) reporting on Mexican independent and countercultural film production in surprisingly celebratory terms.[19] Written almost exclusively by men, film reviews in the pages of these magazines stand out from most of the other sections in terms of the kind of aesthetics they project. They do, however, maintain a certain thematic and rhetorical consistency in their absolute preference for foreign (US, French, British, and Italian) cinema over Mexico's, and in the predominance of the discourse of Mexican cinema's crisis.

 While the breakdown of the traditional family and masculinity, much discussed in the pages of these magazines, is framed as a global crisis, Mexican cinema is likewise framed in terms of its decline, but in national terms—reflecting the poor taste of the public. Thus, in a rare case of a woman writing about cinema, one of *Kena*'s lead contributors, Esperanza Brito de Martí, lending the magazine by far its most progressive feminist voice, laments the absence of high-quality scripts— and the demise of the beloved figure of the *charro*—in an article paradigmatically entitled "Mexican cinema in crisis."[20] This same sentiment is reflected throughout the discussions of cinema in the pages of these magazines: thus, Jacqueline Andere laments in the pages of *Claudia* in 1969, two years before starring in *Yesenia*, that

FIGURE 14. Tao Izzo's tarot card series of María Félix in *Kena*, 1972. Hemeroteca Nacional de México.

despite her higher artistic standards and aspirations, the poor aesthetic tastes of the Mexican public force her to act in low-quality productions: "The people are asking for bad movies (*churros*): so, there you have it, Mexico does not make good cinema."[21] This same discourse is persistent throughout the decade—appearing somewhat at odds with the same magazines' celebration of Mexican star actors and actresses, whose careers almost inevitably display a crossover among cinema, television, and, often, music. But just as reviews of Mexican music in the pages of these journals continuously return to the romantic music of Lara and its contemporary incarnations, such as the Spanish Julio Iglesias, the movie stars of the Golden Age—Dolores del Río, Cantinflas, and María Félix—feature prominently, frequently posited as a counterweight to the crisis of the cinema of the present.

In the midst of these affirmations of nostalgia, *lo cursi* emerges with a vengeance—best manifested in the art sections of these journals. Most striking within them is the artwork depicting the same stars of film and television melodrama, but done in even more archaic romantic styles. They feature paintings and

CHÁVEZ MARION
continúa

entre otros. Debe tener alrededor de 20 retratos en toda su casa.

—¿Por qué crees que le gusta tanto el tuyo?

—Porque yo la pinté tal como es María, María sin nada de fantasía. Ese retrato está colgado sobre la chimenea de su biblioteca.

—¿No te gusta la fantasía?

—La fantasía siempre me ha inquietado, pero a mí me gusta la personalidad retratística en interpretación y línea, dentro del academismo, sin llegar al academismo del siglo pasado... Sin embargo, cuando supe de esta entrevista, llamé a María para hacerle algo fantasioso y aceptó.

—¡Debe de encantarle posar!

—María nunca posa para nadie. Pero conmigo es muy linda.

—¿Y cómo la fantaseaste?

—María con toda esa riqueza de perfil viendo al observador y, en vez de cabello, ramas de hojarasca poblada de insectos, mariposas, escarabajos, arañas, y por la parte posterior de la cabeza, una lagartija, mientras que un colibrí revolotea en su busto.

—¿Y le gustó?

—Está feliz. ¡Le encantó!

—¿A quién más has pintado últimamente?

—A Fanny Cano. Es un desnudo de cuerpo entero, velado solamente por un manto. También, para seguir con gente de cine y teatro, a Amparo Rivelles, cuando hizo una telenovela llamada "La mujer dorada", en la que por única vez, apareció como rubia. También le hice un retrato a Begoña Palacios.

Fanny Cano la sensacional estrella del cine mexicano en un atrevido retrato de Chávez Marión.

FIGURE 15. Mario Chávez Marion's pinups of María Félix (left) and Fanny Cano (right) in *Kena*, 1971. Hemeroteca Nacional de México.

drawings by contemporary artists, most memorably those depicting María Félix in various historical ornamentalist and Orientalist settings and styles, from the tarot card extravaganza of Tao Izzo's paintings of La Doña as the Queen of Saba and Scheherazade to "tastefully erotic" pinups by Mario Chávez Marion.[22] The article on Chávez Marion also features paintings of Fanny Cano, the star of the telenovela version of *Yesenia*, in a similarly provocative pseudoclassical rendition.[23]

These artworks further exoticize and eroticize the actresses, but the difference between them and the pinup art or centerfolds in men's magazines like *Playboy* is not in the degree of nudity on display. Instead, the cursi feminist artwork in *Kena* remediates the images of the movie and television stars through painting, a more traditionally respectable art form, rendered through a veritable mise-en-abyme of stylistic anachronisms (reviving neoclassical or Orientalist styles, which were themselves attempts at revivals of imaginary earlier aesthetic modes). They glorify the stars' femininity and sexuality, endowing them with quasi-mystical power, recasting them as goddesses—entirely consistently with the kind of women-centered discourses and representational models that appear in these journals in advertisement, fashion, and literary sections alike.

In this, despite the class differences of their intended audiences, cursi feminist aesthetics and ideology emerge from *Kena* and *Claudia* as remarkably consistent with cursi melodrama and telenovela articulations, informing each other and creating a shared discourse and style. Their consistent engagement of earlier forms and styles, in particular, allows for a normalization of ahistorical representations of femininity as markers of the universality of women's condition and of false solidarity, rooted in the presumptions of their essential sameness. An example of this in a more popular genre is the figure of the maid, *la criada*, in telenovelas, as the presumed shared point of identification for the upper-class women and their domestic help, who are watching telenovelas together—an image that constitutes part of the mythology of telenovela viewing as overcoming class barriers.[24]

The political ambivalence of such "late feminist cursi" as reflected in *Yesenia* is further highlighted in its 1970s Soviet reception—and its transnational resonance speaks to both some underlying historical similarities and a shared cultural logic of its global moment.

CURSI vs. POSHLOST'

In its historical formation, rooted in its ambivalence toward or rejection of revolutionary and modernizing state practices (in particular, those of the early part of the twentieth century), the discourse on the Mexican cursi aesthetic demonstrates surprising parallels with its Soviet correlate—a cluster of equally culturally specific terms: *poshlost', byt,* and *kul'turnost'* (the latter discussed in the prelude and chapter two). The Russian word *poshlost'*, famously discussed by Vladimir Nabokov, points to a category of bad taste that combines banality with vulgarity and sexual undertones—an attitude toward the sentimental realm as much as toward mass culture, marked as artistically trivial and spiritually or morally deficient.[25] As much as Monsiváis's designation of *lo cursi* as a dominant national aesthetic, both Nabokov's and cultural critic Svetlana Boym's explorations of the term construct it as intrinsic to Russian self-understanding: "Poshlost' and its vehement critique are at the core of the definition of Russian identity, both national and cultural."[26]

Importantly, Boym links *poshlost'* to another culturally specific Russian term, *byt*—which signifies simultaneously the domestic sphere and the drudgery of the everyday. With its unmistakable connotations of the feminine sphere, the negative connotations of *byt* historically tap into a particular category of bad taste—such as in reference to excessive and/or old-fashioned home décor—"domestic trash" as Boym terms it.[27] Heroic opposition to byt constructed both the Russian and the Soviet intelligentsia's cultural ideals and, periodically (in the 1920s and 1960s) official Soviet cultural policies designed to minimize its spread and impose a more ascetic lifestyle enhanced by functional design, free of clutter or frivolities. Together with the more officially constructed cultural category of *kul'turnost'*, which demarcates the contours of good taste in the broadest sense of educational, behavioral, and, ultimately, moral standards, Boym argues that the terms *poshlost'* and *byt* form a semantic and cultural cluster that is key to understanding the historical transformation of Russian and Soviet culture in the twentieth century.[28] At the same time, as we will see, it can shed light on the specificities of the cultural translation of Mexican cursi feminist icons, like Yesenia, into the Soviet milieux.

In their respective Hispanic and Russian contexts, scholars see the emergence of such categories of bad taste—and their cultural and political force in the battle for national self-definition—as first and foremost a reaction to the belatedness of their encounter with modernity (and the creation of middle-class culture), pointing to the gap between the appearances and the reality of development, in particular in its uneven temporality.[29] Boym traces the etymology of *poshlost'* as originally linked explicitly to the past, meaning simply "old and common."[30] In this, it is remarkably close to Monsiváis's emphasis on the Mexican cursi as "that which brings us closer to previous sensibilities at their peak."[31] In nineteenth-century Russia, Boym argues, this notion began to intersect with the fear of everyday sexuality and sentimentality, both offensive in their excesses: much like byt, which threatens to envelope and suffocate the heroic revolutionary asceticism with meaningless everyday routinization, poshlost' "risks 'prostituting' national culture, turning tradition into fashion, love into sexuality, spirituality into triviality."[32] Mass culture in its various forms is held up as the culprit, and differentiating and delineating between bad mass culture and postrevolutionary, state-mandated, democratic (therefore, also mass) cultural practices and forms becomes a major point of contention for much of the twentieth century in both Mexico and the Soviet Union.

Unsurprisingly, in Russia as elsewhere, the aesthetic regime of both production and consumption of mass culture was frequently femininized—thus, *poshlost'* was understood early on as an intrinsic quality of "women's genres" (or even of all artistic productions accessible to women). It became particularly pronounced in the first quarter of the twentieth century at the moment when urban vernacular culture, from the burlesque to the overtly sentimentalist, rose to greater visibility while being commercialized and reified—part of the same process that activated cursi aesthetics in Mexico in roughly the same period. And, as we will soon see, in Russia as in Mexico, popular music—even more than the literary or other artistic spheres—reflected this new vernacular aesthetic.

The revolution made poshlost' a politically charged terrain. Despite the original revolutionary fervor, embodying a valiant attempt to destroy the daily grind and elevate petit bourgeois private emotions to a higher and purer spiritual plain, very quickly the state began to simultaneously coopt and delineate the contours of poshlost' in its policies and practices. As in Mexico, it became the space where the agency of the popular could become expressed—and the disdain for it did not prevent hegemonic cultural institutions from incorporating its many elements into the mainstream. In the 1930s through 1950s, as Vera Dunham famously explored, "this process culminated in a peculiar pact between the Stalinist state and the new Soviet middle class"—coded, in particular, through the notion of *kul'turnost'*, which elevated poshlost' to a middlebrow status.[33]

During those very decades, the state was particularly vigilant over its borders—keeping sentimentalist and burlesque vernacular expressions out of the officially accepted realm. As we explored in the prelude, the cult of Lolita Torres, which occurred precisely at the end of that period, brought together the long-standing cultural norms of *kul'turnost'* with the post-Stalinist liberalization and inclusion of "private feelings." Twenty years later, *Yesenia's* reception in the Soviet Union tapped into an even longer history of this aesthetic cluster, which was being revitalized, yet again, right at that moment.

Boym states decidedly that "the war against poshlost' is a cultural obsession of the Russian and Soviet intelligentsia from the 1860s to 1960s"—thus raising the question of what happened in the 1970s.[34] She sees that decade as the moment when, just as with the Western postmodernist embrace of kitsch and camp, the Soviet intelligentsia likewise conceded to these previously debased values and their ongoing cultural vitality.[35] This included the ever-increasing passion for consumerism (which certainly marked the aesthetic regime of poshlost'): more than ever, in the 1970s, mass-produced foreign goods, from vinyl records to plastic shopping bags, become "the fetish and the desirable black-market commodities" of all sociocultural groups, increasingly forming part of the texture of everyday life, albeit in its informal manifestation.[36] The result, however, as several cultural scholars have argued, was not a "lowering" of the cultural standards but a new ambivalent aesthetic regime that characterized late socialism (what Alexei Yurchak termed *outsidedness*, or *vnye*, and Peter Schmeltz explores through the notion of *polystylism*).[37]

This description produces a certain contradiction: both poshlost' and *lo cursi* entail not only an aesthetic associated with particular objects or genres, but a mode of consumption and a relationship to art—a relationship that can only be described as too immediate, where the consuming subject judges aesthetic value as doubly determined by its induction of strong sentiments (therefore irrational) and by its presumed direct link to reality (therefore naïve).[38] At best such an approach is at odds with, and at worst it is incompatible with, either irony or polystylism as articulated by the scholars of late socialism. The earnest popular reception of the 1970s melodrama—and the dismay it caused the equally earnest Soviet film critics—testifies to the fact that while this ironic and ludic attitude was certainly typical of the intelligentsia and artistic elites (especially the younger ones), it did not fully extend across sociocultural classes and generations. Moreover, even for the intelligentsia, guarding the boundaries of taste and specific aesthetic regimes was as serious a business as ever before—it's just that these boundaries were shifting, and, in the Soviet case in particular, the state was increasingly less invested in dictating them. The artists—including filmmakers—were quite willing to test them, as often out of a desire to revitalize the old as to experiment with the new.[39] This shifting attitude was particularly evident in the dynamics of the return of both melodrama and romantic popular songs to Soviet screens, whose aesthetics reflect the shared dynamics of both Russian poshlost' and Mexican cursi.

THE RETURN OF ROMANCE

The increasing engagement of Soviet filmmakers (who were undoubtedly full-fledged members of the intelligentsia), in the mainstream middlebrow cinematic culture of the 1970s, with what would have been considered unacceptable poshlost' just a decade before is evidenced in the reappearance of the formerly denigrated genre of domestic melodrama, discussed in chapter 2. But even more so, it is evident in the dominance of historical romantic dramas and musicals on both large and small screens. The most celebrated examples of films belonging to these genres include *The Flight* (Aleksandr Alov and Vladimir Naumov, 1970), *Lautary* (Emil' Loteanu, 1972), *The Station Master* (Sergei Soloviov, 1972), *The Captivating Star of Happiness* (Vladimir Motyl', 1975), *A Slave of Love* (Nikita Mikhalkov, 1975), *Gypsies Are Found Near Heaven* (Emil' Loteanu, 1975), *An Unfinished Piece for the Mechanical Piano* (Nikita Mikhalkov, 1977), and *A Hunting Accident* (Emil' Loteanu, 1978). Most of them were literary adaptations, including several of Chekhov—a writer whose oeuvre was entirely dedicated to the theme of the inescapable and undefeatable powers of poshlost' and byt. Their tone, unlike that of historical film adaptations of the previous decades, is unapologetically nostalgic vis-à-vis the prerevolutionary past, as expressed in their loving treatment of the very details of its everyday (byt) and its private feelings. Nearly all of them feature suffering women who embody "the epoch," at once as icons of the lost prerevolutionary culture (the object of nostalgia) and yet also as major points of audience identification. And all of them—whether categorized as musicals or not—are particularly remembered by their soundtracks, featuring memorable melodies and romantic songs, written for the screen, which thereafter entered the broader cultural domain to be rerecorded and performed by popular stars and amateurs alike. Whether diegetic or nondiegetic, these songs and musical themes came to express the overall tone of those films. And, regardless of the genre of the movie, this tone was decidedly sentimental.

Marking this cultural shift was the return to the realm of official culture of romances (*romansy*), songs that have their origins in eighteenth-century French recitations of "poems of ancient love and gallantry" to music, nineteenth-century German romantic *Lieder*, Russian folk melodies, and, most significantly, Romani musical production, aka "gypsy music." At the turn of the twentieth century, their vernacular versions—so-called *gorodskie/bytovye romansy*—were the most popular form of music in prerevolutionary Russia. Urban romances were associated simultaneously with amateur performances that were part of everyday Russian culture—byt—and with the demimonde of cabaret and street cafés.[40] They were frequently performed by Romani musicians, and even when they were not, this musical style was still associated with them—while fully consistent with the broader stylistic norms for expressing authenticity. As Anna Fishzon demonstrates in her analysis of the nineteenth-century Russian gramophone culture, authenticity was conceived in emotionally intense, confessional terms and expressed in an operatic style.[41] Romances operated within this register, usually expressing "the yearning for a past, departed or unrequited love that had fizzled out, together with dreams about some other 'mighty passions' or a celebration of gypsies' unimpeded lifestyle."[42] Just as lamentation over lost or impossible love and/or crushed hopes and dreams was a dominant motif of both tangos and boleros, "gypsy" or urban romances functioned within the same affective register—linguistically cued by the frequent use of the word *toska*, which expresses intense and desperate yearning, longing, melancholy, and anguish.[43]

For much of the Stalinist and post-Stalinist period from the late 1920s into the 1950s, urban and "gypsy" romances were associated with petit bourgeois, decadent, or criminal culture and, to varying degrees, were decried in official culture, eager to separate the more academic classical variant from the vernacular form. But, as David MacFadyen emphatically concludes in his survey of Russian popular song of the first half of the twentieth century, "the passion of romance survived politics (although some of [it] survived only in exile)."[44] In the 1970s, romances made a triumphant comeback, fully reincorporated into the official popular music sphere, particularly through cinema. Renditions of the old romances and a whole range of new ones entered popular soundtracks of the 1970s, both diegetically and nondiegetically, and many of the popular romantic songs from the Soviet period come from the movies of that period.

This shift arguably also allowed for the surprisingly continuous popularity of the Latin romantic songs, from Lolita Torres's performances to "Bésame Mucho." If, in the 1950s, these songs stood out as vibrant examples of exciting foreignness, so appealing to the generation of the Thaw, by the 1970s they had become utterly ubiquitous, part of the country's sonic landscape. Thus, upon his return from the Soviet Union in 1974, Rodolfo Echeverría was quick to report the total omnipresence of "Bésame Mucho" (as well as the Russians' constant mispronunciation of its lyrics), performed virtually everywhere music was played during his trip (which took place the same year that *Yesenia* was released).[45] Consumed without clear national denominations, as a regional monolith, Latin American popular music—emblematized by "Bésame Mucho"—connoted various registers of excessive emotions, from sentimental melancholy to unrestrained passions— overlapping with the local vernacular romantic music tradition (including "gypsy music") in Russia, despite their somewhat different musical roots. In its Soviet reception, the melodic structure and basic harmony of "Bésame Mucho" were recognized as identical to those of "gypsy" and "criminal" romances—albeit combined with Latin rhythmic structure, thus acquiring an even greater affective charge through its exotic associations.[46] Both, after all, were anachronistic renditions of European lyrical (or operatic) music and local exotic vernacular (Romani or Afro-Caribbean) influences, resulting in heart-rending romantic hits. The conflation, within the twentieth-century Soviet context, between vernacular (pseudo-gypsy or pseudo-Russian) music and "salon music" (the closest Russian equivalent of the cursi bolero)—is apparent, for example, in this Soviet account of prerevolutionary Russian music: "There was indeed a time (which we recall with a smile) when on the Russian pre-revolutionary estrada heart-rending romances were popular. They had a somewhat 'harsh' intonation, as in the pseudo-gypsy or pseudo-Russian songs 'My Heart Is Broken,' 'Booze-Up, What a Booze-Up,' 'Marusia Got Poisoned' and so on. During the First World War the bourgeois public also loved salon songs about refined feelings, exoticism, and eroticism: 'I'm Tired of Life,' 'Lady Coke-Head,' 'Kitty Dear' and others. Performers sang these works with a languid limpness."[47]

After a long hiatus, Soviet heart-rending *romansy* returned to the mainstream in the 1970s, visible even in the titles of many films—*Urban Romance* (*Gorodskoi romans*, Piotr Todorovskii, 1971), *A Lover's Romance* (*Romans o vliublennykh*, Andrei Konchalovskii, 1974), *Cruel Romance* (*Zhestokii romans*, Eldar Riazanov, 1984)—along with the cognate *roman*, meaning a love story or a romantic novel, consistent with the more common usage of "romance" in English, for example *Sentimental Romance* (*Sentimental'nyi roman*, Igor Maslennikov, 1976) and *Office Romance* (*Sluzhebnyi roman*, Eldar Riazanov, 1977), which, incidentally also feature famous *romansy*—including "gypsy" ones—in their soundtracks.

"THE GYPSY AESTHETIC" IN SOVIET
HISTORICAL MELODRAMA

In many of these 1970s Soviet historical romances, "the gypsy theme" emerges not only in its latent form, embedded in the very history of the genre of Russian vernacular romantic music, but as built into the films' diegesis, as a crucial part of the cultural landscape of nostalgia for the prerevolutionary past. Romani musical performers are at the narrative center of two films by the Moldovan director Emil Loteanu, *Lautary* and *Gypsies Are Found Near Heaven* (*Tabor ukhodit v nebo*). And while their presence in both Eldar Riazanov's and Nikita Mikhalkov's historical melodramas of the period functions primarily as part of the background, they are nevertheless crucial to establishing the affective and expressive core of these films.

Indeed, the association between Romani culture and sentimentalism in Russia was so pronounced that another term for bad taste and "vulgar sentimentality" was the untranslatable *tsyganshchina*. It was most commonly applied to the style of musical performances—but extended to sentimentalism in "boulevard" literature and early film melodrama (which did, indeed, often feature "gypsy passions"), as well as more generally excessive behavior, décor, or fashion—whether flamboyant, decadent, blasé, or fervent.[48] This mirrored the relationship established by the French term *la bohème*, a term for vagabonds and marginals attributed to the Roma (who were mistakenly believed to come to France from the region of Bohemia), and which expanded in the nineteenth century to mean all those, especially the "artistic" set, who adopted unconventional social habits, associated with the margins of romanticism.[49] It is not surprising, then, that one of the myths surrounding the etymology of the Spanish term *cursi* likewise attributed it to "gypsy slang" in Spain.[50] The productivity of this cluster of terms underscores its vitality as a vibrant cultural phenomenon and an aesthetic category.

Its placement on a scale of aesthetic judgment and cultural power (even in a low or negative position) served a complex function: assuring its lower status while paradoxically acknowledging and legitimizing the presence of Romani cultural production within Russian life. This also coincided with the decline of the patronage of the courts, church, and nobility, and with the transformation of the artist's labor vis-à-vis new spheres of media, which demanded education but did not yet have a firm foothold in capitalist enterprise. At the same time, these myths perpetuated the racialization of the Roma people by attributing to them essential social qualities, while simultaneously reinforcing and naturalizing the traditional (imperial and class-based) aesthetic hierarchies.

By the 1920s and 1930s, *tsyganshchina* became a particular and commonly used accusation against popular singers *tout court*—which nonetheless did not diminish Romani musical tradition's inextricability from popular Soviet romantic music. At the same time, the actual Roma's performances remained a constant presence in the public sphere. As Anna G. Piotrowska, a Polish historian of Romani music, affirms, it "can be credited for shaping the urban sonic space of those places" and should be "viewed as instrumental in negotiating the centrality of the Romani aural presence in Russian public spaces."[51] A Romani section of the Ethnographic Theater having opened in Leningrad in 1929, and the Romen Theater having been founded in Moscow in 1929, throughout the Soviet period Romani performance culture became integrated within the system of state support and state control. Crucially, the campaigns against *tsyganshchina* were not geared toward eliminating Romani music culture, but rather toward delineating the contours of its legitimacy and defining its precise role in the state's creation of an assimilated Soviet collectivity.[52] The official reverence for the "right kind" of Romani performance culture kept racial hierarchies distinct, creating a designated space for the Roma and their role in Soviet public life (as performers), while invertedly perpetuating the "nonofficial" romantic vision of "the gypsies" as an ongoing cultural mythology. At the same time, it provided the Roma (specifically, Russka or Xeladytka Roma, who formed the majority of these official elite cultural institutions, such as the Romen Theater) exceptional and unprecedented security and visibility.[53]

From the 1970s into the 1980s, with the revitalization of melodramatic modes on Soviet screens, films thematically centered on the Roma—inevitably foregrounding their musical and dance performances—also become increasingly frequent: apart from the already mentioned *Lautary* and *Gypsies Are Found Near Heaven*, as well as *Gypsy Happiness* (*Tsyganskoye shchaste*, Sergei Nikonenko, 1983), there were several made-for-TV film productions: *Gypsy* (*Tsygan*, Alexander Blank, 1979) and its sequel *The Return of Budulai* (*Vozvrashchenie Budulaia*, Alexander Blank, 1985), an enormously popular miniseries about a Roma villager struggling to regain his memory and reunite with his family.[54] Employing, to varying degrees, romantic stereotypes and actual Romani performers, the "gypsy" figure in these films functioned similarly to that in the Hungarian context, where, according to Anikó Imre, it offered "metaphorical screens . . . onto which the East Central European nation projects its own repudiated or idealized images—those that contradict or exceed, and therefore cannot be contained within, the nationalist rhetoric of universal brotherhood, equality, and democracy."[55]

In the Soviet case, however, these symbolic negotiations were inseparable from the ongoing attempt to reclaim and redefine the "private" and affective sphere within the developed socialism of the Brezhnev era. These fantasies of nonassimilation under the modern nation-state and socialist internationalism gestured toward the creation of new collectivities of sentimental publics via industrial mass media. The supposedly "unruly sentimentality and sensuality" of "the gypsy" served as metaphors of and proxies for the popular and populist impulse of those who felt themselves positioned outside of dominant and approved forms of collectivity. As such, they created an aesthetic that critically underscored the stigmas of gendered and racialized dimensions of the state's hegemonic control, while reinforcing them at the same time. *Yesenia*'s image—in both its Mexican production and its Soviet reception—reflects this contradictory combination of highly conservative gender norms with liberatory impulses, mixing the still predominant ideals of social (and racial) equality and the correspondingly complex set of community allegiances with an emerging (neo)liberal aspiration for individual heteronormative self-realization.

As is evident from the preceding discussion, *Yesenia*'s reliance on "gypsy culture" as an international marker of a cluster of emotional authenticity and intensity, music and dance, and social and cultural exclusion was undoubtably one of the reasons for its easy cultural translatability in the socialist world, resonant with the return of the figure of "the gypsy" to Soviet screens. And in the Soviet Union, as we have already seen, representations of the Romani culture were extremely popular, especially in the 1970s, thus forming an immediate cultural context for *Yesenia*'s reception. The year after *Yesenia* broke all box office records in 1975, the highest-grossing film, with some 64.9 million tickets sold, was *Gypsies Are Found Near Heaven*, based on romantic, Orientalist stories by Maxim Gorkii in his early, pre-socialist-realist phase. During the prerevolutionary period, Gorkii was one of the fiercest ideologues of anti-philistinism (*meshchanstvo*, yet another cognate term with *poshlost'* but with a much more unambiguous class designation), and within his romantic vision the Roma people serve, above all, as the alternative to the materialism and utilitarianism of the modern age.[56] The film takes place in late nineteenth-century Bessarabia and is set within a Romani camp. While its romantic leads were played by Moldovan non-Roma actors, the film featured many artists from the Romen Theater, with songs that had formed the theater's first repertoire in the 1930s, performed in the original language.[57] In fact, the costumes and musical performances in both this film and *Yesenia* show remarkable similarities and are, indeed, consistent with Romani folkloric self-representation both in Mexico and the Soviet Union. And, along with *Moscow Does Not Believe in Tears*, to which we will return at the end of this book, *Gypsies Are Found Near Heaven* was one of the rare successful Soviet cinematic exports to Mexico in the early 1980s.[58]

LA GITANA IN MEXICAN CINEMA

Romani culture, of course, had its own vexed history on Mexican screens. Initially part of the Spanish cinematic vocabulary, in the 1940s through 1960s the figure of "the gypsy woman"—*la gitana*—became particularly visible in Mexico's numerous coproductions with Spain. These films usually adopted the narrative structure typical of Spanish folkloric musicals of Franco's era (*españoladas*, discussed briefly in the prelude). Most of them centered on the union between a male protagonist belonging to a higher socioeconomic stratum (landowner, military, or lawyer) and a woman of lower standing—working class or Lumpenproletariat, typically presented as an Andalusian "gypsy." The main original ideological function of these films was to serve as a cultural mediation, appropriating and pacifying the earlier Popular Front ideologies to present an idealized image of Spanish hegemony and nonantagonistic class relations.[59] Jo Labanyi analyzes this exploitation of an image of an Andalusian "gypsy" culture as a projection of Spain's response to modernization during cultural homogenization and integration into the capitalist market.[60] The marriage as the ultimate outcome of such narratives represents the triumph of both.

Mexican-Spanish coproductions, as well as Mexican films taking place in Spain or with the significant participation of Spanish filmmakers, which became prominent in the late 1940s, retained this formula—and the "gypsy" protagonist (almost always female) in these films functions as a stand-in not only for Andalusian folklore, but for Spain at large. In these Pan-Hispanic variants, Spanish nationalism gave way to narratives that underscored a Spanish-Mexican fraternity through "a nationally inscribed romance . . . whose most emblematic protagonists were the Mexican macho, embodied in the figure of a charro . . . and the Spanish gitana and flamenco dancer."[61] The latter (whose *bailaora* and Romani identities often seem to be interchangeable) was best known in Mexico through the performances of Lola Flores, while the most famous *charro* was none other than Jorge Negrete, one of Mexico's biggest stars.[62] This reconfiguration ultimately reversed the traditional geopolitical power hierarchies between Spain and Mexico, with the latter "conquering" the former, as these films' international reception was driven, at least in part, by Negrete's international popularity. Some of the other coproductions starred María Félix, thus inverting the formula by focusing on a Mexican femme fatale.[63] As such, this genre played into the construction of the Mexican national-popular imaginary, more than the other way round, thereby subsuming both the Andalusian and "gypsy" identity within it.

Narratively, rather than constructing a fantasy of social mobility through marriage, as was typical of *españoladas*, these films instead affirm the social status quo, whereby marriage between nonequals becomes credible to the viewer only when the two turn out to be, in fact, of the same social class. This is realized through the trope of unexpected inheritance and/or newly discovered family ties as part of the common melodramatic trope of mistaken identity (which is central to *Yesenia*'s narrative as well).[64] Yet the mediation between the two opposed models of class and cultural belonging, while central to all these narratives, is realized differently in different films. In such classics of the genre as *Two Charros and a Gitana* (*Dos charros y una gitana*, Antonio Román, 1956), the opposition between the upper-class, well-mannered and mild-tempered love interest and a temperamental and passionate lower-class ingenue with no regard for social conventions allows for the Pygmalion motif, whereby "the gypsy" is reeducated through the erasure of all characteristics of popular class (and/or "gypsy") identity, which is common to many of these films and also evident in *Yesenia*. But sometimes this dynamic is reversed, making "the gypsy" the force that transforms and liberates the (weak and prepressed) male protagonist—usually using music and dance as acceptable signifiers of inherent freedom and expressivity of the "gypsy" and/ or Andalusian identity. And as the genre evolved, it acquired increasingly more self-parodic attributes, whereby the stereotypes are fully acknowledged as such, providing the comedic core of the spectacle. Unlike that of the more apparently reactionary *españoladas*, the gender politics of these Pan-Hispanic films was more complex, as the very image of a strong, successful, and (to a point) independent woman—which was always at the center of such narratives—stood in considerable contrast, in the context of Franco-era Spain, to the country's extremely conservative religious gender politics.[65]

Beyond the specific subgenre of the Mexican-Spanish coproductions, an even older figure of the exotic, passionate, but ultimately dangerous "gypsy woman" in Mexico had also been historically mediated by its French models, most famously embodied in the character of Carmen from Prosper Mérimée's eponymous novella, which provided the libretto for the perhaps even more famous Bizet opera.[66] As already seen in the example of the very term *la bohème*, French associations with the "gypsy" culture constituted a shared cultural reference point far beyond France or even Europe. In the Soviet Union, Mérimée's *Carmen* likewise provided a common template for the representation of a "gypsy woman," not least through its many cinematic versions, from a trophy 1943 French-Italian film adaptation, which was screened from 1954 on, to the enormously popular 1983 Carlos Saura film. In the 1970s, however, it had a very specific point of reference: the ballet *Carmen Suite*, which was created by the choreographer of the Ballet Nacional de Cuba, Alberto Alonso, for the Soviet *prima ballerina assoluta* Maia Plissetskaia in 1967. When first performed, the ballet was banned by the Ministry of Culture for its "eroticism" and "deviant technique." As both of these official critiques referred to the specifically Cuban elements of its choreography, the scandal furthered Soviet associations between the Spanish "gypsy" and contemporary Latin American (dance) culture as erotically charged and thus subversive vis-à-vis official Soviet cultural norms. When the ban on the ballet was lifted three years later, in 1970, its film version was both frequently shown on Soviet TV and exported internationally. Plissetskaia was, after all, as one of the world's most renowned female ballet dancers, a key player in Soviet cultural diplomacy abroad.[67]

It is hardly a coincidence, then, that just as *Yesenia* was being purchased for exhibition in the Soviet Union, Sonia Amelio was negotiating the terms for the Soviet-Mexican coproduction (as discussed in chapter 1). This film was supposed to be based on none other than Bizet's *Carmen Suite*, scripted by the head of the Soviet-Mexican Cultural Association, Lev Kulidzhanov—and to star Amelio herself. It was meant to inaugurate the entry of Latin America into the subsequent edition of the Tashkent festival (which until then officially included only Asia and Africa).[68] Amelio's fame as a player of the castanet, an instrument strongly associated with flamenco and, by extension, with Andalusian Romani performances, perfectly positioned her for this role—and she was, no doubt, hoping to assume the same cultural role for Mexico as Plissetskaia did for the Soviet Union. Although, like so many other planned coproductions, the Soviet-Mexican *Carmen* never materialized, this choice speaks to its recognition as a shared cultural text with numerous versions and reappropriations in both countries. Nor was the image of the Romani exceptional on Mexican TV screens at the time (or to this day)—in fact, the direct competition to *Yesenia* in 1970 was another "gypsy"-themed telenovela, *Renzo el Gitano*.[69]

Reflecting a similar peculiar transculturation, Yesenia's "gypsy" identity in Vargas Dulché's depiction mixes Spanish Calé Roma elements with distinctly Eastern European Ludar ones. The character first appeared in Vargas Dulché's earlier historietas of the 1940s as Zorina, a Slavic name associated in particular with Eastern European heritage. In 1965, renamed Yesenia (a Spanish name with Arabic origins), she became the main character in an eponymous historieta. Such confusion in some ways reflects the reality, given that many Roma did initially arrive in Mexico in the early twentieth century from the Balkans and the Russian empire (hence the misnomer *húngaros* in the Mexican vernacular), many coming from Ludar communities.[70] And the film version of *Yesenia* made an unusual effort to create a level of cultural authenticity by engaging a group of local Romani performers to act in all the scenes in the film that focus on the Romani camp to which Yesenia initially belongs.[71] Andere also claims to have picked the costumes for her character in the film directly from Romani sellers in Mexico City who provided her with clothes, jewelry, and even shoes (this was after Fanny Cano refused to allow Andere to use the wardrobe from the telenovela).[72] Claims to such a relationship with the production may appear dubious, given the virtual invisibility of the real Romani and other nomadic peoples in the country to date. But from the turn of the century, and especially between the 1940s and 1980s, the most common occupation among members of the Romani communities in Mexico was mobile film projection—which required obtaining many official permits, thus entailing considerable institutional familiarity and regular contacts with film authorities.[73]

A common motif associated with the figure of "a gypsy" as a cultural text shared between Mexico and the Soviet Union—in addition to its associations with sentimentality, sensuality, and anachronistic, nostalgic visions of the vernacular culture—is the molding of unruly female sexuality into a civilized, modern, "national" body through marriage. In the Mexican case, this national-hegemonic plot is more pronounced—and it is no wonder that only the charismatic symbol of the proud Mexican *charro* could be a true match to the Andalusian "gypsy." In the Soviet case, however, the image of the gypsy tends to foreground its primary markers of emotional authenticity and of the utopian possibility of social and political *non-belonging*, at odds with or in excess of the dominant Soviet models.[74] In the following discussion of *Yesenia*, I attempt to bring together these slightly divergent cultural readings as nonetheless pointing to the larger stakes of the shared transnational imaginary the film produces.

YESENIA'S IDENTITY

The narrative identity of Yesenia as a "gypsy" (albeit a mistaken one, "corrected" in the course of the narrative) underscores her marginalized position, shared by those other Global South icons of Soviet screens: Raj Kapoor's Vagabond in *Awara* (1955) and the eponymous protagonist of the Brazilian TV series *The Slave Isaura*, whose stories are likewise those of outcasts, and/or of social and racial "passing" and mistaken identities. The tension between the protagonist's experience of social and cultural non-belonging and its ultimate resolution through the restoration of the correct bloodlines, so central to melodramatic plotting, was clearly crucial to the emotional impact of these cultural texts. *Yesenia*'s casting of a nonracialized actress (which prefigures the popularity of *Isaura*—whose character, a mixed-race, light-skinned slave, was played by a white actress) underscores this tension, symptomatic of the disavowal of nonwhiteness within the countries' respective media industries—which no doubt eased their reception and assimilation in the Soviet Bloc.

In this respect, too, *Yesenia*'s textual politics are obviously problematic. It has become commonplace to show how melodramas powerfully expose conflicts and contradictions that require a more radical transformation—in their narrative resolution offering instead either solace through compassion, by way of a cathartic tragic ending, or the fantasy of a happy ending reconstituting the very natural order that created the problems in the first place. Along these same lines, there is no doubt that *Yesenia*'s emotional impact relies on its foregrounding and celebration of the socially marginalized status of its protagonist and her community. Yesenia repeatedly mocks and subverts (at times through physical violence) the pretensions of the higher classes who deny her entry into their ranks, thus allowing for projections of the emotional experience of the audience's own disfranchisement and its cathartic release. As a "gypsy," Yesenia exists outside the assimilable space of the nation-state: a rare, almost impossible situation for either the Mexican or the Soviet cultural and political imaginary (this is underscored by her ignorance of the Virgin of Guadalupe, an enduring symbol of Mexican identity—the fact used by García Riera is his review as the final proof of the narrative implausibility of the script). Yet this melodramatic narrative ultimately restores Yesenia's "natural" belonging to the very aristocracy she mocked earlier and to the national (and religious) hegemony she had blissfully ignored—to her rightful place within a colonial hacienda and a Catholic church that is experienced as the ultimate fulfillment of her true desires. The question then becomes, to some extent: What exactly is offered in this fantasy of fulfillment, especially in its transnational reception?

As was increasingly the case with Soviet melodramas of the 1970s, the ultimate horizon for *Yesenia* is not the public space of the street but the private space. Lolita Torres's two characters in *The Age of Love* are singers whose careers are at odds with the class status of their beloved's or their parents' expectations, and whose reconciliation between private and public desires takes place as self-realization on stage. Such compromises, while compelling in the earlier moment of socialist-populist reconstruction (of Perón's Argentina or Khrushchev's Soviet Thaw), are no longer symbolically available in the 1970s. *Yesenia*'s ecstatic moment of conflict resolution takes place in the most traditional manner, through a church wedding, and is geared entirely toward the domestic. The wedding, however, plays a complex narrative role, reconciling the earlier "gypsy" marriage (complete with the ritual of the mixing of bride and groom's blood) with the Catholic one, thus in some ways legitimizing both while eliminating any potential incompatibility between these divergent sources of the law, neither of which is directly articulated through the state.

For Soviet audiences, this finale was all the more phantasmagoric in that it was geographically, historically, and politically removed, with no possible equivalent in their contemporary socialist society—thus hardly functioning as meaningful restoration of a hegemonic order, but rather pointing to the shared fantasy of a prerevolutionary past with its imported (French) aristocratic culture.[75] Anecdotally, some fans of *Yesenia* in rural parts of Russia did not even identify it as Mexican, Latin American, or foreign more generally—the combination of "gypsy"

FIGURE 16. *Yesenia*'s depiction of the Roma camp—note the samovar. DVD screen grab.

and "aristocratic" milieux was visually so generic and consistent with the conventions of Soviet period dramas, and its dubbing (which was a common exhibition practice) so convincing, as to convincingly "domesticate" its reception.

As such, the stereotypical iconicity of characters and settings secures their familiarity and typicality across the national and cultural divides and, as Jane Tompkins argues in the context of American sentimental fiction, "rather than making them bankrupt or stale, are the basis of their effectiveness as integers in a social equation."[76] Likewise, the film's score is so generic that it was perceived as "universal" in its combination of romantic and "gypsy" melodic structures—at once memorable (as evidenced by the many comments below the YouTube clips of the theme music) and utterly ubiquitous. As such, it formed part of a global affective vernacular whose very form—perceived as excessive or otherwise at odds with official cultural norms—foregrounds the passions and, most importantly, the suffering of those positioned outside of cultural, political, and economic hegemony (which, by the 1970s, included the hegemony of the intelligentsia). In Mexico, the affects similarly tapped into the sense of cultural marginalization of the popular classes combined with radical redefinitions of feminine agency, clearly mediated by the increasing power of mass cultural industries and the needs of global capital. Thus, the cultural geopolitical particularity of the experience of marginalization (Mexican/Romani) in the film ensures its emotional authenticity for the viewer—while the transcendency of its cultural markers (their stereotypical generic quality) allows for its claim to universality, but a new kind of universality that stems from the very initial exclusion from it. Such alternative political orientation is articulated by Lauren Berlant as a search for a new vernacular language: "The centrality of melodrama and comedy in sentimental publics expresses a desire for a new vernacular, a new realism to be established in the dominant public: it speaks to the thinness of common sense. Processes of vernacularization are always struggles over the consensual terms in which nondominant ordinariness is expressed."[77]

The idea of melodrama as "a new (vernacular) realism" perhaps helps explain the frequency with which the Soviet publics explain their preference for Indian popular cinema by asserting its "realism"—a claim that is hard to understand using conventional aesthetic categories, as Neepa Majumdar points out.[78] The same claims of emotional verisimilitude are noted by Turovskaia in her description of the audiences' understanding of *Yesenia* as a film that is "about them"—and therefore experienced as "realistic." Such audience experiences lead us to understand melodramatic conventions and stereotypes as expressing the "nondominant ordinariness" of sentimental publics whose very existence is unacknowledged by the hegemonic culture, forming a new vernacular language that is "realist" insofar as it can finally express this universal collective. Such a demand for universalism in the face of persistent rejections and exclusions (at the geopolitical level, within the global world order, and within the nation, of those marginalized within it) from the universal is, similarly, what is at stake in Monsiváis's analysis of *la cursilería*. As Brandon Bisbey notes, citing Monsiváis, "The ferocious sentimentalism locked in the ghetto of cursilería proves that one Pure Sentiment is equal to any Pure Sentiment, if sincerity is the norm and there is no reason for it not to be"—such emphasis on sentimentality is then, at least in part, "an expression of a desire for full modern subjecthood."[79] This "realism" is finally achieved through identification with the foreign character, creating a global-popular icon.

Significantly, however, this new universal vernacular, produced from within the hegemonic mainstream and seen in its transnational Mexican-Soviet dimension, presents a remarkable shared projection of alterity as signifier of authenticity, passion, and emancipatory non-belonging embodied in the image of "the gypsy." As such, this image stands in an ambiguous position vis-à-vis the nation—at once meant to represent its "true spirit," molded into its national body, and yet celebrated and mourned for its very unassimilability and exclusion from that body. On the one hand, this image has its roots in shared Orientalist iconographies, with their projections of irrationality and excesses onto the "Others" of the European Enlightenment. On the other, it also speaks not only to the status of those marginalized within the national culture, but also to the national culture's own simultaneous belonging to and marginalization from the West (as constructed through the shared culture of Enlightenment values, capitalism, and colonialism), reflecting the respective peculiar geopolitical positioning of the two countries.

As discussed in the introduction, both Mexico and Russia have historically been constructed as "Others" of the European culture—and, in the twentieth century, of the US empire—while having developed their own modes of conceptualizing this relationship both to European culture and intellectual traditions and to US modernity, in a way that is significantly distinct from most postcolonial discourses. Such a complex form of entanglement produced their respective senses not only of national specificity, but also of the universal. Russia's—as well as Mexico's—imaginary engagement with the Romani (or "gypsy") identity is best seen as a reflection of such complex positionality. As Piotrowska notes in her discussion of romances, Russia's "elites positioned themselves as part of the European legacy, at the same time feeling the urge to emphasize their distinctiveness by means of a self-imposed and self-oriented idea of otherness. When blurring the lines between the 'Russian' and 'Gypsy' vocal romances, Russian intellectuals clearly embraced the fluidity of their own self-definition, as both types of romances alluded to the same aesthetic categories of nostalgia and melancholy."[80]

Bisbey makes a similar point about the function of the aesthetic of *lo cursi* in Mexico to argue for "the persistence of exaggeratedly sentimental romantic/modernista discourse in Mexican culture as a sort of 'failed attempt' of the culture of the entire nation to imitate the cultural codes of the Global North."[81] The aesthetic modality—*lo cursi* in Mexico and poshlost' in the Soviet Union, finding its manifestation in the melodramatic mode and its focal point in the figure of "the gypsy"—is a productive articulation of the sense of exclusion from or marginality to the European/US modernity from within its own codes of commercial mass culture. This exclusion is expressed both globally, via the geopolitical status of the nation, and locally, as marginalization within the nation-state. This non-belonging, both desired and mourned, speaks via the figure of "the gypsy" who is at once more "us" than "us," and yet isn't "us"—gesturing to a different construction of what is at the center of such popular modes of cultural expression: the people. But doing so brings particular attention to the inherent fissures and increasing conflicts embedded in the very categories that were meant to constitute one shared body—of "people," "nation," and "the masses"—and the cultural and political anxiety this process triggered.

To understand these divisions and their impact further, it is worth taking another musical detour. In his discussion, in *Noise Uprising*, of vernacular music around the globe in the 1920s (with the new market synthesis between radio, gramophone, and nightlife), Michael Denning goes so far as to argue that the discourse on "gypsy music" that emerged in the early twentieth century was paradigmatic for this broader phenomenon. His category of "vernacular musics" includes a wide range of genres emanating from colonial ports around the world, including "son, rumba, samba, tango, jazz, calypso, beguine, fado, flamenco, tzigane, rebetika, ṭarab, marabi, kroncong, hula."[82] Denning does not explicitly mention the bolero in his discussion (admittedly, the smoothness of bolero would be difficult to reconcile with the perception of "noise" crucial to Denning's analysis of the unruliness of such vernacular forms).[83] Nor does he include Soviet 1920s "vernacular musics"—understandably, for although Soviet sites such as Odessa played a similar cultural function musically as the other ports in his global narrative, they were no longer part of the same commercial and colonial circuit. Yet his discussion of "gypsy music" as paradigmatic for the meaning of vernacular culture is relevant to both bolero and Soviet vernacular music.

Through Béla Bartók's writing and other examples, Denning demonstrates that "gypsy music" in European discourses—like Black music in the US and South Africa—was understood not as a form of folk music (a category reserved for rural *national* peasantry) but rather as necessarily a commercialized hybrid, constructing "gypsy" performers as "outcast urban entertainers, virtuoso on other people's music"—and, above all, as "commercial musicians."[84] On the one hand, this devalues the creative originality and refuses the very status of "the people" to racialized groups. On the other, this emphasis on the mass-cultural core of these various "vernacular musics" also exposes the anxiety of artistic and intellectual elites in the face of such "impure" manifestations of the modern vernacular. We see this same anxiety expressed in the formation of both cursi and poshlost': Boym elucidates this point by noting that the latter "refers to a whole variety of 'impure' phenomena such as the mixed and eclectic low-brow urban culture—neither the aristocracy-intelligentsia nor the people—and in fact it jeopardizes the clear contrast between the two and threatens the intellectual's idealization of the people's culture and its national purity."[85]

Not that there was any such idealization remaining by the 1970s. The unruly vernacular cultures of the 1920s had, by the post–World War II period, largely been absorbed into the mainstream, recreating both poshlost' and cursilería within the official culture in yet another round of anachronisms. And indeed, both Boym and Monsiváis in their discussions focus on those expressions of cooptation of these categories by the Establishment, which become emblematic of the respective official state rituals as false claims to the state power's connection to the people. But the persistence of the more vernacular popular tastes remains equally unbearable for the Soviet intelligentsia. The reception of *Yesenia* demonstrates the profound state of the cultural division between the tastes of the majority of Soviet citizens and those of the Soviet cultural elites and intelligentsia, who aspired to middlebrow and highbrow "Western" (largely European) cultural standards and mocked or lamented the poshlost' of the masses moved by the doubly uncouth (lowbrow *and* non-Western) Mexican, Indian, and Egyptian films.

The rift would widen further in the subsequent decades. Writing in the 1990s, twenty-five years after she first wrote about the film, Turovskaia sums up her discussion of *Yesenia* (see chapter 1) in the following way: "The preference given in those years to the films originating in the Third World over the temptations of the not-so-infrequent commercial films from the West [speaks to] the degradation of the Soviet lifestyle to the level of the 'underdeveloped' countries."[86] This claim is factually incorrect, as the Soviet standard of living in the 1970s was dramatically improved over that of earlier decades—and, for most, was considerably higher than in the immediate post-Soviet period, when Turovskaia was writing this. Yet it clearly speaks to a sense of degradation among the intelligentsia, who saw their loss of the war against poshlost' as a victory not of Western (capitalist) mass culture or the "society of the spectacle," but of those very local, vernacular cultural forms coopted by Soviet state power.

Turovskaia explicitly links the popular taste for films like *Yesenia* to the criteria of Russian folkloric culture—which she understands as the archaic modes of collective artistic production embedded in everyday life, reaffirming traditional cultural codes—as opposed to art, rooted in individual creation by an auteur, aesthetic distance, and an orientation toward innovation.[87] The few Soviet reviews of *Yesenia* upon its release make this distinction clear as well: if one critic suggests that Soviet cinema needs to produce more—and better—films about love to "overcome Yesenia," another wonders why the more subtle and ironic versions of romantic films, namely those from France and Japan (the ultimate cinematic embodiments of auteurism and good taste for the cinephiles of the 1970s) did not earn the same appreciation among the popular audiences as the "artless" *Yesenia*.[88]

But it's the other leading Russian scholar of Soviet popular cinema, Neiia Zorkaia, also writing retrospectively in the 1990s, who puts this in the most explicit terms, calling Soviet popular taste "undeveloped, infantile and provincial": "This taste and the aesthetic behind it belong more to the Third World than to the West, whose lawful offspring cinema is. In this taste and aesthetic, forming a constant, we can clearly see traditions of folkloric taste and the aesthetic system typical of folk creations. To be even more exact, it's the aesthetic of *lubok*, the late-folkloric, adapted to the urban: the *lubok* lithography, festive booths and fairground attractions, pulp fiction from the fin de siècle, penny dreadfuls like *Nat Pinkerton*."[89]

Zorkaia, like Turovskaia, sees *Yesenia* as purely "a fake," an amateurish imitation of Western models—"Esmeralda for the poor played by a Mexican Gina Lollobrigida for the even poorer"—rather than as a product of a film industry, however "underdeveloped," with its own mixture of state and commercial interests.[90] To these critics, *Yesenia* is a direct expression of a shared archaic popular taste, an extension of vernacular practices of *lubok*, the nonindustrially produced "artisanal" (*kustarnye*) objects of mass consumption of the early twentieth century, a close cultural equivalent to "gypsy songs."[91]

What is particularly striking about this set of observations is their internal contradictions. They combine unquestioning assumptions about progressive historical development and the centrality and originality of European cultural models (vis-à-vis both Russia and Mexico), while acknowledging and even arguing for the very nonlinearity and hybridity of cultural forms. And they offer a disdainful and patronizing view of "the great Soviet nation and its whole population" that nonetheless assigns a great sense of agency to "the popular"—as an expression of a collective enduring will to exercise the people's own taste. Zorkaia blames her contemporary critics for the failure to analyze the "integral and mass success" of *Yesenia*—which, she insists, was not gendered, for she saw the film in the provincial town of Voronezh, where the theater was full of working-class men who watched the film in silence and, when leaving, kept repeating, "Well done, Mexicans."[92] She concludes that had "they" (presumably, film critics and scholars) analyzed this phenomenon at the time, they wouldn't have been shocked, some twenty years later, by "the avalanche of popular love for the tiny Verónica Castro," a television actress and singer, and wouldn't have assumed that all those telenovelas, such as *Simplemente María* and *Rosa salvaje*, "are forced on unarmed television audiences by some villains from the TV channels," but would see that they were instead a reflection of a "deeply felt, time-honored, stable passion of all the population of all our territory."[93]

Ironically, this understanding of the dynamics of "the popular" aligns Zorkaia and Turovskaia with the subaltern studies scholars—albeit from the opposing political position. Both Soviet critics clearly affirm what Bishnupriya Ghosh terms "a chaotic field of power" around the collective aspirations expressed in such passionate reception of global icons—a power, however, that is clearly seen by these critics as destructive rather than emancipatory.[94] If there is one thing Turovskaia and Zorkaia were right about, it is certainly the need to analyze and theorize more rigorously the notion of the popular within the Soviet and post-Soviet context.

But, if historically lacking in the Soviet context, such analysis has certainly been at the center of much of Latin American and Mexican criticism of the twentieth and twenty-first centuries, from Monsiváis and Roger Bartra to Néstor García Canclini (as discussed in the introduction). Varying in the degree of their appreciation of and generosity toward popular or mass cultural products, these Latin American critics nonetheless have been particularly attentive to the shifting historical contours of the category of "the people." However, unlike our (post-)Soviet scholars, eager to disavow any vestiges of Marxism in their analysis, they have been considerably more aware and attuned to the specifically market-industrial aspects of these seemingly "nonindustrial" (or *lubok*) cultural products.

In the concluding chapter, taking a cue from both these approaches, we will turn to *Yesenia* as reflecting the intersections between mass-produced imaginaries of fashion and glamour on the one hand and informal cultural production and consumption on the other. These spheres in both countries, I argue, occupied a crucial transitional space between the collapsing nationalist and state-socialist collectivities of the past and the impending neoliberal (postsocialist) regimes of the future—the transitional and transnational space that characterizes *Yesenia*'s cultural history.

4

The People, the Gray Market,
and the Ballroom Gown

There are many historical reasons why the discourses on "the popular" and "the people" reached a certain fever pitch in the 1970s, in countries as geographically remote, and politically and economically distinct, as Mexico and the Soviet Union. The aftermath of the global 1960s, exacerbated by the events of 1968 (the Prague Spring in the Soviet Union and the Tlatelolco student massacre in Mexico), brought to a head the state's crisis of legitimacy. At the same time, the vibrancy of the counterculture that arose from the same period, and its demands for radical democratization of all spheres of life, exercised considerable pressure on all aspects of cultural production. And yet, unlike in the earlier (postrevolutionary) periods that demanded—and succeeded in bringing about—a mass restructuring of society, it was no longer clear either who would be leading such a project or what "mass" entailed, in human terms. In both countries, the gaps between the notion of "people" as conceived by the socialist state the or nation-state, "the masses" as they were derogatively and despairingly conceptualized by the cultural elites, and the actual collectivities formed by all those marginalized by these respective hegemonies became increasingly visible.

Dismissed within traditional Marxism as the Lumpenproletariat, celebrated in postcolonial studies as the subaltern, its collective power conceptualized in autonomism as the multitude—this new non-hegemonic polity has come to stand, in recent decades, as an alternative to the earlier leftist vision of political organization of "the people."[1] In the 1970s, it was already evident that this emerging collective identity could no longer be easily mapped out through unproblematic identification with the nation-state, traditional class structure, or party affiliation, all of which provided its earlier cohesion. The promises that these institutions made in the subsequent decades were increasingly failing. Even in the Soviet Union, despite the absence of capitalist class exploitation, a growing sense of inequalities and radically different accesses to privilege further increased. The late capitalist shift to immaterial labor, globalization, the debt economy, and the collapse of state socialism (aka "The End of the Cold War") would irrevocably transform social organization everywhere in subsequent decades; in the 1970s, however, these developments were far from overdetermined. The transitional nature of the period makes the questions of how to understand and where to locate "the popular" during that decade, in both Mexico and the Soviet Union, particularly challenging. Yet it is evident that the members of this polity exercised their agency through a wide range of political, cultural, and artistic practices and preferences—and it was to them that *Yesenia* apparently spoke so powerfully.

In Mexico, on the militant end of the spectrum, the impact of the eruption of state violence of 1968 pushed many activists and artists to seek independence from both state and market forces, or a "singular form of relating the autonomous and the political," as argued by Susana Draper and others. These attempts found their cinematic expression not in the Echeverría-supported film industry but outside of it, through groups such as the Cooperative of Marginal Cinema and other Super 8 experimentations.[2] These attempts, however, remained at best disconnected and at worst perceived as antagonistic by a nonradicalized majority that was drifting further away from the projections of the new political Mexican culture they could offer. Soviet dissident culture, while powerful in its own right, likewise remained at best marginal to the majority of the people. Thus, rather than the utopian space in the making, or the public sphere in its liberal-democratic iteration (itself barely existing under Mexican *dictablanda*, let alone under Soviet socialism), the mainstream polity operated largely through and within the gray zone of informal practices and shadow economies, albeit inseparable from the state itself. In turn, this sphere shaped its collective identity in many ways. Variously theorized as pirate modernity, the black or gray market, globalization from below, or the penumbra, the development of informal practices of (re)production and circulation that form part of this social space are usually associated with the 1980s and 1990s.[3] Within the mediasphere in particular, it has been linked to the availability of audiovisual recording technologies such as VHS. At the same time, these informal modes of media reproduction were furthered by neoliberal globalization with its imposition of punitive structures of legal and economic governance, such as the World Trade Organization and the World Intellectual Property Organization. As such, they were inseparable from the breakdown of state structures (culminating in Mexico's debt crisis of the 1980s and the collapse of the Soviet Union), which made informal economic activity one of the only available ways for many people to stay afloat—while, at the same time, its status was increasingly criminalized, especially with the introduction of antipiracy campaigns.[4]

It is certainly the case that such informal economic activity intensified with the arrival of neoliberal globalization and its "legitimate" consumer culture of shopping malls with international brands, credit cards, and, increasingly, the digital economy, and its legal status changed drastically. Yet one often forgets that prior to these changes, especially under the regime of import-substitution (which characterized both Mexico and the Soviet Union in the 1970s), various informal economies—from popular markets to domestic DIY practices—and their corresponding modes of sociability and cultural expression were firmly embedded in everyday lives in much of the world, and certainly in Mexico and the Soviet Union. From our contemporary perspective, therefore, the 1970s appears to have been a crucial transitional phase, in which the state still attempted to both subsume and mediate the spheres of (re)production and consumption but was ultimately unable to address the social and cultural fragmentation, with new forms of populism emerging on its margins. Crucially, the state itself was enmeshed in this informal black or gray market on both the macro and micro levels, and this dynamic was equally visible in both Soviet and Mexican film and media cultures.

The history of *Yesenia*'s international circulation belongs to just such a transition zone: produced in the period of fragmentation of the previously unified film industry and the rise of the new media hegemony of Televisa, it was purchased through a minor distribution company by the Soviet state for a flat sum without royalties. For decades, the Soviet state suppressed information about its exhibition and box office revenues, in fear that Mexico might challenge the legal terms of its export.[5] In the Soviet Union, *Yesenia* was exhibited in theaters fully controlled by the state, but whose profits often relied on informal practices by the local exhibitors—such as switching the prints to increase the number of screenings of more popular foreign movies.[6] The appeal of such productions depended not least on their distinctive styles of personal apparel, simultaneously reflecting and promoting global fashion trends—but in a way that required considerable mediations in both Mexico and the Soviet Union. The audiences relied on the informal or black markets for realizing the desires fueled by films like *Yesenia*. Much of this chapter, then, examines the specific modes of (re)production and consumption of fashion associated with *Yesenia* as another major area of resonances enabling the film's transnational reception and its affective community—modes that belonged to the gray area between market and traditional economies and state socialism, and that relied on a wide range of informal practices, technologies of individual self-realization, and communal sociability.

The relationship between melodrama, alongside other presumed "women's genres," and the production and consumption of clothing and fashion has been at the center of much scholarship in the past several decades.[7] Positioned at the intersection of feminism and cultural studies, the turn to fashion and other forms of consumption was itself an attempt to redirect film studies away from highbrow questions of aesthetics and art cinema and toward the ways in which

FIGURE 17. *El Informador* ads, 1971: "Yesenia wig" (top left); "Gypsy haircut, layered or curly" (left center); "Gypsy dresses, Yesenia-style" (right center). Hemeroteca Nacional de México.

cinema penetrated the everyday experiences of mass audiences. At first glance, however, *Yesenia*'s nineteenth-century period and "ethnic" costumes couldn't be further away from the everyday fashion of the 1970s, either in Mexico or the Soviet Union.[8] Nor were the Soviet and Mexican economies of the time attuned to or capable of the kind of corporate synergies that characterized film and fashion industries in the West.[9] And yet, the most enduring cultural impact of *Yesenia* in both countries is, indeed, associated with fashion and personal care: it persists in the names of hairstyles, clothing shops, and beauty salons, as well as in designs for dresses, including homemade knitting and dress-making patterns.

In 1971–72 alone, the Guadalajara newspaper *El Informador* featured— alongside numerous retail items, from scarves and baby bottles to washing and sewing machines (the latter will be crucial for our discussion later in the chapter)—advertisements for "Gypsy dresses, Yesenia-style," "Yesenia" wigs, and a "gypsy haircut, layered or curly."[10] Its lifestyle section described children's costumes at a dress-up party as "Hungarian Yesenia outfits."[11]

These articles establish a clear link between Yesenia (as a brand or a fashion icon) and women's consumer culture, and announce its appropriateness and apparent availability for middle-class clients in local venues, though, in both Mexico and the Soviet Union, consumption fueled by the trends in "international" fashion seen on screens was more readily available through the more informal commercial spheres. These informal spheres capitalized on (re)selling American (or, in the Soviet case, generic "Western") goods or their locally, often nonindustrially, produced versions: the kind of consumer "culture of the copy" that was equally characteristic of Second and Third World countries in the 1970s and 1980s.[12] This was especially the case with women's consumer products and fashions. The Soviet Union couldn't offer anything comparable to US department stores (so closely associated with the rise of women's culture—and the Hollywood women's film in particular—in the American 1930s) or British or European "high street" fashion shops with their industrially produced emulation of couture fashion for women.[13] In Mexico, the US department stores did exist—but were affordable only to the middle-class consumers whose numbers decreased dramatically over the course of the 1970s. Moreover, President Echeverría's economic policies strongly favored local production of consumer goods, but development in that area proved slow and limited in many parts of the country.[14]

More available in both countries were street markets with locally, "artistically" produced versions of the fashion items or knock-offs brought from abroad by entrepreneurial black marketeers. By the 1970s, DIY domestic production (especially of clothes and domestic consumer objects) was virtually the norm— creating more intimate relationships to these consumer goods and greater possibilities for self-fashioning. At the same time, because these practices were highly gendered, as Lilya Kaganovsky reminds us, they had the effect of further increasing the demands on women's domestic labor.[15] Like sheet music, which in the Soviet Union was still published and circulated in the face of gradually dominant bootlegged tapes (of various formats) and smuggled vinyl records, the paper patterns for dress making were published in magazines, passed around, and used to recreate domestic versions of international favorites. The sewing machine advertised right next to Yesenia wigs on the pages of *El Informador* is a casual illustration of this relationship. This mode of production and circulation was indeed both reflexive and productive of the kind of populist or subaltern collectivity that emerged in this period—positioned somewhere between the aspiration of individual neoliberal self-realization through consumption and the social interdependency of the communal network of producers and consumers characteristic of societies peripheral to "fully developed" consumer capitalism.[16]

This cultural formation is successfully reflected in the aesthetics of the films and TV serials of the era, which certainly contributed to audiences' affective engagement with them. The (relatively) low budget of *Yesenia*—and, subsequently, of the Latin American telenovelas—certainly contributed to the perception of its inferior status as "trashy." Yet this look affirmed its audiences' cultural practices and aspirations, furthering a sense of recognition, playing a key role in the creation of emotional authenticity and intimacy, which the melodramatic mode relies on. This was the very affect that was frequently perceived as missing from the

European and North American cultural products whose high production values mirrored their respective geopolitical and economic privileges—lacking that very *cursi* regime of the copy that was both recognizable and, ultimately, imitable. To fully explore this dynamic, we need to turn once again to the relationship between melodrama and consumer culture—in its historical and comparative dimensions.

CONSUMER CULTURE AND MELODRAMA

The relationship between melodrama and consumer culture (as an extension, more broadly, of women's culture as rooted in consumerism) has been the subject of numerous studies: in the US context, star glamour in Hollywood women's pictures has historically been connected to the rise of department stores; soap opera, in turn, takes its name from assumed associations between gender, genre, and cleaning supplies, alluding to women's domestic labor.[17] The assumed givenness of the precise implications of this relationship, however, deserves to be challenged. First, for Latin America, the primacy of gender in this context has been much debated—insofar as melodrama has historically functioned in relation to broader nation-state ideologies and global market forces, thereby necessitating address to audiences of all genders. And unlike soap operas, the telenovela in Latin America has been linked primarily to class—although likewise aspiring to a broader, cross-over audience.[18] Neither should we assume the primacy of industrial consumption (of fashion or otherwise) as being at the core of the relationship dynamic between gender and consumption in melodramatic media. Thus, while in the case of US cinema, as Michelle Tolini Finamore explores, the shift from films that emphasized the production of fashion to those that encouraged its consumption took place in the first decades of the twentieth century, such a neat division, as this chapter will demonstrate, had not taken place as of the late 1970s, either in Mexican or Soviet cinema—or in their respective cultures.[19]

Given this conventional emphasis on gender and consumption, scholarship on this topic, like much of feminist cultural studies, has been divided. One approach is characterized by critiques of such practices as vehicles of passive consumption and the subjugation of women into normative gender self-expressions. The other espouses them as a liberating force for women's modern self-realization, an exercise of agency, and the emancipatory expression of gender fluidity with other identities available through the act of dressing up. While the problem of gender and consumption remains of crucial importance to our understanding of the politics of Yesenia's reception as a global icon, my approach to its analysis is more influenced by what Daniel Miller demonstrates in his study of the reception of the US soap opera *The Young and the Restless* in Trinidad.[20] Miller argues that the relationship between media reception and consumer culture needs to be understood through its mediations by distinctive local cultural frameworks. He focuses in particular on the dynamics of Trinidadian audiences' identification with style (in distinction from the consumption of mass-produced street-wear), as well as the multiple functions of informal social communication engendered by it.[21] While the latter is more pronounced for serialized melodrama (which will prove to be the case in the Soviet Union as well), *Yesenia*'s reception provides an interesting variant on Miller's Caribbean-specific observations.

Indeed, Neia Zorkaia begins her discussion of the apparently inexplicable popularity of *Yesenia* by pointing to the centrality of informal networks for "spreading the word" about the film in the context of a total lack of official promotion. Zorkaia identified such word-of-mouth publicity using the Russian term *sarafannoe radio*—literally, a sarafan (referring to a traditional Russian peasant sundress) radio, a term usually reserved for gossip, with unmistakable gender and class connotations. She sees this mode of informal communication, "secret channels, unknown to sociologists, film critics, and Goskino employees, spreading its unprecedented advertisement to the whole country," as yet another manifestation of the "late-folkloric" (nonindustrialized) mode of cultural and social production that, according to her, constitutes the core of such popular cinema, emblematized by *Yesenia*.[22] But the very informality of this mode of reception, as we'll see, speaks more precisely to its contemporary moment. And the term *sarafannoe radio*, too, through its invocation of earlier technologies (radio) and peasant dress, uncannily encapsulates both the anachronistic but highly mediated temporality of the collective at play and its link to women's fashion.

Miller's observations concerning what he describes as a "special relationship" between fashion and transnational soap opera reception in Trinidad are particularly relevant here: "Clothing and style have for a long period had a much more significant position in many Trinidadians' conception of themselves and their identities than may be the case in other regions. This may be directly linked to the dualism of transcendence devoted to the domestic regime, the interiorization of values, and the cultivation of 'roots' or religiosity, as against the transience associated with individualism, the outside or exterior, and a refusal of institutionalization."[23]

While rooted in entirely different histories, Soviet publics certainly had their own special relationship to commodities, "cultivation of style," and material culture more broadly. Cultural historian Alexey Golubev argues that Soviet citizens' social and cultural experiences were characterized by particular "attentiveness to human-object relations—a product of particular historical conditions shaped by the planned economy, welfare state, and socialist discourses."[24] Borrowing from Engels, he terms this relationship "elemental materialism": "a set of spontaneous and situational cultural forms that gave Soviet people ways to make sense of this social agency."[25] Soviet objects and spaces, Golubev argues, "interfered in the processes of subjectivation by suggesting forms of selfhood that fell out of the civilizing frameworks of the Soviet enlightenment project."[26]

Beyond such philosophical and *longue durée* aspects of the Soviet relationship to commodity culture—some aspects of which we encountered in the discussions of *byt* and *poshlost'* in chapter 3—in the 1970s, consumption began to loom especially large in the Soviet imaginary and everyday realities, as Natalya Chernyshova demonstrates: "Soviet sociologists in the early 1980s found a strong link between material prosperity and one's perceptions of self and others. One study showed that over 70 percent of those respondents who negatively assessed their current life situation and prospects were those who found fashionable clothes largely beyond their means."[27]

This is merely one illustration of Chernyshova's overall argument that "rapid growth in private consumption and consumerism became a defining social characteristic of the era, inviting recently the suggestion that Brezhnev-era society was the scene of nothing less than a consumer revolution."[28] As is evident from the cited study, "fashionable clothes" featured particularly prominently within this consumer revolution—much more so than, for example, domestic appliances, which might rationally seem like more desirable objects given the "double burden" faced by Soviet women, which such technology was designed to alleviate. Chernyshova's chapter on fashion in her book *Soviet Consumer Culture in the Brezhnev Era* begins with this statement: "There was hardly any other consumer item in Soviet history that aroused as much controversy and passion as clothes."[29] She describes a culture consisting of shops that were full and yet unable to meet consumer preferences, and shoppers who were highly discriminating, attuned to the latest changes in fashions, and eager to go to great lengths to obtain the desired outfits. They relied largely on informal networks of tailors and black marketeers, their own dress-making abilities, secondhand trade among friends and strangers, and designs obtained abroad or in fashion magazines and foreign cinema as a reliable source of information and inspiration.[30] The aesthetic and cultural translation and instrumentalization of the look of a Mexican "gypsy" melodrama set in the nineteenth century into wearable fashion, or, more generally, the "deciphering" of the relevant information from a culturally obtuse film, was a mechanism that for Soviet viewers was part of a familiar hermeneutic practice.

It appears that as in Miller's observation about Trinidad, commodities as markers of fashion and style ultimately performed a particularly complex, culturally and socially symbolic function. This is especially true in regard to gender politics. Personal styling—dependent on material goods and services—in the Soviet Union, as elsewhere, was a screen onto which individual and collective fantasies, aspirations, and frustrations were projected. The interactions with the material world in this process entailed—nay, required—a great deal of skill, imagination, and social and political savvy. This was often experienced as a battlefield, a fight not only for status or comfort but for essential selfhood.

Cinema provides a perfect projection for such masquerades, so it should not be surprising that a survey conducted in the Soviet Union in 1969 showed that television and movies were the most influential means of the diffusion of fashion.[31] Foreign films, in particular, were similarly important models for femininity: specifically the hyper-feminized and sexualized ones. This dynamic is visible even in the reviews of *Yesenia*. The protagonist's wardrobe was even noticed by the film's first (male) Soviet reviewer, Iurii Smelkov—who, characteristically lamenting the poor taste of the audiences, mentions "beautiful dresses" several times, as both an attribute of bad melodramatic movies and an explanation for their popularity.[32] And despite her critiques of "fairground" popular taste evidenced by *Yesenia*'s popularity, Turovskaia makes an exception for this mode of gender representation as "natural," given "a sharp deficit of normal life and of eroticism of women's image" in Soviet cinema.[33] In an essay published in English in the 1990s, "Notes on Women and Film," she further elaborates on this "deficit," linking it to what she perceives to be a form of "radical alienation" of the Soviet woman from the "sphere of simple material consumption."[34] It is worth quoting Turovskaia at length here again. Her discussion implicitly elucidates the logic governing the reception of *Yesenia* as linked to fashion, notions of gender, and material culture at large.

In identifying differences between the idea of liberation as understood by a Soviet woman (like herself) and the Western feminist one, Turovskaia recounts an anecdote a German feminist filmmaker cited as an example of sexism: being asked to appear at a film festival wearing an evening gown. In response, Turovskaia reflects that "a mean thought occurred to me—that a Soviet woman would have gone crazy with happiness to have received such a proposal. But the difference consists not only in the fact that a Soviet woman—even a director—would not always have a dress to wear for such an occasion. . . . In her everyday life there simply is no chronotope for such a dress. . . . In the crude life of the Soviet woman a ball gown is not provided for, not only materially, but morally."[35]

She elaborates on the total lack of "the institution of fashion, advertisement, cosmetics, perfumes, and jewelry" in the life of a Soviet woman—the lack of "normalcy," which, she argues, renders Western feminist critique not only inapplicable to Soviet (and post-Soviet, since the piece was written in 1995) reality, but makes its exact reversal the only possibility for the Soviet version of feminism. Turovskaia summarizes her point with a saying from her grandmother: "One woman cries because she has thin pearls, another because she has thin soup"—interpreting it for the readers by concluding that "for each, the tears are equally salty and bitter."[36] As with many folk sayings, the actual meaning of this proverb is rather ambiguous: one can see it either as a claim that emotions are a kind of surface phenomenon, covering the more fundamental rift between the rich and the poor; or that all women suffer from injustice, regardless of their class, constructing emotions and especially tears as a shared space—the very melodramatic community Berlant talks about. Of course, for the context we are considering, both are simultaneously true. And an evening dress—or, more specifically, a ball gown—within this discourse functions as a symptom not only of luxury per se, but also of leisure time away from the dual demands of work and domestic labor, a manner of self-realization as well as basic self-preservation. But, foreshadowing the logic of "self-care" within third-wave feminist discourse, a "ball gown" became the ultimate point of cathexis within Soviet women's culture, both from "above" and from "below." In its associations with the prerevolutionary aristocratic culture of balls, which, indeed, in many ways defined the Russian cultural imaginary of the eighteenth- and nineteenth-century aristocracy, the desire for a ball gown is a highly anachronistic and nostalgic gesture, which, as we have seen in chapter 3, coincided with the 1970s Soviet intelligentsia's idealization of prerevolutionary Russian life as a period before the gender crisis brought about by the Soviet regime.

It is worth pointing out that Turovskaia's claims about the absence of such feminine attire from Soviet life can only be understood in the most literal terms. It is certainly true that throughout the Soviet period, many prominent film and television stars dressed themselves—as neither stylists nor ball gowns or properly fabulous stage apparel were provided by the state entertainment industry.[37] Thus, Soviet realities, even in the case of the very elite—stars, who projected the fantasy of glamour and luxury—were not entirely removed from the struggles of everyday consumers. At the same time, throughout the existence of the institution of Soviet (and socialist Eastern European) fashion, highly conventional evening wear was extremely prominent and projected as its essential component. In fact, from the 1960s on this marked a significant and much-commented-on difference between socialist and Western fashions, since the latter during that period became less formal and structured, and more oriented toward youth culture.[38] The expectation of and demand for such formal evening women's wear was, indeed, fueled by the Soviet state institutions themselves, as an indispensable part of Soviet gender ideology. At the same time, for much of the intelligentsia this was yet another proof of the regime's hypocrisy and/or of the philistinism of the official culture.

This highly contradictory and phantasmagorical significance of a gown may be one of the reasons for the exceptional popularity, in the Soviet Union in 1976, of the otherwise utterly unremarkable Egyptian melodrama *The White Gown* (*Al-Reda'a al-Abiad* / الرداء الأبيض, Hassan Razmi, 1974). One of many Egyptian melodramas released in the Soviet Union, and one whose status in Egypt's national film history is considerably lower than even that of *Yesenia* in Mexico's, its plot revolves around the female protagonist's desire for a fancy dress in the window of a shop in post-Nasser, economically liberalized Cairo. The dress, indeed, serves as a narrative catalyst for the whole film, which proved to be one of the highest-grossing films of the Soviet 1970s and the most popular Egyptian film in Soviet history.

An excessive and almost obsessive attention to dress, however, has long been something that melodrama and costume drama are known for—to the extent that spectators' reverie for the "design extravagance" of these genres seems to somewhat distract, if not detract, from melodramatic affective charge—what Jane Gaines has called "the costume idiolect" independent of narrative codes.[39] Thus, it should not be surprising that the number of dresses Yesenia wears in the movie draws attention to itself. Used in one instance to demarcate the passing of time early on in the film (when she makes Oswaldo wait for her for three days, while looking at

FIGURE 18. Yesenia's dresses. Collage of DVD screen grabs.

him from afar—each day alluded to by a different dress she wears), such variety of clothing is otherwise in excess of meaning. If we associate having a lot of clothes with a certain class status, this is certainly not the case in *Yesenia*, as these scenes take place early in the film, while she is part of the "gypsy camp"—forcing one to contemplate where she keeps these dresses, given the close quarters she shares with her mother and grandmother, and their famously mobile lifestyle.

In fact, despite the fact that her new dresses are thematized as a diegetic object of marvel and attention in the second half of the film, changes in her wardrobe once she joins her biological aristocratic family are no more or less frequent than earlier in the film, and they look considerably stodgier, more generic, and less connected to contemporary fashion—while remaining very much on display.

Such attention to wardrobe, however, and especially to dresses, was highly resonant with Soviet audiences—while constituting a crucial part of the expectations of pleasure associated with the genre of historical melodrama everywhere, but in Soviet times extending to any foreign movie or TV program.[40] The obsession with evening-wear played out as comedy even in *Holidays in Prostokvashino* (*Kanikuly v Prostokvashino*, Vladimir Popov, 1980), one of a series of enormously popular late-1970s to early-1980s animated films for children. The fashionable mom of the boy-protagonist refuses to spend their holiday at the dacha in the countryside. Her response to

FIGURE 19. *Holidays in Prostokvashino*: Mom and her closet of evening-wear. DVD grab.

her husband's and son's pleas to go to the country is "And what am I going to do with all my evening dresses there? Chop wood in them?" Instead, she insists on going to a resort where she can wear a different evening dress every night of the week. This line became a much-quoted joke owing to its obvious misogyny—as "Mom" is clearly expected to overcome such outrageous desire for a glamorous vacation and settle for a simple life of domestic labor in the countryside. But it was probably also due to a certain bitter irony embedded in it, as most Soviet women in the 1970s couldn't possibly have had so many evening dresses, as much as they would have loved to (as we know from Turovskaia). At the same time, embedded critiques of such desires were increasingly common in official discourses as part of the Soviet fight against philistinism (as we have seen in the discussion of the category of *poshlost'* in chapter 3), which intensified in the 1970s precisely because of increased consumerism, when, as Chernyshova describes, "the ranks of the intelligentsia had swelled to include much broader segments of the population, and new arrivals often strove to assert their membership in this ideologically anti-materialistic class by means of conspicuous consumption. Consequently, the intelligentsia now found itself under pressure to defend its own moral integrity as a group. Fighting against materialism came to mean fighting within one's own expanded class for a kind of purity and for the intelligentsia's ethical right to retain its traditional perception of itself as society's moral guardians."[41]

This position, however, was particularly vexed for women within the intelligentsia, such as Turovskaia and Zorkaia. On the one hand, as Soviet film critics, they occupied the position of guardians of good taste and antimaterialism against the philistine culture (as is evident in their attack on the "cheap" melodramatic genres). On the other, as Turovskaia's later writing makes clear, privately they saw the lack of material resources and personal styling choices—crystallized in the image of the evening dress—as a crucial part of the oppression of women by the Soviet apparatus. And in the 1970s, for the Soviet Union, as we have seen in earlier chapters, the desired liberation of the self from the oppression of the state was seen as regaining one's essential status as a "real woman"—despite or against the "desexualizing" Soviet ideological norms.[42] Following the common logic of "femininity as masquerade," so often discussed by Western feminist and film scholars alike, such an "essence," therefore, not only was externalized but was best found "elsewhere"—in the past, or abroad, or among the internal ethnic or cultural "others"—thus offering both a stable sense of self-realized essential selfhood and an imaginary escape and freedom from it.[43]

This dialectic is, of course, far from unique to Soviet women. For example, Pam Cook, in her discussion of British postwar costume drama, links the genre to popular adventure and historical women's fiction: "'Escapist' literature of this sort, populated by gypsies, pirates and smugglers, and featuring heroes and heroines dedicated to wandering over land and sea, was prevalent during the 30s and resurfaced in the 40s with the wartime intensification of social mobility. This vagrant spirit provided the inspiration for the Gainsborough costume romances."[44]

Beyond any presumed limitations of a costume drama, both Yesenia's "gypsy" look and her "high society" dresses strongly resonated not only with the cultural obsessions of late socialism but with those of the Mexican 1970s, as well as the global fashion trends they were mediating. Combining European ballroom gowns and the opulence associated with Empress Carlotta (of Maximilian-era Mexico), the hippie free spirit and "natural femininity" of the "gypsy style," and the self-possessed sexuality of a modern liberated woman (and the endless consumer choices confronting her), the so-called "boho-chic" and "ethnic" fashions of the 1970s served as a powerful cultural context for *Yesenia*'s production and reception.

ETHNIC AND BOHO-CHIC FASHION COME
TO MEXICO AND THE SOVIET UNION

Combining the hippie image of a "flower child"—colorful floral prints, maxidresses, big skirts, ruffles, abundant inexpensive jewelry—with various eclectic "folk" elements, the ethnic and boho-chic trends were, indeed, some of the most prevalent elements of 1970s European and US fashion, equally visible in both haute couture and mainstream clothing, as well as, of course, in movies. The adoption of the so-called "gypsy style" was part, and an extension, of this larger trend.[45] It began to

FIGURE 20. "Let Yourself Go Gypsy" photo shoot, *Look*, 1967.
Public domain.

flourish in high fashion in the late 1960s, as is evident from a 1967 issue of *Look* magazine, featuring a photo shoot titled "Let Yourself Go Gypsy"—with two Italian models apparently dressed to represent the high-end fashion take on the Roma.[46]

In some ways, this style and its chain of cultural appropriations—already familiar to us from the cinematic histories discussed in chapter 3—culminated in the fall of 1976, with an Yves Saint Laurent show that has been referred to interchangeably as "Carmen," "Russian," "Peasant Rive-Gauche," or "Opéras-Ballets russes" (brought back the following year as "Les Espagnoles et les Romaniques" ready-to-wear collection). Mixing toreadors and models in black corsets, lace, and Bermuda shorts with fur-clad "Ballet-Russe-inspired" kaftans, turbans, and bright multicolored shawls, with banded and fitted high-hipped full maxiskirts, the collection was meant to evoke Cale Roma, Andalusian folkloric figures, and czarist-era Russian peasants in one look.[47]

Nor was such conflation of various signifiers of exotic ethnicity in any way exceptional. For example, a 1968 issue of *Vogue* featured a so-called "Mexican" photo shoot titled "Fashion at the Zenith of the Sun": models with long, flowing hair, wearing "bohemian" maxidresses in bright colors with shawls, scarves, and oversized and ornate costume jewelry pose at various Mexican archaeological sites as a way to reference Mexican folk and indigenous culture—with an inclusion of virtually every element of "gypsy style."[48] The high echelons of "ethnic fashion" thus indiscriminately, and at times virtually interchangeably, mixed national markers and stereotypes of primitivism—whether identified as "gypsy," "peasant," "Russian," "Mexican," or "indigenous"—with the more countercultural image of a hippie or a bohemian.

Indeed, in Mexico, "ethnic fashion" was most visible within the social stratum seemingly most opposed to global fashion trends: the counterculture. At the same time, the Mexican *jipies* began to include indigenous elements (sandals, huaraches, Oaxacan shirts and beads) in their clothing in imitation of their Western counterparts—"the reabsorption of styles that youth from abroad had already appropriated in their mutual yet quite distinct flights from and expressions of modernity," as described by Eric Zolov in *Refried Elvis*. "In rejecting their own middle-class lifestyles," he writes, "Mexican youth were simultaneously embracing its transnational manifestation, literally embodied in the countercultural practices of foreign hippies. This embracement, in turn, stimulated a nationalist gesture reflected in a return to the land and the revalorization of indigenous cultures. It was in this way that Mexican youth adopted the gestures of a postmodern cultural politics guided toward a counterhegemonic strategy of popular (versus 'official') nationalism."[49]

"Official nationalism," however, also used ethnic clothing as a marker: thus, María Esther Zuno de Echeverría, the wife of the Mexican president, was known to appear at public functions wearing traditional indigenous clothes—although, as Mexican essayist José Agustín notes, instead of the intended associations with Frida Kahlo, these clothes brought to mind the uniforms of waitresses in the middlebrow Sanborns chain.[50]

At the same time, as is extremely clear from the pages of women's magazines during the time, ethnic motifs in all their manifestations were prominent in Mexican fashion: as discussed in chapter 2, Mexican clothing line Verona's 1970 collection—"Mexican Contrast '70"—featured a mix of folkloric dresses, evidently inspired by regional costumes, mixed in with miniskirts and jumpsuits. Nor was the ethnic element limited to Mexico's own heritage: thus, *Kena*'s 1972 selection of its "romantic and sophisticated style for youth fashion" features entirely incongruous "Russian-style" head scarves—demonstrating that the imaginary of an exotic Russianness was an equal part of the "ethnic" repertoire.

In many ways, these ethnic, indigenous, folkloric styles culminated, once again, in the notion of "the gypsy style"—which, as *Kena*'s review of the latest fashion trends of 1971 affirms, is "without a doubt, the big success story of contemporary fashion . . . adopted all around the world."[51] Later that year, *Kena*'s own clothing line, Kena, sold in the department store El Palacio de Hierro, featured two dresses "in the popular gypsy style."[52] *Yesenia* was released that same year, and its protagonist's iconic look is certainly a perfect reflection of these trends.

FIGURE 21. "Romantic and sophisticated," Russian-style, *Kena*, 1972. Hemeroteca Nacional de México.

In the Soviet Union, however, "ethnic" or "folkloric" fashion was not only already well known by the 1970s, but had a much longer history than in the West. Its deployment was one of the crucial ways that the Soviet establishment tried to reconcile the growing desire for Western cultural consumer models within official socialist parameters. Just as folk-dance elements were introduced into ballroom dance routines and folk melodic roots were emphasized in popular music (as discussed in the prelude), from the 1950s onward the "folk elements" were consistently incorporated into socialist fashion, from formal evening wear to the most casual. This incorporation performed a number of ideological functions: to claim a connection to national folk culture as a way to diminish its mass-produced status and differentiate it from its Western bourgeois capitalist origins; to infuse fashion with "politically-imposed historical references" to national cultures and demonstrate their vitality within a multination socialist state; to underscore the connection of the fashion industry with "genuine peasant art" and encourage collaboration between professional urban artists and "the countryside."[53] Thus, a showcase of formal linen dresswear in the Lithuanian fashion magazine *Banga* would be accompanied by an article on the importance of traditional fabrics in socialist production of clothing titled "Linen: the Pride of Lithuania."[54] And despite announcing that "folkloric style converges with romantic style, and national costume elements

FIGURE 22. "Without a doubt, the big success story of contemporary fashion has been the gypsy style, adopted all over the world." *Kena*, 1971. Hemeroteca Nacional de México.

FIGURE 23. Summer fashion as seen in the pages of the Soviet Lithuanian magazine *Banga*, 1980.

FIGURE 24. Dresses for summer resort vacations, *Banga*, 1976.

are used more moderately than before,"[55] a photo shoot depicting "combinations for sunny summer days" in the very same issue of *Banga* seems to defy that claim.[56]

By the 1970s, however, even in the Soviet context these folkloric elements became detached from any such officially imposed signifiers, blending in with international fashion trends. We see this in the clothing collection of Soviet premier couturier and fashion ideologue Viacheslav Zaitsev, nicknamed in the 1970s "the Red Dior." His writings from the period reflect the usual cult of *kul'turnost'* with programmatic discussions of Soviet "culture of clothing" (*kul'tura odezhdy*), as opposed to the Western notion of "fashion" (*moda*), along with his prerequisite critiques of Western hippie and ethnic fashions and their "ridiculous imitations by boys and girls on Soviet streets."[57] Yet it is hard to reconcile his continuous rhetoric of aesthetic restraint in defining the socialist culture of clothing with the eye-popping look of his 1975 collection, which seems to mirror precisely the "boho ethnic chic" and the *Yesenia* look in the very year the film took the Soviet Union by storm. Its less extravagant variations appeared on the pages of the various Soviet women's magazines, although with a caveat that they were recommended to young women only.[58]

BALLROOM GOWN, WEDDING GOWN,
AND *QUINCEAÑERA* DRESS

It wasn't only the "ethnic" or "gypsy" style that was characteristic of fashion in the 1970s. Despite all the emphasis on freedom and on youthful and informal wear, evening gowns remained firmly within the repertoire of both Soviet and Mexican fashion. Thus, *Kena*'s "indispensable fashion items of 1970" included not one but two options of "essential" women's evening wear: one identified as "gala" (and resembling most closely a ball gown), and the other simply as "maxidress."[59] In fact, much of the ethnic/gypsy fashion itself entailed elaborate long dresses—but its romantic associations were meant to connote freedom and nature, as well as unabridged passion and sensuality as definitive femininity.

But just as in *Yesenia*'s narrative, bright chiffon dresses eventually gave way to formal empire wear, culminating in a wedding gown. And in Mexican fashion and culture, a formal gown occupied a very particular place. With its stylistic signifiers of complex class and historical dimensions, it remained most visible in Mexico through the persistence not only of the wedding gowns, but also of the *quinceañera* tradition: a celebration of a girl's fifteenth birthday, which entails not only a lavish party and dancing, but also a special dress. The *quinceañera* dress code (like the wedding dresses in much of the West to date) is specifically associated with the imaginary of European nineteenth-century ballroom culture—and, in the case of Mexico, specifically the Maximilian era depicted in *Yesenia*, such courtly fashions were brought from France. At the same time, the ritual celebration of a girl's reaching fifteen (*quince*) years of age as a rite of sexual maturity in Mexico has been persistently understood as an expression of national identity and "national roots"—therefore frequently attributed both to pre-Columbian indigenous practices and to the Virgin of Guadalupe. The latter as a national symbol likewise plays an important role in the narrative of *Yesenia*: Yesenia's true family—and Christian identity—is restored due to a locket depicting the Virgin; the film's last scene depicts Yesenia's (church) wedding and her praying to the Virgin, signifying her integration into the body of the nation.

While the associations between the Virgin of Guadalupe and Mexican national identity would have escaped the film's Soviet audiences, the symbolic significance and the very iconicity of her image would be equally powerful, especially as the ornamental ritual elements of worship (referred to in Russian Orthodoxy as *obriadnost'*) became an object of widespread fascination in the Soviet 1970s. This public interest, fueled by Soviet official prohibition on religion, was focused in particular on the ritual and aesthetic elements of service, including the emphasis on icons, especially of the Virgin Mary (albeit referred to in the Orthodox context as the Mother of God). Thus, such imagery became increasingly common in Soviet 1970s cinema as well.[60]

And in the absence of the *quinceañera* tradition in the Russian culture, on the level of lived experience it was the traditional wedding dresses that for many in the Soviet Union became an important attribute of religious ritual, conveying authenticity of feeling in contrast to the reified bureaucratic rituals of civil marriage—while also invertedly connoting the aristocratic culture of the ballroom dress as well. In Mexico, against the ubiquity of religious culture, even more so than weddings, *quinceañera* celebrations are important across economic classes, playing a wide range of social symbolic functions. These are particularly class-coded affairs, as the choice and quality of the dress is intensely scrutinized (easily earning the pejorative description not only of being *cursi* but of being *naco*, that other culturally specific, racially inflected Mexican category of bad taste, now referring specifically to urban lower classes, as is evident even in contemporary online social media).[61]

The expressions of class differences through formal dress are highlighted in one of the earlier films by the director of *Yesenia*, Alfredo B. Crevenna's *Quinceañera* (1960). This film, in turn, provided a blueprint for several subsequent teen telenovelas made by Televisa in the 1990s through 2000s.[62] In addition to illustrating once again the direct link between Mexican film melodrama and the telenovela genre, the drama of Crevenna's film—which follows three girls, one lower-class, one middle-class, and one upper-class, in their preparation for this important party—is visually marked through the characters' party dresses and narratively through the challenges of their acquisition.

In the title sequence, the three actresses are introduced one by one, dancing in their fancy *quinceañera* frocks (as seen in the film's poster). The culminating sequence of the film features two girls who appear resplendent in their gowns, while the lower-class girl, María Antonia, whose parents cannot afford the celebration, is wearing a casual dress, self-consciously pulling on its plain collar, clearly heartbroken. But María Antonia's father informs her that everyone contributed money to make sure she could have her *quinceañera*; and as the white gown is carried across the ballroom while everyone applauds, she is told that her friend's aunt made the dress for her, while the other friend gifted the fabric for it.

While the melodramatic lessons of the story—that virtue triumphs over misfortune, and that a true community, despite its internal discords, can come together to help a young girl's dreams come true—are articulated through the image of

FIGURE 25. Alfredo B. Crevenna's *Quinceañera*. DVD cover.

this dress, underscoring the symbolic importance of the (*quinceañera*) ball gown to Mexican culture, it is rather the mode of its making that particularly interests me here. The fact that the dress was literally made through communal efforts, of course, carries metaphorical meaning within the film's narrative. But it also reflects the realities of production and consumer practices in Mexico in 1960—realities that would carry into the 1970s. If, in the North American or European context of the 1960s, "high street fashion" was indicative of middle-class status, and "tailor-made clothing" pointed to higher-class positionality through its proximity to haute couture, in Mexico (as in the rest of Latin America—and, indeed, much of the world) the more artisanal modes of production were prevalent and persisted across class lines.

RETAIL, INFORMAL ECONOMIES,
AND DIY PRACTICES

In Mexico, the period of transition to the market dominance of global retail took place primarily in the second half of the 1970s. While a handful of American department stores that opened in the late 1940s set the standards (and aspirations) for middle-class consumerism during Mexico's economic boom, and advertising agencies in their use of nationalist rhetoric successfully reconciled revolutionary goals with those of prosperity and consumerism, the existing industrial manufacturing infrastructure simply couldn't keep up with the demand.[63] In the late 1940s and early 1950s, the US retail company Sears became the model for a new kind of apparel industry centered on readymade clothes—and women's dresses quickly became the most popular item in the store (making Mexican Sears an exception compared to its US chain, which largely specialized in hardware and big-item retail).[64] Yet the purchasing power of what Sears identified as its target consumers—the Mexican middle class and those aspiring to that status—was entirely at the mercy of the volatile economy, and even at the height of the economic boom of the 1950s and 1960s, this kind of readymade retail could never become a dominant form of consumption for the majority of the population, due to its relatively high cost. Moreover, as hard as the company tried to reconcile its commercial practices with the rhetoric of consumer nationalism, the store was continuously associated with US economic and cultural primacy—a feeling that became further magnified in the increasingly politicized 1960s and 1970s.

On the other end of the retail spectrum, in 1967, the creation of the International Salon in El Palacio de Hierro was a big gesture toward Mexico's opening up to international luxury brands. But this gesture was entirely symbolic—and the openness was rather short lived, as for much of the decade during Echeverría's presidency the fashion industry and retail market, from haute couture to street wear, remained a closed system.[65] Over the course of the decade, while various local brands (such as Verona and Kena, as we have seen in their advertisements) began to gain ascendence, the international fashions were promoted largely through the women's magazines, movies, and television—while remaining largely inspirational and adapted through local practices. With price hikes on basic and luxury goods in the 1970s, Mexicans were expected to "kick their addiction to luxury goods," which had become the expectation of the middle class—a government-held position that was entirely at odds with the increasing advertisements in the multiplying lifestyle magazines.[66] At the same time, government-sponsored consumer credit (Fonacot) and bank credit cards were introduced to encourage spending but were largely available only to the middle classes. Essentially acknowledging that even a middle-class income was not sufficient to support the "modern" lifestyle that was so tirelessly advertised and ardently desired, at the same time, these policies further aggravated the disparities in standards of living (and began developing the economy of debt, which would fully flourish in the 1980s); however, the line between "essential" and "luxury" goods was virtually impossible to categorize.[67] The government consumer credit program, Fonacot, sponsored design competitions "with the dual goal of reducing production costs and increasing style by imitating (with cheaper materials, to be sure) high-end products."[68] Mirroring these national industrial practices—which were themselves "copies" of the desired high-end, foreign-made luxury goods—was the persistence of homemade "luxury" items such as women's dresses and evening gowns.

FIGURE 26. Making dresses out of scarves, *Tarybinė Moteris*, 1979.

Within the Soviet context, ironically, an object comparable to a ball gown in desirability was, in many ways, its opposite: denim blue jeans. And yet, both of their meanings as markers of cultural and class status were entirely different from those in the West and/or Mexico. As Chernyshova notes, "jeans may have been the ultimate symbol of classlessness in the United States during the 1960s and 1970s, but in the Soviet Union they had become a symbol of class" and "increasingly became a prerogative of the educated urban middle classes with material aspirations."[69] The fantasy of a ballroom gown apparently cut across various social strata, unlike jeans, the acquisition of which required both considerable skill and economic viability. The ballroom gown or "fancy dress," however, was a fetish that was everywhere and nowhere, and this was particularly true for the "ethnic-inspired" kind of dress we see Yesenia wear. In Bartlett's words, "An opulent dress adorned with ethnic-inspired decoration was a mythical object par excellence within the socialist fashion narrative. Visually, the lavishness of the ethnic motif fulfilled the myth's aesthetic criteria. Moreover, due to the richness of its complicated handmade embroidery and lace ornaments, which involved highly skilled techniques, such an outfit could not be mass-produced. Instead it languished in an everlasting, perfect mythical world."[70]

This aura of handmade artisanry was dialectically opposed to jeans, the symbolic value of which depended almost entirely on their being mass produced—and in the US. As Chernyshova explores, there were, indeed, many local attempts to produce denim jeans in the Soviet Union, as well as import them from countries that had friendlier trade relations with the Soviet Union. But such attempts were in vain, because "real" jeans, which could fulfill the symbolic function of social and cultural distinction, had to be from specific US brands, and consumers and local marketeers alike were highly attuned to the minute indications of inauthenticity.[71]

This, however, was not the case with other fashion items, whose variations and permutations were perfectly acceptable. One of the most ingenious solutions to the difficulties involved in the production of fashionable clothes is presented on the pages of the Soviet Lithuanian magazine *Tarybinė Moteris* in 1979, which proposes "to sew very playful clothes out of colorful shawls that are plentiful in our stores."[72] Consistent with the aesthetics of "gypsy fashion," the article urges readers to "not be afraid to combine fabrics and shawls of different patterns" to achieve the desired results. We can see how the kind of fashion inspired by *Yesenia* did lend itself more easily to creative reproduction, allowing for freedom that rested not only on the fluidity of style and self-definition, but on adaptability to specific material conditions.

Despite very different overall economic systems, the creative ingenuity of Soviet consumption culture in the 1970s was surprisingly similar to its Mexican counterpart. Of course, the Soviet economy notoriously produced scarcity and consumer deficit, and did not have Sears, or any other American companies, to provide even the upper classes with readymade US street fashion. But on the level of an average citizen's experience, the difference was a matter of degrees, as they struggled to meet their desires for fashionable self-styling through a range of nonindustrial and informal practices: mediating Western or American consumer imagery through domestic reproduction, repurposing, or tinkering. These practices also often depended on resorting to the black market or other informal arrangements, from acquiring fabrics and designs to the more advanced domestic technologies and prototypes. This, in turn, was often enabled by the elites' travels abroad, which also increased during this period—due, somewhat ironically, to the promotion of Third-Worldist (in the case of Mexico) or cross-socialist (in the case of the Soviet Union) ties. José Agustín recounts with hilarity the shopping craze of the top echelons of the Mexican intelligentsia on the way back from a writers' conference in Argentina, when the plane had a stopover in Panama, whose Canal Zone was at the time US territory and therefore offered a full array of consumer goods.[73] Similar accounts are of course plentiful in Soviet memoirs—in addition to the more systematic smuggling of goods but also, crucially, fabrics and designs, and their subsequent circulation through the black markets and other forms of informal economy enabling alternative local production and resale of clothes.

In addition to the more fluid relationship between production and consumption in the 1970s, even the more recognizably "developed capitalist" forms of consumer culture in Mexico and the Soviet Union were, above all, communal practices that relied on highly developed social skills and forms of cooperation. As Chernyshova puts it, "A Soviet consumer was a dynamic and skillful social operator, not a loner browsing boutiques or department stores at leisure. . . . [C]onsumption was a way to engage with the Soviet collective rather than isolate oneself from it."[74] Unlike postfeminist self-fashioning and self-care as a form of neoliberal self-reliance, consumption in these contexts was embedded in community and depended on the ability to navigate its various contours and negotiate its needs. For the popular classes, in Mexico and in the Soviet Union, the primacy of the community and communal values was, more generally, still the prevailing *habitus* and the dominant cultural model—in the face of the increasingly evident betrayal of these very values by the ruling elites.[75]

In the Soviet case, those ruling classes, however, still enforced the normativity of such collective practices. Golubev and Smolyak demonstrate, in their analysis of Soviet media's construction of women's "homemade" culture through advice columns, how "these practices established a normative basis of social communication: the norm was to exchange designs and patterns, as well as to ask each other's advice."[76] They further underscore the crucial role of the broader visual regime, and in particular of foreign cinema, for the construction of such communal culture as a distinctly modern practice. This was specifically the case with the adoption of "ethnic fashions"—such as those embodied by *Yesenia*. "The discourse of Soviet women's magazines transferred do-it-yourself practices from the traditional rural domain to the normative urban culture, since ethnic patterns in one's dress or apartment proved, as the magazine claimed, 'an excellent taste: not a sign of backwardness, but that of the Soviet modern.'"[77] While necessarily collective, this "Soviet modern," however, was not merely gendered as a way to produce rationally organized social space, through which gender was defined. The distinctive collectivities and spaces of collective DIY production and consumption corresponded to the reciprocally exclusive social functions men and women were supposed to perform, thus further essentializing gender identities. And such everyday gender essentialism further affirmed, and was affirmed by, the melodramatic worldview projected in *Yesenia* and other popular favorites.

In short, a quick glance at the various imaginaries and practices within the Mexican and Soviet cultures of the 1960s and 1970s, which constitute the broader context for the *Yesenia* production and its subsequent Soviet reception, attests to a more complex and distinctive relationship between melodramatic media and women's consumer culture—one that defies many simplistic assumptions based either on the conventional US model or on the more contemporary globalized flows of commodity culture, which came to be dominant in much of the world from about the 1980s onward. While profoundly influenced by cinema and television, the social and cultural dynamics of this transitional consumer culture were deeply rooted in collective and interpersonal social networks, and in forms of individual and communal labor. In the 1970s, they were also characterized by profound ambiguities in the status of the original and the copy: a distinctive regime of mediation between state and official culture and the Western (or, in the Mexican case, often specifically American) imaginaries.

Nor can the kinds of transnational affinities activated by *Yesenia* be easily reduced to familiar forms. It does not fit within earlier forms of Third-Worldist internationalism or identifiable notions of political solidarity. The concept of "vernacular modernism" developed by Miriam Hansen, which has frequently been used to account for the international circulation of popular cinema, rooted as it is in the exemplary role of early Hollywood, clearly cannot account for this formation either. Despite the evident relevance of the legacy of vernacular cultural practices for both Russia and Mexico, their relationship to Hollywood is, if anything, reversed as compared to Hansen's concept (see chapter 3).[78] What emerges at this moment of the 1970s, then, as seen in the example of *Yesenia*, is a highly hybrid formation, mediating its earlier models of reception and circulation with new emerging forms of global media. It not only predates but also, in some ways, sets up the later patterns of what Ghosh and Sarkar theorize as the global-popular: cultural productions that are a clear extension of the commercial entertainment industry with its own patterns and interests, and yet, in their consumption, circulation, and reproduction, continuously mediated by bottom-up cultural practices relying on DIY cultures and informal economies.[79]

Thus, these shared dynamics of consumer culture and fashion, as refracted in *Yesenia*'s reception, offer a framework for understanding its transnational affective power and the desires, aspirations, and attitudes that shaped its complex and contradictory politics—as well as the new potential polities it evokes. These new aspirations, practices, and communities, however, extended to the mediasphere not only via the impact of the representations projected by films and TV programs. It is through the mode of the material (re)production of media that we can locate a particular kind of collective agency, constituted through a series of social exchanges that render the subject part of the community of creative coauthors rather than a mere individual consumer. This informal circulation—first of images, texts, and music and then, with the introduction of VHS recorders and tapes, of audiovisual media at large—through its cycles of transformations further enhanced the powerful intimacy of transcultural appropriations. At times, such exchanges further solidified some of the hegemonic (patriarchal) norms and affective economies and, increasingly, reaffirmed and reproduced the unequal economic relations and power hierarchies. At other times, though, they could trigger unexpected openings, at odds with the original producers' or distributors' motivations. Such "unruly" collective agency is recognizable to us through the familiar discourses on fandom—and here, too, most of the scholarly discussions of this phenomenon tend to focus on contemporary, internet-era creative economies, but their earlier iterations likewise offer unexpected insights. While the audiovisual media of the 1980s, with the widespread availability of VHS recorders, provides the best example of these dynamics, informal music circulation and (re)production had already set these patterns in place, as we have seen in the prelude.[80] Like fashion, which offered its virtual models through its representations within media, but whose reproduction and circulation depended on informal social circuits, music, too, was embedded in the representational regimes projected by audiovisual media—and yet its material infrastructures of circulation likewise reflected and reshaped those same social and cultural regimes.

"BÉSAME MUCHO" AND *MOSCOW DOES NOT BELIEVE IN TEARS*

The specificities of this aspect of the Soviet cultural sphere are particularly well demonstrated by the reception and circulation of that ultimate hymn of Mexican melodramatic sensibility, "Bésame Mucho"—a history that reframes *Yesenia*'s, tying together many of the strands this book explores. Its popularity in the Soviet Union, unlike that of *Yesenia*, is far from unique: the song, written by a young, unknown Mexican composer named Consuelo Velázquez and first performed in Mexico in 1941 by Emilio Tuero, quickly became a hit worldwide after its US cover first reached number one on the Billboard charts of 1944. That same year, the song appeared in two "entertaining the troops" Hollywood films—*Follow the Boys* (Edward Sutherland, 1944) and *Cowboy and the Senorita* (Joseph Kane, 1944), and over the years it has been featured in dozens of films and performed by musicians ranging from Frank Sinatra to the Beatles, from Lucho Gatico to Il Divo, from Dalida to Luis Miguel. It is frequently cited as the most popular Spanish-language song of all time and a song that has generated the largest number of versions in history.

What sets the Soviet covers of "Bésame Mucho" apart from this broader history, however, is the fact that unlike their Western counterparts, they did not pay licensing fees or royalties to Velázquez. Already in the late 1940s and early 1950s, the song was performed by several Soviet singers—Gleb Romanov, Nikolai Nikitskii, and, perhaps most famously, by Ruzhena Sikora (whose career we discussed in the prelude). Given the similar popularity of Rio Rita on the Soviet music scene throughout the 1930s and 1940s, we can assume that the inspiration for the Russian versions of "Bésame Mucho" likewise came from the song's US covers, reflecting the US Latin boom of that period, which arrived in the Soviet Union via Hollywood wartime imports and the so-called trophy films (also discussed in the prelude).[81]

But after the International Festival of Youth and Students in Moscow in 1953, where the song was memorably performed by several groups from Latin America, Spanish-language versions of "Bésame Mucho" came to dominate the Soviet soundscape. In 1956 the song was included on the record released by the Trio Los Panchos, a group that was originally formed in New York City but that had relocated to Mexico (where two of its original members were from) by the 1950s, alongside a selection of other boleros, some originally written by the Trio and another by Lara. Los Panchos were themselves a crucial part of US-sponsored Cold War cultural diplomacy. Having performed for the US Army, thereby earning US citizenship, they toured not only the Soviet Union but Japan and Korea under those auspices.[82] Thus, even these Spanish-language versions of the songs were still heavily mediated by the US mediasphere.

Velázquez's name as the composer of "Bésame Mucho" was included on the Soviet record, and this was the version of the song that remained the standard in the Soviet Union throughout subsequent decades, while it continued to be performed everywhere by a wide range of musicians, both foreign and local, as noted by Rodolfo Echeverría on his 1972 visit.[83] The song's popularity was further revived when it was included on the soundtrack of the highly successful (and Oscar-winning) Soviet melodrama *Moscow Does Not Believe in Tears* (1979). On the film soundtrack the song is performed by another famous trio, Los Paraguayos, with a similar genesis as official representatives of cultural diplomacy: the group was first sent to Europe in 1953 on a cultural mission to promote the music of their native Paraguay. Once in Europe, they signed on to the record label Philips, with which they would eventually sell over twenty million records, which included a range of popular Latin American romantic standards: their 1960s album is appropriately titled *The Ambassadors of Romance*.[84]

This was certainly a perfect choice for the soundtrack of a film that turned out to be the most popular Soviet melodrama (selling seventy-five million tickets upon release, and securing a long life on television), and evidently the most internationally known one: the film's Oscar for best foreign language film ensured its worldwide international distribution, which included Mexico, where it became the most successful Soviet film since the days of Eisenstein and was screened commercially and broadcast on TV.[85] The film tells the story of a young woman, Katerina, and her two girlfriends over the course of twenty years—from their arrival in Moscow in the 1950s to Katerina finally finding true love, all the while raising a child as a single mother and working her way up to become a factory's executive director. "Bésame Mucho" plays an important narrative function in the film. The song appears as a leitmotif accompanying Katerina's history of failed love affairs: from her first, which results in her pregnancy, to a failed relationship with a married colleague some twenty years later. In addition to serving to cue the emotional (and moralist) interpretation of these relationships as passionate but doomed, the song also serves as a link between the two epochs. When the song is first heard in the film's diegesis, it stands in as a marker of the period of the 1950s associated with the Thaw and emblematized by the Festival of Youth and Students, which is also featured in the film. When the audience hears its more contemporary instrumental version in the film's second part, which takes place in the 1970s, it provides additional continuity between these two historical periods and parts of Katerina's life.

Much has been said about *Moscow Does Not Believe in Tears* as a paradigm for the gender relations of the late Soviet period. On the one hand, it's a story of a self-made woman who comes to the capital as a provincial outsider and a factory worker and, through hard work and dedication, rises to the position of the factory's executive director, despite the challenges of being a single mother.[86] On the other hand, Katerina ultimately finds true happiness only when she finally meets Gosha, a "good decent man"—one who believes in traditional gender roles, refuses to be criticized or contradicted by a woman, and even breaks off the relationship when he realizes that Katerina earns more than he does, providing for the film's last bit of dramatic suspense. The narrative resolution, as many critics have noted, comes across as particularly successful because the heroine, in the end, can have it all: a professional career that comes with a high standard of living, motherhood, and a "real" man who can finally let her be a real woman. Gosha is a relic of Thaw-era Soviet romanticism—played, appropriately, by Aleksei Batalov, the protagonist of such seminal Thaw-era films as *Cranes Are Flying* and *Nine Years of One Year*. He is an antimaterialist (he lives in a room with barely any conveniences and has no interest in fashion or design) but also a "master builder" in his work as a mechanic, inventor, and tinkerer—all highly prized qualities of a member of the Soviet technical intelligentsia, perfectly corresponding to the gender divisions of Soviet society (he is also, inexplicably, very good at karate, as seen when he "neutralizes" a group of teenagers threatening Katerina's daughter Aleksandra and her boyfriend).[87]

The characters in the film are all marked by their musical associations: thus, Katerina's affective life for much of the film is expressed through "Bésame Mucho"—passionate, romantic, and decidedly *cursi*, as befits a provincial girl in search of happiness. Her teenage daughter in the 1970s listens to Boney M, the Euro-Caribbean disco group, marking her generational belonging and hinting at the more updated international version of "bad taste" and consumerism (associated with Western music and disco in particular)—a choice that likewise would have been fully recognized by Mexican viewers in the early 1980s, when the band was enormously popular in Mexico (as in much of the world, except for North America). On the other hand, Gosha, the ultimate Soviet good guy, enjoys the Russian singer-songwriter/guitar music of *bardy* (a movement akin to the Latin American *Nueva Trova* or Italian *Canta-Autore*), a choice that is specifically associated with the previous generation of Soviet intelligentsia (of the 1960s, to whom he certainly belongs).[88] It is Gosha's choice that ultimately frames the film as a whole: the title of the main theme song, "Aleksandra"—which belongs to the same

FIGURE 27. Spanish-language poster for *Moscow Does Not Believe in Tears*. Personal collection.

genre of bard music—references the name of Katerina's daughter. The song thus serves as an integration of Katerina's whole family under this cultural formation, subtly directing the bildungsroman of the protagonist's sentimental education—as well as her daughter's!—into a more appropriate, at once more tasteful and patriotic, Soviet cultural norm.

Despite the primacy of the song to the film's soundtrack, the producers of *Moscow Does Not Believe in Tears* never asked for Velázquez's permission to use it or paid fees associated with it, despite its international distribution or the fact that, in 1973, the Soviet Union had officially revised the Soviet copyright laws to conform with the Universal Copyright Convention—whose main objective was to extend copyright protection to foreign authors.[89] Velázquez granted her permission retroactively, after her trip to Moscow in the early 1980s, where she became confronted with the ubiquity of the song in the Soviet Union—and finally received official recognition as the song's author. Velázquez, who was well known in Mexico as an advocate for authors' intellectual rights, served as president of the Association of the Authors and Composers of Mexico (Asociación de Autores y Compositores de México) and as the vice-president of its Panamerican Guild Organization, and seemed to have delighted in accounts of Soviet interpretations of her work.[90] According to one interview given decades later, she first heard her song immediately upon arrival in Moscow, when her taxi driver kept whistling it during the trip, and when she told him that she wrote the song, he explained to her that it was just included in *Moscow Does Not Believe in Tears*—and refused to take any money from her, as a gesture of gratitude for her musical creation.[91] In another interview, she remembers hearing "Bésame Mucho" in Moscow, performed by the Soviet Army choir as the final concert at the International Tchaikovsky Competition, where it was announced as a "Cuban folksong," leading to her confronting the Soviet minister of culture regarding her authorship of the song, of which he was apparently unaware.[92]

This purported lack of awareness of Velázquez's authorship conflicts with the oral accounts included in the Russian TV film *Kiss Me Stronger, or Operation Bésame Mucho,* which not only reconstructs the story of the attempt by a Velázquez fan to hijack a plane (which opens the introduction of this book), but also includes accounts of how, in the 1960s, postcards featuring Consuelo Velázquez were produced on the black market and circulated all over Russia. Gennadii Mitrofanov, a deaf-mute who in the 1960s was making money by selling postcards and calendars on commuter trains, recounts in detail how he found foreign magazines with Velázquez on the cover at the house of his neighbor who was a sailor and thus traveled abroad. Mitrofanov was so taken with the photos—and even more so once he found out who this beautiful woman was—that he had another friend print them as postcards. These postcards, he claims, were "more popular than pornography and sold at higher prices," providing him with steady income for years.[93] Thus, not just the song, but even the image of its composer entered into the informal economic circuit, partaking in the emotional charge—and extending the sexuality and romanticism of the music not to the performer but to the author (which, of course, was already inscribed in the original photo taken from an American magazine). In the best *cursi* style, the black-and-white postcards were decorated with hand-colored drawings of flowers or hearts, a total throwback to turn-of-the-century low-class commodity culture.

As such, this mode of circulation stands in a dialectical relationship to official Soviet efforts to similarly integrate "Bésame Mucho" into the representational regime by rendering it as a military march performed by the Soviet army choir—serving as its opposite, yet intrinsically related. Such militarization of sound is both a mode of disciplining its subaltern origins through a European nationalist/colonialist and socialist military framing and a way of imposing the collectivist

FIGURE 28. A homemade postcard featuring Consuelo Velázquez in *Kiss Me Stronger or Operation Bésame Mucho*. DVD screen grab.

and public onto the "personal" and private aesthetic. A perfect example of "the colonization of the ear"—particularly striking in the context of the Soviet invasion of Afghanistan, which was taking place exactly at that time, and of the military's overall role in Soviet society more broadly—such a rendition is as terrifying as it is ridiculous.[94] Indeed, by the late 1970s, such juxtapositions couldn't be perceived as anything but kitschy; the pathos was as exaggerated as in the song's performances by Andrea Bocelli and Plácido Domingo, but not as likely to generate strong positive feelings among audiences. Instead, the reception of the song's more conventional versions, such as the ones used in *Moscow Does Not Believe in Tears*, is anything but ironic—instead, the nostalgia it evokes endows the song with additional markers of sincere, if misplaced, affections and desires.

All in all, Velázquez, who was PRI deputy at the time and was married to the vice-president of the Mexican branch of RCA Records, Mariano Rivera Conde, for many years—and who, according to numerous accounts, traveled with a handbag full of diamonds, much to the dismay of Soviet customs and the various composers asked to receive her as a guest in their humble Soviet apartments—took these Soviet copyright infringements in good cheer. Velázquez's authorship of the famous song was publicly celebrated in Russia in the early 2000s, at the international celebration of its sixtieth anniversary (occasioning many interviews and the film *Operation Bésame Mucho*). More surprisingly, her trip(s) to Moscow in previous decades had not generated the kind of publicity that could be expected of the famous composer's visit.

What emerged clearly in the 2000s, however, was the link in the Russian public consciousness between the song and broader Latin American melodrama production, at the very moment when Mexican telenovelas had just reached their peak on post-Soviet TV. Asked about this relationship—her song's "preparing the population of the planet for the reception of telenovelas"—Velázquez responded merely by saying that she herself did not watch television except for classical music programs, but was not ashamed of having contributed music to telenovelas over the years.[95] Post-Soviet cultural and film critics likewise arrived at a consensus that the passions and a particular sense of recognition that "Bésame Mucho" generated in the Soviet Union were directly transformed into those the late Soviet audiences had for Latin American telenovelas. The latter was equally perceived as "far removed from the ethos of Protestant ethics and capitalism" of American culture on the one hand and from the drabness of Soviet life on the other.[96] Although they do not mention *Yesenia*, the filmmakers and critics interviewed by the makers of *Operation Bésame Mucho* perceptively construct a shared cultural and affective field of reception and its uneven nonlinear temporality—which, as I have argued here, constitute, together with the mixed informal/state-created mode of reproduction, a peculiarly socialist mode of circulation of Latin American melodramatic media.

Coda

Yesenia *in China and the Arrival*
of Telenovelas in the Socialist World

The pattern of reception detailed in this book, while quite distinctive in its Soviet iteration, was limited to the Soviet Union neither in geography nor in historical periodization—and the film's reach, however transformed, extends to the present day.

In 1976, as a result of *Yesenia*'s box office success in the Soviet Union, Chinese film authorities visited Mexico to arrange for screenings to form part of the first week of Mexican cinema and purchased "several dozen copies" of the film, as well as meeting with Jorge Lavat to discuss his visit to China.[1] The film was, indeed, screened in the open-air cinema in Shanghai's Zhabei Park in July 1979, along with two films by Tito Davison: *Corazón salvaje* (1968) and the Mexico-Columbia coproduction *María* (1972), reportedly watched by more than ten thousand people.[2]

All three films were subsequently released commercially, and *Yesenia* was particularly popular with viewers, who were delighted by the film's depiction of romance, which had been entirely absent from Chinese cinema of the Cultural Revolution. In keeping with its original history, upon the film's release in China, a *lianhuanhua* (serialized photo-novel) of *Yesenia* was published—a big departure from the use of *lianhuanhua* for educational and political propaganda purposes that was typical of Chinese media just a few years prior. Overall, the popular reception of the film in China appears similarly framed by the discourse on "free love" and the feminization of women's screen representations—seen as distinctly Western, with heroines depicted as exuberant, defiant, and sexually forward (evidently, "the Mexican gypsy's" red dress was especially memorable in this respect).[3]

FIGURE 29. Advertisement for *Yesenia* as part of the week of Mexican cinema in Beijing, 1977. Personal collection.

FIGURE 30. A more recent cover for a pirated Chinese copy clearly foregrounds the eroticism of *Yesenia*.

Yesenia became even more of an icon after Jacqueline Andere visited the country in 1983 with her husband, Mexican author José María Fernández Unsáin, who was received by China PEN Center. During her much-publicized visit, Andere met the Chinese voice actor Li Zi, who dubbed Yesenia in Chinese. Li Zi contributed a great deal to her character's iconic status and is responsible for her much-quoted

FIGURE 31. Poster art for *Yesenia*. Personal collection.

lines, perceived as particularly sexually risqué.[4] Li was also known for her dubbing of Gina Lollobrigida's Esmeralda in *Notre-Dame de Paris* (Jean Delannoy, 1956), which was also released in China in the late 1970s, furthering associations between these movie "sex symbols" within postreform China's reconsiderations of gender and sexuality.

Yesenia continued to be popular in China throughout the 1980s and into the 1990s, when the 1987 adaptation of the previous telenovela was broadcast on CCTV-8. In the 2000s, Yesenia was repeatedly evoked in official Chinese programming, now through the lens of nostalgia for the immediate postreform era: first in the 2001 CCTV-6 program *The Best*, a TV broadcast of the film that

FIGURE 32. Poster art for *Yesenia*. Personal collection.

included extended analysis by the host; again, in 2007, when CCTV-6's World Film Report released a special filmed in Mexico, "Looking for Yesenia," which included an interview with Andere; and again in 2014, when the Beijing TV Spring Festival Gala invited Andere as part of a "childhood memories" section of the event.[5] As recently as 2021, CCTV-6's *The Best* screened *Yesenia* with an accompanying two-part discussion of the film and what it meant for the Chinese viewers.

We may speculate on the geopolitical motivations of the Chinese government–sponsored revivals of these instances of Chinese-Mexican affinities, or on the postreform moment of opening toward the world, but this was considerably different from Russian critics' continuing disdain over non-Western forms of entertainment (in the face of their government's anti-Western stance). It is evident that the specific cultural and political dynamics of the circulation and reception of Mexican melodramatic media differed considerably across the "socialist world," with each instance deserving a separate detailed examination. And *Yesenia* is not an isolated case, but a broader historical cinematic phenomenon, the significance of which extends beyond the contours of the 1970s Soviet Union. Tracing this pattern will reshape our understanding of the subsequent phase of media globalization flows in the 1980s and 1990s, providing indispensable clues to the gender dynamics of global postsocialism and its complex relationships with the world beyond Europe and North America.

The belated popularity of *Yesenia* and other popular Mexican films in China, which continued throughout the early 1980s, was in many ways responsible for Chinese TV executives' decision to purchase the rights to broadcast the Brazilian TV telenovela *The Slave Isaura* (*A Escrava Isaura*, Globo, 1976). Once shown on Chinese television in 1984, in the midst of an ongoing love affair between Chinese audiences and Mexican melodramas, the series was not only the first foreign program shown on national television, but remains one of the most beloved: three hundred thousand viewers purportedly voted to nominate its star, Lucélia Santos, for China's prestigious Golden Eagle Award, making Santos the first foreign actress to receive this honor. In subsequent years, *Isaura* conquered TV audiences in China, Albania, Poland, Hungary, and Cuba. Eventually sold to a total of 104 national markets, it turned out to be Globo's breakthrough international success and Brazil's biggest TV export.[6]

Isaura finally arrived on Soviet televisions in late 1988, where it held center stage in fierce cultural debates among critics and audiences, replaying and magnifying those triggered by *Yesenia* a decade earlier. Only this time, rather than being voiced by a handful of film critics, the concern over what *Isaura*'s popularity meant for the state of Soviet culture and media reached the mainstream. A very cursory search for 1989–1990 reveals the mention of *Isaura* in over twenty articles in major Soviet newspapers such as *Pravda, Sovetskaia kul'tura*, and *Literaturnaia gazeta*, in addition to mentions in specialized publications such as *Iskusstvo kino, Sovetski ekran*, and *Televidenie i radioveshchanie*. These publications were inundated with letters from viewers, expressing their love for the show and asking for more information—much to the reviewers' and journalists' dismay.

Like the Mexican melodramas that came before it, *Isaura* was a historical romance. The series was adapted from Bernardo Guimarães's nineteenth-century abolitionist novel *A Escrava Isaura*, which was subsequently translated and published in both China and the Soviet Union. Thus, *Isaura* came complete with a politically progressive antislavery message and deeply conservative race and gender representational politics.[7] In many ways, *Isaura*'s global reception fits remarkably well within the cultural dynamics described in this book—albeit taking them to a truly global level. Its success was inseparable from its racial politics: nominally progressive and antiracist, yet not only stereotypical in its representations of Afro-Brazilian culture but highly problematic in its reliance on the figure of a "white" slave, paradoxically detaching slavery from race.[8]

And while *Yesenia* as a cultural and cinematic phenomenon remained largely unacknowledged by the Soviet cultural institutions at large, *Isaura* found its place at the center of some of the fiercest public cultural debates, especially because within two years its popularity was matched by new Latin American imports such as Mexican Televisa's *Los ricos también lloran*. It would become the most-watched program on TV, with an estimated two hundred million Russians and ex-Soviets tuning in to the series finale, quickly to be followed by *Simplemente María*, another

FIGURE 33. Poster art for *Yesenia*. Personal collection.

Pimstein-produced telenovela, which attracted an average of 140 million viewers.[9] From that point on, for at least two decades, post-Soviet television, whose domestic production lagged significantly behind, was dominated by Latin American telenovelas. But both *Isaura* and *Los ricos* marked a real turning point not only in the Soviet but in international media flows, establishing Latin American telenovelas' prominence beyond their original Latin American and US-diasporic media circuit. This development both foreshadowed and demonstrated the potential for a truly global circulation of serialized melodramatic media originating outside of the Global North—realized more recently by the worldwide commercial and popular successes of Turkish *dizi*, South Korean dramas, and Indian serialized TV.

In the post-Soviet space, the synergy of Latin American telenovela and popular music culminated in the creation of yet another global-popular icon, Natalia Oreiro. "Nasha Natasha"—"our Natasha," as she is known thanks to the eponymous Netflix documentary—is an Uruguayan-Argentinian singer and telenovela star who enjoyed unparalleled on- and off-screen popularity in the former Soviet Union in the 2000s and continued touring the region so much that she was recently granted Russian citizenship.[10] Oreiro's acting and singing career had a powerful reboot triggered by the Netflix documentary: after decades of relative obscurity, at the moment of this book's writing she is the star of several major Argentinian made-for-streaming media productions, playing none other than Eva Perón in the recent popular serialized biopic (currently distributed through DisneyPlus). Oreiro's story in many ways takes us back to Lolita Torres, where this book began—and yet it also positions us firmly in the present, when cinema, television, and music industries are virtually inseparable from streaming platforms and digital piracy as modes of production, circulation, and consumption that shape new global media cultures. Both public debates and ardent fandom, too, take place largely in the virtual space of social media.

There is no doubt that a lot has changed—and these new global icons, as well as the geographies and infrastructures for their circulation, deserve a separate close study. This brief coda is therefore merely a teaser, an invitation to consider new questions arising from the history this book constructed. It is also a glimpse intended to demonstrate how despite these changes, many of the same dynamics become increasingly relevant to our new media landscape. And to critically engage with this new landscape, we need to go beyond some of the traditional binary thinking about national and global, North and South, East and West, socialism and capitalism, reactionary melodrama and progressive avant-garde. As such, the story of *Yesenia* can provide us a better understanding of one manifestation of the global-popular media and the way such cultural icons succeeded in addressing the changed affective regime of the post-1968 global landscape. Their popular transnational resonances foreground the various failures of cultural politics in both Mexico and the Soviet Union—failures that can be seen as paradigmatic of the inability of both state-led efforts and those of a cultural intelligentsia to engage the persistent importance of popular culture. This, in turn, speaks to their inability to face the actually existing historical conditions of "the people" they were meant to represent.

Beyond its ability to tap into unaddressed grievances and utopian imaginaries that resonated across the borders, *Yesenia* did not offer anything like a valid alternative for emancipatory politics of its time. A close reading of the various cultural resonances mobilized by the film's transnational reception points to both the persistence of older colonial and patriarchal epistemologies and the emergence of neoliberal and postfeminist frameworks of the subsequent decades. And yet neither of these two overlapping modalities could fully contain the cultural intimacies triggered by these global icons. And however problematic the populist imaginaries of alternative communities mobilized through these histories, and however flawed the strategies for their realization in everyday life, politically they are not reducible either to reified visions of state socialism or to consoling passions of capitalist consumption. In this very excess they may retain the potential for alternative modes of global solidarities that sidestep the seeming inevitability of global neoliberalism or the critical impasse of the Left. To mobilize them for new liberatory politics of popular culture would entail neither a full rejection of earlier models nor the savoring of sacred talismans of supposedly progressive moments of media histories, but a more attentive reckoning with the messiness of the past and the unanswered questions it still holds.

NOTES

INTRODUCTION

1. *Kiss Me Stronger or Operation Bésame Mucho* (*Tselui menia krepche ili operatsiia Bésame Mucho*, Maksim Vasilenko, 2005).

2. See, for example, Leslie Woodhead, *How the Beatles Rocked the Kremlin: The Untold Story of a Noisy Revolution* (London: Bloomsbury, 2013) and TV movie (2009); *Wind of Change: With Patrick Radden Keefe* (podcast series) (London: Pineapple Studios, 2020–2022).

3. Fatima Bhutto, *New Kings of the World: Dispatches from Bollywood, Dizi, and K-Pop* (New York: Columbia Global Reports, 2019).

4. Lisa Parks and Shanti Kumar, *Planet TV: A Global Television Reader* (New York: NYU Press, 2003); D. Y. Jin, "Transformation of the World Television System under Neoliberal Globalization, 1983 to 2003," *Television and New Media* 8, no. 3 (2007): 179–96; Tasha Oren and Sharon Shahaf, *Global Television Formats: Understanding Television across Borders* (New York: Routledge, 2013).

5. Bishnupriya Ghosh and Bhaskar Sarkar, "The Global-Popular: A Frame for Contemporary Cinemas," *Cultural Critique*, no. 114 (Winter 2022): 1–22.

6. Alexander Fedorov, *200 Foreign Leaders of Soviet Film Distribution: A Selected Collection* (Moscow: OD "Information for All," 2023); Kristin Roth-Ey, *Moscow Prime Time: How the Soviet Union Built the Media Empire That Lost the Cultural Cold War* (Ithaca, NY: Cornell University Press, 2011), 43–44.

7. In the English-language context, however, it was not the Mexican telenovela but the American show that gave rise to the iconic scholarly work on soap operas' international appeal: Ien Ang's *Watching Dallas: Soap Opera and the Melodramatic Imagination* (London: Routledge, 1982).

8. It is worth pointing out that the term *Soviet*, which I use throughout the book, can be quite misleading in its implications of homogeneity within the enormous cultural and political space it refers to. Still, based on anecdotal evidence, we can assume that

the dynamics described here were not limited to the Russophone urban centers such as Moscow or Leningrad, or to the Russian republic. Indeed, the overall box office statistics I rely on would have been impossible had the popularity of films and figures I discuss been limited to any one part of the Soviet Union. And yet, the immense cultural heterogeneity among the Soviet republics doubtless resulted in highly diverse patterns of local reception and forms of cultural and political engagement that this book cannot possibly account for. At the same time, in many other instances, the official discourses and practices described here stemmed "from above"—originating in the center (i.e., Moscow), thus imposing a model of a supposedly shared Soviet culture. This model, despite its highly uneven and conflictual applications across the regions of the Soviet Union, exercised a great deal of pressure on local conditions, resulting in a de facto hegemony of Russian cultural models, and diverse iterations and responses to them. This complexity is extremely hard to capture in a book that is focused more broadly on a transcultural, international context. Yet it must be acknowledged, lest we continue to ignore and therefore normalize the assumptions of equivalence between the denominations "Soviet" and "Russian," however difficult they may be to disentangle in each instance.

9. For a discussion of *dictablanda* in the Mexican context, see Paul Gillingham and Benjamin T. Smith, eds., *Dictablanda: Politics, Work, and Culture in Mexico, 1938–1968* (Durham, NC: Duke University Press, 2014). For a discussion of the political and historiographic implications of the term *late socialism*, see Dina Fainberg and Artemy M. Kalinovsky, "Introduction: Stagnation and Its Discontents: The Creation of a Political and Historical Paradigm," in *Reconsidering Stagnation in the Brezhnev Era: Ideology and Exchange*, ed. Dina Fainberg and Artemy M. Kalinovsky (London: Lexington Books, 2016).

10. For a discussion of a similar dynamic in a more contemporary context, see Paloma Duong, "*Postsocialismos de Bolsillo*: Women and Fashion in Secondhand Time," in *Portable Socialisms: New Cuban Mediascapes after the End of History* (Austin: University of Texas Press, 2023), 113–40.

11. Another example of this is "Lambada," the French-Brazilian music hit whose popularity across the collapsing Iron Curtain in 1989 heralded the end of the Cold War and the beginning of the integrated globalized market for popular—and "world"—music. It resonated, in its Soviet reception, with that of Brazilian telenovelas.

12. Jesús Martín-Barbero, *De los medios a las mediaciones: Comunicación, cultura y hegemonía* (Mexico City: Ediciones G. Gili, 1987), 126; quoted in Marvin D'Lugo, "Luis Alcoriza; or, A Certain Antimelodramatic Tendency in Mexican Cinema," in *Latin American Melodrama: Passion, Pathos and Entertainment*, ed. Darlene J. Sadlier (Urbana-Champaign: University of Illinois Press, 2009), 115.

13. See Ravi S. Vasudevan, "Melodrama," *BioScope: South Asian Screen Studies* 12, no. 1–2 (2021), 125–28; Vednuti Duggal, "Intermediality," *BioScope: South Asian Screen Studies* 12, no. 1–2 (2021), 113–16.

14. See Marvin D'Lugo, "Aural Identity, Genealogies of Sound Technologies, and Hispanic Transnationality on Screen," in *World Cinemas, Transnational Perspectives*, ed. Nataša Durovicová and Kathleen E. Newman (New York: Routledge, 2010), 160–85; Ana M. López, "Of Rhythms and Borders," in *Everynight Life*, ed. Jose Muñoz and Celeste Fraser Delgado (Durham, NC: Duke University Press, 1997), 310–44; Jacqueline Avila, *Cinesonidos: Film Music and National Identity during Mexico's Época de Oro* (London: Oxford University Press, 2019).

15. Jesús Martín-Barbero, "Memory and Form in the Latin American Soap Opera," in *To Be Continued . . . Soap Operas around the World*, ed. Richard C. Allen (New York: Routledge, 1995), 382–83.

16. Anahid Kassabian, *Ubiquitous Listening: Affect, Attention, and Distributed Subjectivity* (Berkeley: University of California Press, 2013). For the many functions of music in Mexican cinema, see López, "Of Rhythms and Borders"; D'Lugo, "Aural Identity"; Avila, *Cinesonidos*.

17. Daya Kishan Thussu, ed., *Media on the Move: Global Flow and Contra-flow* (New York: Routledge, 2007).

18. On media capitals, see Michael Curtin, "Media Capitals: Cultural Geographies of Global TV," in *Television after TV: Essays on a Medium in Transition*, ed. Jan Olsson and Lynn Spigel (Durham, NC: Duke University Press, 2004), 270–302.

19. See Iuliia Glushneva, "Sentimental Education across the Borders: Hindi Soap Opera and Translation Cultures on the Russophone Web," *Feminist Media Studies* (2023), in press.

20. A paradigmatic approach in this regard is articulated in Joseph Straubhaar, "Beyond Media Imperialism: Asymmetrical Interdependence and Cultural Proximity," *Critical Studies in Mass Communication* 8, no. 1 (1991): 39–59.

21. Ana M. López, "Our Welcomed Guests: Telenovelas in Latin America," in *To Be Continued . . . Soap Operas around the World*, ed. Richard C. Allen (New York: Routledge, 1995), 256–75; D'Lugo, "Across the Hispanic Atlantic: Cinema and Its Symbolic Relocations," *Studies in Hispanic Cinemas* (new title: *Studies in Spanish & Latin American Cinemas*) 5, no. 1–2 (2009): 3–7; Robert Irwin and Castro Ricalde, eds., *Global Mexican Cinema: Its Golden Age* (London: Palgrave, 2013).

22. Diana Rios and Mari Castañeda, eds., *Soap Operas and Telenovelas in the Digital Age: Global Industries and New Audiences* (New York: Peter Lang, 2011).

23. Timothy D. Taylor, *Global Pop: World Music, World Markets* (New York: Routledge, 1997); Ed Morales, *The Latin Beat: The Rhythms and Roots of Latin Music, from Bossa Nova to Salsa and Beyond* (New York: De Capo Press, 2003).

24. Robert Hanke, "Yo quiero mi MTV! Making Music Television for Latin America," in *Mapping the Beat: Popular Music and Contemporary Theory*, ed. Thomas Swiss, Andrew Herman, and John Sloop (Malden, MA: Blackwell, 1997), 219–45; Mary Beltrán, *Latina/o Stars in U.S. Eyes* (Urbana-Champaign: University of Illinois Press, 2009); Benjamin Han, *Beyond the Black and White TV: Asian and Latin American Spectacle in Cold War America* (Rutgers, NJ: Rutgers University Press, 2020).

25. Michael Denning, *Noise Uprising: The Audiopolitics of a World Music Revolution* (London: Verso, 2015); Andrew F. Jones, *Circuit Listening: Chinese Popular Music in the Global 1960s* (Minneapolis: University of Minnesota Press, 2020).

26. Thomas Lamarre, "Regional TV: Affective Media Geographies," *Asiascape: Digital Asia* 2 (2015): 94. See also Joshua Neves, "Southern Effects: *Kaiju*, Cultural Intimacy, and the Production of Distribution," *Cultural Critique* 114 (2022): 127–52.

27. Lamarre, "Regional TV," 94.

28. I use the term *postfeminist* in the way it was articulated by Angela McRobbie as marked by, among other things, ideology of personal choice, self-improvement, willing self-hyper-sexualization, and individual professional advancement combined with sexual confidence. Angela McRobbie, "Post-feminism and Popular Culture," *Feminist Media Studies* 4, no. 3 (2004): 255–64.

29. For a detailed discussion of this, see Anna Ledeneva, *Russia's Economy of Favours: Blat, Networking and Informal Exchange* (Cambridge: Cambridge University Press, 1998); Susan Reid and David Crowley, eds., *Style and Socialism: Modernity and Material Culture in Post-war Eastern Europe* (Oxford: Berg, 2000); David Crowley and Susan E. Reid, eds., *Socialist Spaces: Sites of Everyday Life in the Eastern Bloc* (Oxford: Berg, 2002); Lewis H. Siegelbaum, ed., *Borders of Socialism: Private Spheres of Soviet Russia* (New York: Palgrave Macmillan, 2006); Natalya Chernyshova, *Soviet Consumer Culture in the Brezhnev Era* (London: Routledge, 2013); Dina Fainberg and Artemy M. Kalinovsky, eds., *Reconsidering Stagnation in the Brezhnev Era*; Timo Vihavainen and Elena Bogdanova, eds., *Communism and Consumerism: The Soviet Alternative to the Affluent Society* (Leiden, The Netherlands: Brill, 2016).

30. Brian Larkin, "Indian Films and Nigerian Lovers: Media and the Creation of Parallel Modernities," *Africa* 67, no. 3 (1997): 406–40, 408–09.

31. Bishnupriya Ghosh, "Looking through Coca-Cola: Global Icons and the Popular," *Public Culture* 22, no. 2 (2010): 333–68, 341.

32. Ignacio M. Sánchez Prado, "Latin America, Uneven Development, Political Economy & Global South," in *The Global South and Literature*, ed. Russell West-Pavlov (Cambridge: Cambridge University Press, 2018), 61–62.

33. Louise Walker, *Waking from the Dream: Mexico's Middle Classes after 1968* (Stanford, CA: Stanford University Press, 2013), 48.

34. Ghosh, "Looking through Coca Cola," 345; Ghosh and Sarkar, "The Global-Popular."

35. For an insightful discussion of politics of fandom in intermedial contexts, see Aswin Punathambekar, "'We're Online, Not on the Streets': Indian Cinema, New Media, and Participatory Culture," in *Global Bollywood*, ed. Anandam P. Kavoori and Aswin Punathambekar (New York: NYU Press, 2008), 282–99.

36. Alexei Yurchak, *Everything Was Forever, Until It Was No More: The Last Soviet Generation* (Princeton, NJ: Princeton University Press, 2005); Kristin Roth-Ey, *Moscow Prime Time: How the Soviet Union Built the Media Empire That Lost the Cultural Cold War* (Ithaca, NY: Cornell University Press, 2011); Eleonory Gilburd, *To See Paris and Die: The Soviet Lives of Western Culture* (Cambridge, MA: Harvard University Press, 2018).

37. Mark Betz, *Beyond the Subtitle: Remapping European Art Cinema* (Minneapolis: University of Minnesota Press, 2009); Ross Melnick, *Hollywood's Embassies: How Movie Theaters Projected American Power around the World* (New York: Columbia University Press, 2022).

38. Ruth Vasey, "Foreign Parts: Hollywood's Global Distribution and the Representation of Ethnicity," *American Quarterly* 44, no. 4 (1992): 617–42.

39. Thomas Elsaesser, *European Cinema: Face to Face with Hollywood* (Amsterdam: Amsterdam University Press, 2005).

40. Tamara Falikov, *Latin American Film Industries* (London: British Film Institute, 2019).

41. Rielle Navitski, *Transatlantic Cinephilia: Film Culture between Latin America and France, 1945–1965* (Oakland: University of California Press, 2023).

42. Marina Kosinova, "International Relations of the Soviet Cinema in the Years of the Thaw," *Modern Research of Social Problems* 6, no. 50 (2015): 638.

43. Kosinova, "International Relations," 237.

44. Kosinova, "International Relations," 641, 624.

45. Alexander Fedorov, *200 Foreign Leaders of Soviet Film Distribution: A Selected Collection* (Moscow: OD "Information for All," 2023).

46. Nikita Markov, "Sistema gosudarstvennogo upravleniia sovetskim kinematografom, 1963–1968" (PhD diss., Russian State Academic University of the Humanities, 2019), 181–91.

47. See Iuliia Glushneva, "Legitimate Transgression: Home Video Culture and Screen Translation(s) in Late Socialist Russia," *Journal of Cinema and Media Studies* 63, no. 5 (2023).

48. Kosinova, "International Relations," 638.

49. Natalya Chernyshova, "Philistines on the Big Screen: Consumerism in Soviet Cinema of the Brezhnev Era," *Studies in Russian and Soviet Cinema* 5, no. 2 (2011): 227–54, 230.

50. Chernyshova, "Philistines on the Big Screen," 230.

51. For a fuller elaboration of this argument, see Glushneva, "Sentimental Education across the Borders."

52. Ghosh, "Looking through Coca Cola," 359.

53. Pekka Gronow and Ilpo Sauno, *An International History of the Recording Industry* (London: Cassell, 1998), 135.

54. For the history and politics of the Eurovision Song Contest and its role in global music developments, see Dean Vuletic, *Postwar Europe and the Eurovision Song Contest* (London: Bloomsbury, 2018); Adam Dubin, Dean Vuletic, and Antonio Obregón, eds., *The Eurovision Song Contest as a Cultural Phenomenon: From Concert Halls to the Halls of Academia* (London: Routledge, 2022). On Intervision, see Dean Vuletic, "The Intervision Song Contest: A Commercial and Pan-European Alternative to the Eurovision Song Contest," in *Eastern European Popular Music in a Transnational Context*, ed. E. Mazierska and Z. Győri (London: Palgrave Macmillan, 2019); Anna G. Piotrowska, "About Twin Song Festivals in Eastern and Western Europe: Intervision and Eurovision," *International Review of the Aesthetics and Sociology of Music* 47, no. 1 (2016): 123–35.

55. Laura Podalsky, "Cosmopolitanism, Modernity and Youth in the 1960s: The Transnational Wanderings of Teen Idols from Argentina, Mexico and Spain," *Transnational Screens* 20 (2020): 1–19; Richard Dyer, "The Pervasiveness of Song in Italian Cinema," in *Popular Italian Cinema*, ed. L. Bayman and S. Rigoletto (New York: Palgrave Macmillan, 2013), 69–81.

56. For a history of bootlegged x-ray recordings, see Stephen Coates, *X-Ray Audio: The Strange Story of Soviet Music on the Bone* (London: Strange Attractor Press, 2015) and *Bone Music: Soviet X-Ray Audio* (London: Strange Attractor Press, 2022); Marsha Siefert, "Entrepreneurial Tapists: Underground Music Reproduction and Distribution in the US and USSR, 1960s and 1970s," in *Music and Democracy: Participatory Approaches*, ed. Marko Kölbl and Fritz Trümpi (Vienna: mdw Press, 2021), 19–60.

57. See Coates, *Bone Music*; Siefert, "Entrepreneurial Tapists."

58. Kaveh Askari, *Relaying Cinema in Midcentury Iran: Material Cultures in Transit* (Oakland: University of California Press, 2022), 8.

59. Peter Schmelz, *Sonic Overload: Alfred Schnittke, Valentin Silvestrov, and Polystylism in the Late USSR* (London: Oxford University Press, 2021).

60. Matthew Jesse Jackson, *The Experimental Group: Ilya Kabakov, Moscow Conceptualism, Soviet Avant-Gardes* (Chicago: University of Chicago Press, 2010), 7.

61. Néstor García Canclini, *Hybrid Cultures: Strategies for Entering and Leaving Modernity* (Minneapolis: University of Minnesota Press, 2005); Yurchak, *Everything Was Forever*.

62. The descriptions of indigenous South Americans and of natives of Slavic lands in European travel writings are characterized by similar terms, exemplified by Madame de Stael's observations, as discussed in Gražina Bielousova, "Western Disorientations: The Vanishing East of South America and Eastern Europe," *Acta Academiae Artium Vilnensis* 105, no. 105 (January 18, 2022):18.

63. Michael Herzfeld, *Cultural Intimacy: Social Poetics and the Real Life of States, Societies, and Institutions* (New York: Routledge, 2016), 3.

64. Rahul Rao, "Before Bandung: Pet Names in Telangana," in *Meanings of Bandung: Postcolonial Orders and Decolonial Visions*, ed. Quỳnh N. Phạm and Robbie Shilliam (London: Rowman and Littlefield, 2016), 86.

65. This predicament is productively explored in Kuan-Hsing Chen, *Asia as Method: Toward Deimperilization* (Durham, NC: Duke University Press, 2010). For the Russian context of this dynamic, see Mark Lipovetsky, "The Progressor between the Imperial and the Colonial" in *Postmodern Crises: from* Lolita *to Pussy Riot* (Boston: Academic Studies Press, 2019), 53–87.

66. Jeffrey James Byrne, *Mecca of Revolution: Algeria, Decolonization, and the Third World Order* (Oxford: Oxford University Press, 2016), 10.

67. See Ignacio M. Sánchez Prado, *Strategic Occidentalism: On Mexican Fiction, the Neoliberal Book Market, and the Question of World Literature* (Evanston, IL: Northwestern University Press, 2018); Szabolcs László, "'We Understand Each Other': Writers from Eastern Europe and the Global South at the International Writing Program (1970s)," in *The Cultural Cold War and the Global South: Sites of Contest and Communitas*, ed. Kerry Bystrom, Monica Popescu, and Katherine Zien (New York: Routledge, 2021), 103.

68. Kyrill Kunakhovich, *Communism's Public Sphere: Culture as Politics in Cold War Poland and East Germany* (Ithaca, NY: Cornell University Press, 2022).

69. See Vanessa Freije, *Citizens of Scandal: Journalism, Secrecy, and the Politics of Reckoning in Mexico* (Durham, NC: Duke University Press, 2020).

70. See Chernyshova, "Philistines on the Big Screen."

71. For a cogent summary of many of these debates in relation to culture, see Swati Chattopadhyay and Bhaskar Sarkar, "Introduction: The Subaltern and the Popular," *Postcolonial Studies* 8, no. 4 (2005): 357–63.

72. For an elaboration of this opposition, see Dilip Gaonkar, "After the Fictions: Notes towards a Phenomenology of the Multitude," *e-flux journal* 58 (October 2014), https://www.e-flux.com/journal/58/61187/after-the-fictions-notes-towards-a-phenomenology-of-the-multitude/.

73. On Russian socialism, see Andrzej Walicki, *A History of Russian Thought from the Enlightenment to Marxism* (Stanford, CA: Stanford University Press, 1979).

74. Sánchez Prado, "Latin America, Uneven Development," 61–62.

75. The notion of *communitas* has been much discussed and variously defined in social and political theory and anthropology, from Victor Turner to Roberto Esposito. It is not my goal here to rehash these debates or provide my own unique definition of the term. I am using it here in its broadest meaning of the shared experience of social liminality, rejection of property relations, and a sense of mutual obligation. For another formulation of *communitas*, relevant to this specific context, see Christopher J. Lee, *Making a World after Empire: The Bandung Moment and Its Political Afterlives* (Athens: Ohio University Press, 2010), 25–27; Kerry Bystrom, Monica Popescu, and Katherine Zien, eds., "Introduction," in

The Cultural Cold War and the Global South: Sites of Contest and Communitas (New York: Routledge, 2021).

76. Daniel Bertaux and Marina Malysheva, "The Cultural Model of the Russian Popular Classes and the Transition to a Market Economy," in *On Living through Soviet Russia*, ed. Daniel Bertaux, Paul Thompson, and Anna Rotkirch (London: Routledge, 2004), 25–52.

77. Sudha Rajagopalan, *Indian Films in Soviet Cinemas: The Culture of Movie-Going after Stalin* (Bloomington: Indiana University Press, 2008), 57–61; Aurora Jacome, "The Munequitos Rusos Generation," in *Caviar with Rum: Cuba-USSR and the Post-Soviet Experience*, ed. Jacqueline Loss and José Manuel Prieto González (New York: Palgrave Macmillan, 2012), 29–34.

78. See Engracia Loyo, "La Lectura en México, 1920–1940," in *Historia de La Lectura En México* (Mexico City: El Colegio de Mexico, 1997), 243–94.

79. On the figure of the bazaar in the South Asian context, which I argue is pertinent throughout this book, see Kajri Jain, "Bazaar," *BioScope: South Asian Screen Studies* 12, no. 1–2 (2021): 35–38.

80. Darlene J. Sadlier, ed., *Latin American Melodrama: Passion, Pathos and Entertainment* (Urbana-Champaign: University of Illinois Press, 2009).

81. Exceptions to this are Victoria Ruétalo and Dolores Tierney, eds., *Latsploitation, Exploitation Cinemas, and Latin America* (London: Routledge, 2011); and Olivia Cosentino and Brian Price, eds., *The Lost Cinema of Mexico: From Lucha Libre to Cine Familiar and Other Churros* (Gainesville: University Press of Florida, 2022).

82. Lauren Berlant, *The Female Complaint: The Unfinished Business of Sentimentality in American Culture* (Durham, NC: Duke University Press, 2008); Agustín Zarzosa, *Refiguring Melodrama in Film and Television: Captive Affects, Elastic Sufferings, Vicarious Objects* (New York: Lexington Books, 2012); Ravi Vasudevan, *The Melodramatic Public: Film Form and Spectatorship in Indian Cinema* (London: Palgrave, 2011); Jesús Martín-Barbero and Sonia Muñoz, *Televisión y melodrama* (Bogotá: Tercer Mundo, 1992).

83. Ana M. López, "Calling for Intermediality: Latin American Mediascapes." *Cinema Journal* 54, no. 1 (2014): 135–41.

84. Tobias Rupprecht, *Soviet Internationalism after Stalin: Interaction and Exchange between the USSR and Latin America during the Cold War* (London: Cambridge University Press, 2012), 108.

85. For readings of Boom literature in the Cold War context, see Niel Larsen, "The Boom Novel and the Cold War in Latin America," *Modern Fiction Studies* 38, no. 3 (1992): 771–84; Rafael Rojas, *La polis literaria: El boom, la Revolucion y las otras polémicas de la Guerra Fría* (Mexico City: Taurus, 2018).

86. Ilshat Saetov, "Populiarnost' turetskih serialov u russkoiazychnyh zritelei," *Vostochnaia analitika*, no. 4 (2020): 249–57; Valerii Burt, "Bollivud protiv Gollivuda. Budem pet' i smeiat'sia kak deti," *Russkaia Planeta*, March 24, https://rusplt.ru/kulturnaya-rossiya/bollivud-protiv-gollivuda-mi-623c17c64d.html.

87. Evgenii Margolit, "Melodrama v sovetskom kino," in *Noveishaia istoriia otechestvennogo kino: 1986–2000*, vol. 6, ed. Luibov' Arkus (St. Petersburg, Russia: Seans, 2006), 227–37.

88. Evgenii Margolit, "Melodrama v sovetskom kino"; Joshua First, "Making Soviet Melodrama Contemporary: Conveying 'Emotional Information' in the Era of Stagnation," *Studies in Russian and Soviet Cinema* 2, no. 1 (2008): 21–42.

89. Olga Gurova, "The Ideology of Consumption in the Soviet Union," in *Communism and Consumerism: The Soviet Alternative to the Affluent Society*, ed. Timo Vihavainen and Elena Bogdanova (Leiden, The Netherlands: Brill, 2016), 77.

90. First, "Making Soviet Melodrama Contemporary"; Alexander Prokhorov and Elena Prokhorova, *Film and Television Genres of the Late Soviet Era* (New York: Bloomsbury Academic, 2017).

91. Ignacio M. Sánchez Prado, "The Golden Age Otherwise," in *Cosmopolitan Film Cultures in Latin America, 1896–1960*, ed. Rielle Navistki and Nicholas Poppe (Indianapolis: Indiana University Press), 242; Carlos Monsiváis, *Aires de familia: Cultura y sociedad en América Latina* (Barcelona: Anagrama, 2000), 11–12.

92. Kuan-Hsing Chen, *Asia as Method: Toward Deimperilization.*

93. Vasudevan, *The Melodramatic Public*, 16.

94. Mitsuhiro Yoshimoto, "Melodrama, Postmodernism, and Japanese Cinema," in *Melodrama and Asian Cinema*, ed. Wimal Dissanayake (Cambridge: Cambridge University Press, 1993), 101–26.

95. Elena Lahr-Vivaz, *Mexican Melodrama: Film and Nation from the Golden Age to the New Wave* (Tucson: University Press of Arizona, 2016), 21.

96. Lahr-Vivaz, *Mexican Melodrama*, 21.

97. Ghosh, "Looking through Coca Cola," 338.

98. Martín-Barbero, "Memory and Form," 277.

99. Ghosh and Sarkar, "The Global-Popular," 19.

100. Ghosh, "Looking through Coca Cola," 342.

PRELUDE: THE SOVIET STARDOM OF LOLITA TORRES

1. Maria Zezina, "Kinoprokat i massovyi zritel' v gody 'ottepeli,'" in *Istoriia strany. Istoriia kino*, ed. S. S. Sekirinskii (Moscow: Znak, 2004), 390.

2. For more on this context, see Eleonory Gilburd, *To See Paris and Die: The Soviet Lives of Western Culture* (Cambridge, MA: Harvard University Press, 2018); Masha Salazkina, *World Socialist Cinema: Alliances, Affinities, and Solidarities in the Global Cold War* (Oakland: University of California Press, 2023), ch. 1.

3. Trophy films consisted of prints taken from the German Reichsfilmarchiv when the Red Army entered Berlin in 1945, which were added to the state film archive in Russia, soon to be reorganized as Gosfilmofond, making it the largest collection of films in the world at that time. K. Tanis, "Trofeinoe kino v SSSR v 1940–1950e gg: k istorii formirovaniia fenomena," *Kul'tura i iskusstvo*, no. 17 (2017): 85–91.

4. For various accounts of this, see Sudha Rajagopalan, *Indian Films in Soviet Cinemas: The Culture of Movie-Going after Stalin* (Bloomington: Indiana University Press, 2008); Kristin Roth-Ey, *Moscow Prime Time: How the Soviet Union Built the Media Empire That Lost the Cultural Cold War* (Ithaca, NY: Cornell University Press, 2011); Rossen Djagalov, *From Internationalism to Postcolonialism: Literature and Cinema between the Second and the Third Worlds* (Montreal: McGill-Queen's University Press, 2020); Salazkina, *World Socialist Cinema.*

5. These include *Pueblerina*, 1951; *Maclovia* and *Rio Escondido*, 1955; *Maria Candelaria* and *Espaldas Mojadas*, 1956; *Una Cita de Amor*, 1958; and *La Perla*, 1961. Alexander

Fedorov, *200 Foreign Leaders of Soviet Film Distribution: A Selected Collection* (Moscow: OD "Information for All," 2023), 197–98.

6. Matthew B. Karush and Oscar Chamosa, eds., "Introduction," in *The New Cultural History of Peronism* (Durham, NC: Duke University Press, 2010), 1–19.

7. On Mar de Plata, see Clara Kriger, "Inolvidables jornadas vivió Mar del Plata. Perón junto a las estrellas," *Archivos de la Filmoteca*, no. 46 (2004): 118–31; Julio Neveleff, Miguel Monforte, and Alejandra Ponce de León, *Historia del Festival Internacional de Cine de Mar del Plata*, vol. 1 (Buenos Aires: Ediciones Corregidor, 2013); Rielle Navitski, *Transatlantic Cinephilia: Networks of Film Culture Between Latin America and France, 1945–1965* (Oakland: University of California Press, 2023).

8. Valeria Galvan and Michal Zourek, "Artkino Pictures Argentina: A Window to the Communist Europe in Buenos Aires Screens (1954–1970)," *Politické vedy* 19, no. 4 (2016): 36–51, 40.

9. Mario Gallina, *Querida Lolita: Retrato de Lolita Torres* (Buenos Aires: Ediciones Deldragón, 2006), 225.

10. Hugo del Carril's film also enjoyed some level of popular success—for more on that, see Tobias Rupprecht, *Soviet Internationalism after Stalin: Interaction and Exchange between the USSR and Latin America during the Cold War* (London: Cambridge University Press, 2012), 86. On the dynamics of Latin American political cinema in the Soviet Union, see Salazkina, *World Socialist Cinema*.

11. Matthew Karush, *Culture of Class: Radio and Cinema in the Making of a Divided Argentina, 1920–1946* (Durham, NC: Duke University Press, 2012), 217.

12. Gallina, *Querida Lolita*, 229.

13. On female heroines in Argentinian romantic comedies, see Alejandro Kelly Hopfenblatt, *Modernidad y teléfonos blancos: La comedia burguesa en el cine argentino de los años 40* (Buenos Aires: Ciccus, 2019).

14. Eleonory Gilburd, "The Revival of Soviet Internationalism in the Mid- to Late 1950s," in *The Thaw: Soviet Society and Culture during the 1950s and 1960s*, ed. Denis Kozlov and Eleonory Gilburd (Toronto: University of Toronto Press, 2013), 375.

15. Zezina, "Kinoprokat i massovyi zritel' v gody 'ottepeli'," 394; Oksana Bulgakova, "Soviet Thaw Cinema in the International Context," in *The Thaw: Soviet Society and Culture during the 1950s and 1960s*, ed. Denis Kozlov and Eleonory Gilburd (Toronto: University of Toronto Press, 2013), 375.

16. Vladimir Semerchuk, "Smena vekh na iskhode ottepeli," in *Kinematograf ottepeli* (Moscow: Materik, 2002), 129.

17. See Denis Kozlov and Eleonory Gilburd, eds., "Introduction," in *The Thaw: Soviet Society and Culture during the 1950s and 1960s* (Toronto: University of Toronto Press, 2013); David Crowley and Susan E. Reid, eds., "Introduction," in *Pleasures in Socialism: Leisure and Luxury in the Eastern Bloc* (Evanston, IL: Northwestern University Press, 2010).

18. Djurdja Barlett, *FashionEast: The Spectre that Haunted Socialism* (Cambridge, MA: MIT Press, 2010), 198–210; Olga Gurova, "The Art of Dressing: Body, Gender and the Discourse on Fashion in Soviet Russia in the 1950s and 1960s," in *The Fabric of Cultures: Fashion, Identity, Globalization*, ed. Eugenia Paulicelli and Hazel Clark (New York: Routledge, 2009). 78.

19. Barlett, *FashionEast*, 190; Larisa Zakharova, "Soviet Fashion in the 1950s–1960s," in *The Thaw: Soviet Society and Culture during the 1950s and 1960s*, ed. Denis Kozlov and Eleonory Gilburd (Toronto: University of Toronto Press, 2013), 419.

20. As late as the 1960s, after the various other media outlets were more developed, a survey showed that the most influential sources of information about fashion were movies and TV. Quotes in Gurova, "The Art of Dressing," 78.

21. Almira Ousmanova, "Devchata: devech'ia chest' i vozrast lyubvi v sovetskoi komedii 1960x godov," in *Vizual'naya antropologiya: rezhimy vidimosti pri sotsializme*, ed. P. Romanov and E. Yarskaya-Smirnova (Moscow: Variant, 2009), 412.

22. Anna Rotkirch, *The Man Question: Loves and Lives in Late 20th Century Russia* (Helsinki: University of Helsinki Press, 2000), 59

23. See Alexander Prokhorov, "Soviet Family Melodrama of the 1940s and 1950s," in *Imitations of Life: Two Centuries of Melodrama in Russia*, ed. Louise McReynolds and Joan Neuberger (Durham, NC: Duke University Press, 2002), 208–32.

24. See David MacFadyen, *Red Stars: Personality and the Soviet Popular Song 1955–1991* (Kingston: McGill-Queen's University Press, 2001), 44–45.

25. Mikhail Èpshtein, *Vera i obraz: Religioznoe bessoznatel'noe v russkoi kul'ture 20-go veka* (Tenafly, NJ: Èrmitazh, 1994), 98.

26. See Sudha Rajagopalan, *Indian Films in Soviet Cinemas: The Culture of Movie-Going after Stalin* (Bloomington: Indiana University Press, 2009), 51–53.

27. Iuri Murashov, "Liubov' i politika: o medial'noi antropologii liubvi v sovetskoi kul'ture," in *SSSR: Territoriia liubvi*, ed. Nataliia Borisova, Konstantin Bogdanov, and Iurii Murashov (Moscow: Novoe izdatel'stvo, 2008), 18–23; Prokhorov, "Soviet Family Melodrama of the 1940s and 1950s," in *Imitations of Life*.

28. On these heroines, see Josephine Woll, *Cinema of the Thaw* (London: I.B.Tauris, 2000); Antony Anemone, "Tatiana Samoilova and the Search for a New Soviet Woman," in *Women in Soviet Film: The Thaw and Post-Thaw Periods*, ed. Marina Rojavin and Tim Harte (London: Routledge, 2018), 14.

29. Clara Kriger, "El cine del Perónismo, una reevaluación," *Archivos de la Filmoteca* 31 (February 1999): 136–55.

30. Alejandro Kelly Hopfenblatt, *Modernidad y teléfonos blancos*, 49.

31. Kelly Hopfenblatt, *Modernidad y teléfonos blancos*, 37–38.

32. Sudha Rajagopalan, "Emblematic of the Thaw: Early Indian Films in Soviet Cinemas," *South Asian Popular Culture* 4, no. 2 (2006): 85.

33. A similar point is made in Alexander Lipkov and Thomas J. Mathew, "India's Bollywood in Russia," *India International Centre Quarterly* 21, no. 2/3 (1994): 187.

34. Anustup Basu, "Dharmendra Singh Deol: Masculinity and the Late Nehruvian Hero," in *Indian Film Stars: New Critical Perspectives*, ed. Michael Lawrence (London: British Film Institute, 2020), 83.

35. Manishita Dass, "Cinetopia: Leftist Street Theatre and the Musical Production of the Metropolis in 1950s Bombay Cinema," *Positions: Asia Critique* 25, no. 1 (February 2017): 101–24. See also Ravi Vasudevan, *The Melodramatic Public: Film Form and Spectatorship in Indian Cinema* (London: Palgrave, 2011), ch. 3.

36. Richard Dyer, "Entertainment and Utopia," in *Only Entertainment* (London: Routledge, 1992), 178–93.

37. Eva Perón—known as Evita, and immortalized in the eponymous 1976 musical by Andrew Lloyd Webber and Tim Rice—was the First Lady of Argentina between 1946 and her death in 1952. Prior to advancing her public credentials, she had an established career as a stage, radio, and film actress. In the 1940s, she was actively involved in the broadcast performers' union movement.

38. Jessica Stites Mor, *Transition Cinema: Political Filmmaking and the Argentinian Left since 1968* (Pittsburgh, PA: University of Pittsburgh Press, 2012), 56.

39. Karush, *Culture of Class*, 203.

40. For a famous discussion of this aspect of Indian popular cinema, see Madhava Prasad, *Ideology of the Hindi Film: A Historical Construction* (New Delhi: Cambridge University Press, 1998).

41. Bulgakova, "Soviet Thaw Cinema in the International Context," 463.

42. Gallina, *Querida Lolita*, 84.

43. Larisa Zakharova, "Dior in Moscow: A Taste for Luxury in Soviet Fashion under Khrushchev," in *Pleasures in Socialism: Leisure and Luxury in the Eastern Bloc*, ed. David Crowley and Susan E. Reid (Evanston, IL: Northwestern University Press, 2010), 114.

44. For more on Dior in Russian culture and on screen, see Lilya Kaganovsky, "Between Pornography and Nostalgia: Valery Todorovsky's *The Thaw* (*Ottepel'*)," in *Russian TV Series in the Era of Transition: Genres, Technologies, Identities*, ed. Alexander Prokhorov, Elena Prokhorova, and Rimgaila Salys (Boston: Academic Studies Press, 2021), 126–27.

45. See Zakharova, "Soviet Fashion in the 1950s–1960s"; Gurova, "The Art of Dressing."

46. "V gostyakh," *Rabotnitsa*, no. 10 (1957), 32; quoted in Gurova, "The Art of Dressing," 78.

47. See, for example, Donald J. Raleigh, *Soviet Baby Boomers: An Oral History of Russia's Cold War Generation* (London: Oxford University Press, 2011), 59.

48. Kaganovsky, "Between Pornography and Nostalgia," 126–27.

49. Liudmila Gurchenko, *Aplodismenty* (Moscow: Tsentrpoligraf, 2020).

50. *Poiot Lolita Torres* (Moscow: Muzgiz, 1959).

51. Michael Denning, *Noise Uprising: The Audiopolitics of a World Music Revolution* (London: Verso, 2015), 72.

52. Nikolai Ovsiannikov, "Chudesnaiia Koimbra ili Agranovich v Portugalii," *Alef*, March 1, 2013, http://www.alefmagazine.com/pub3188.html (accessed July 23, 2023).

53. Here, I am using the term similarly to Naficy's engagement with what he refers to as "accented cinema" in a specifically diasporic context, extending it to the broader multiculturalism and status of "foreignness" in the Soviet Union. Hamid Naficy, *An Accented Cinema: Exilic and Diasporic Filmmaking* (Princeton, NJ: Princeton University Press, 2001).

54. Iurii Bragin, "Poshlost' meniaet etiketki," *Sovetskaia kul'tura*, March 31, 1955, n.p.

55. Bragin, "Poshlost' meniaet etiketki."

56. On jazz in the Soviet Union, see S. Frederick Starr, *Red and Hot: The Fate of Jazz in the Soviet Union 1917–1980* (New York: Oxford University Press, 1983); *Jazz behind the Iron Curtain*, ed. Gertrud Pickhan and Rüdiger Ritter (Frankfurt: Peter Lang, 2010), 99–116.

57. Francesco Adinolfi, *Mondo Exotica: Sounds, Visions, Obsessions of the Cocktail Generation* (Durham, NC: Duke University Press, 2008), 29–32.

58. MacFadyen, *Red Stars*.

59. MacFadyen, *Red Stars*, 89.

60. Gurchenko, *Aplodismenty*.

61. Gurchenko, *Aplodismenty.*

62. Anisim Gimmervert, *Maia Kristalinskaia. I vsio sbylos' i ne sbylos'* (Moscow: Olimp, 1999), 24.

63. See Gilburd, *To See Paris and Die.*

64. Gallino, *Querida Lolita.*

65. We will return to the genre of *españoladas* in relation to stereotypes of the Romani culture—like the Andalusian "gypsy"—in Mexican melodrama, and *Yesenia* in particular, in chapter 4. See Eva Woods Peiró, *White Gypsies: Race and Stardom in Spanish Musicals* (London: University of Minnesota Press, 2012); José Gallardo Saborido, *Gitana Tenia Que Ser: Las Andalucias Imaginadas Por Las Coproducciones Filmicas Espana-Latinoamerica* (Sevilla, Spain: Fundación Centro de Estudios Andaluces, 2010), 29–30; Jo Labanyi, *Lo andaluz en el cine del franquismo: los estereotipos como estrategia para manejar la contradicción* (Sevilla, Spain: Centro de Estudios Andaluces, 2003).

66. Emeterio Diez Puertas, "Cine español en la Argentina: la exportación del nacionalismo ruralista," *RIHC: Revista Internacional de Historia de la Comunicación* 15 (2021): 42–65.

67. In this they are similar to the more famous examples of this genre, films starring Imperio Argentina. See Laura Miranda y Lucía Rodríguez Riva, eds., *Diálogos cinematográficos entre España y Argentina: Música, estrellas y escenarios compartidos, 1930–1960* (Santander, Mexico City: Shangrila, 2019).

68. For this argument, see Denning, *Noise Uprising.*

69. Karush, *Culture of Class,* 201.

70. This can be contrasted with Yugoslavia, a socialist country with a different trajectory, where the Mexican Golden Age melodramas that were also screened there in the 1950s and 1960s triggered a fashion for Yu-Mex music, with numerous Yugoslavian performers of assorted Mexican classics (with lyrics also adapted into Serbo-Croatian). See Dubravka Suznjević and Robert Irwin, "Vedro Nebo' in Far-Off Lands: Mexican Golden Age Cinema's Unexpected Triumph in Tito's Yugoslavia," in *Global Mexican Cinema: Its Golden Age,* ed. Robert Irwin and Castro Ricalde (London: Palgrave, 2013).

71. Marina A. Aliakrinskaya, "Tendentsii razvitiia massovogo tantsa 1950kh gg: bal'nyi tanets," *Vestnik SpbGUKI,* no. 2 (2019): 135–42.

72. G. Volokhonskaia and A. Okuneva, "Tantseval'nyi sport Rossii," *Omskii nauchnyi vestnik* 1, no. 135 (2015): 25–28.

73. A. G. Kharchev, "Molodezh i brak," *Uchenye zapiski,* vol. 6 (Leningrad: Izdatel'stvo leningradskogo universiteta, 1968), 125; quoted in Nataliia Lebina, *Passazhiry kolbasnogo poezda. Etiudy k kartine byta rossiiskogo goroda, 1917–1991* (Moscow: Novoe Literaturnoe Obozreniie, 2023), 337.

74. Jesús Martín-Barbero, "Memory and Form in the Latin American Soap Opera," in *To Be Continued . . . Soap Operas around the World,* ed. Richard C. Allen (New York: Routledge, 1995), 276–85, 282–83.

75. Rupprecht, *Soviet Internationalism after Stalin,* 90.

76. Benjamin M. Han, *Beyond the Black and White TV: Asian and Latin American Spectacle in Cold War America* (Rutgers, NJ: Rutgers University Press, 2020), 83.

77. Han, *Beyond the Black and White TV,* 77–78.

78. Rupprecht, *Soviet Internationalism after Stalin,* 87.

79. Gerald Drews, *Los Paraguayos: Eine Musiklegende geht um die Welt* (Augsburg, Germany: Weltbild Verlag, 1996), 89–93.

80. See, for example, Pavel Pichugin, "Sil'vestre Revuel'tas i meksikanskii fol'klor," *Sovetskaia Muzyka*, no. 5 (1961); Pichugin, "Tango i ego istoriia," *Sovetskaia Muzyka*, no. 2 (1962); Pichugin, "O gibridnykh muzykal'nykh formakh Latinskoi Ameriki," *Sovetskaia Muzyka*, no. 6 (1965); Pichugin, "Muzyka Kuby," in *Kuba. 10 let revoliutsii*, ed. Viktor Vol'skii (Moscow: Nauka, 1968); Pichugin, *Narodnaja muzyka Argentiny* (Moscow: Muzyka, 1971); Pichugin, ed., *Muzykal'naia kul'tura stran Latinskoi Ameriki* (Moscow: Muzyka, 1974); Pichugin, *Meksikanskaia pesnia* (Moscow: Sovetskii Kompozitor, 1977).

81. Denning, *Noise Uprising*, 221; see also Salazkina, *World Socialist Cinema*, ch. 7.

82. See Pablo Palomino, *The Invention of Latin American Music: A Transnational History* (London: Oxford University Press, 2020); Matthew Karush, *Musicians in Transit: Argentina and the Globalization of Popular Music* (Durham, NC: Duke University Press, 2017).

83. Andrew F. Jones, *Circuit Listening: Chinese Popular Music in the Global 1960s* (Minneapolis: University of Minnesota Press, 2020), 35.

84. See interview with the film's cameraman, Eduard Rozovskii, in A. Ignateneko and V. Gusak, *K vorposu ob ikhtiandre* (Moscow: Direct Media, 2014), 140–41.

85. Jones, *Circuit Listening*, 43.

86. Ignateneko and Gusak, *K vorposu ob ikhtiandre*, 28.

87. A. L. Markhasev, *Andrei Petrov* (Moscow: Kompozitor, 1995), 29.

88. Mikhail Bialik, "Pesennoe tvorchestvo," in *Andrei Petrov: sbornik stateii* (Moscow: Muzyka, 1981), 127.

89. MacFadyen, *Red Stars*, 84.

90. Zezina, "Kinoprokat i massovyi zritel'," 406.

91. For an eloquent description of this affective dynamic, see Gilburd, *To See Paris and Die*.

92. See Mila Oiva, Hannu Salmi, and Brice Johnson, *Yves Montand in the USSR: Cultural Diplomacy and Mixed Messages* (London: Palgrave Macmillan, 2021).

93. On "translation" in this context, see Gilburd, *To See Paris and Die*, 12, 116; Oiva, Salmi, and Johnson, *Yves Montand in the USSR*, 143.

94. "Espiando por la cerradura," *Mundo Radial* 408, April 4 (1957): 26.

95. Quoted in Gallina, *Querida Lolita*, 230.

96. On *The Little Blue Flame*, see Roth-Ey, *Moscow Prime Time*, 124–25.

97. *Mundo radial*, 1955; quoted in Gallina, *Querida Lolita*, 226.

98. *Radiolandia*, August 6, 1955; quoted in Gallina, *Querida Lolita*, 226.

99. Gallina, *Querida Lolita*, 12.

100. Gallina, *Querida Lolita*, 46–49.

101. Paul Vernon, *A History of the Portuguese Fado* (London: Ashgate, 1998), 48; Denning, *Noise Uprising*, 20.

102. Gallina, *Querida Lolita*, 229.

103. Quoted in Gallina, *Querida Lolita*, 251.

104. MacFadyen, *Red Stars*, 104.

105. For recent examples, see https://historiahoy.com.ar/el-dia-que-el-astronauta-yuri-gagarin-conquisto-el-espacio-junto-lolita-torres-60-anos-del-primer-viaje-fuera-la-orbita-terrestre-n3570; https://russkiymir.ru/publications/286528/. This, however, is not the only

known attempt to bring together Soviet space exploration and Latin American music: Rupprecht describes how the Brazilian singer Victor Simón's folkloric shows in the Soviet Union in summer 1966 included "Brazilian dancers in costumes of Soviet cosmonauts sang Rio de Janeiro's samba anthem 'A cidade maravilhosa' (The Wonderful City) and celebrated a 'Carnival on the Moon.'" Rupprecht, *Soviet Internationalism*, 88.

106. Karush, *Culture of Class*, 210.

1. *YESENIA* IN MEXICO AND THE SOVIET UNION

1. For a critique of the term, see Dina Fainberg and Artemy M. Kalinovsky, eds., "Introduction: Stagnation and Its Discontents: The Creation of a Political and Historical Paradigm," in *Reconsidering Stagnation in the Brezhnev Era: Ideology and Exchange* (London: Lexington Books, 2016).

2. Timo Vihavainen and Elena Bogdanova, eds., *Communism and Consumerism: The Soviet Alternative to the Affluent Society* (Leiden, The Netherlands: Brill, 2016).

3. Sari Autio-Sarasmo, "Stagnation or Not? The Brezhnev Leadership and East-West Interaction," in *Reconsidering Stagnation in the Brezhnev Era: Ideology and Exchange*, ed. Dina Fainberg and Artemy M. Kalinovsky (London: Lexington Books, 2016), 88.

4. Ellen Propper Mickiewicz, *Split Signals: Television and Politics in the Soviet Union* (Oxford: Oxford University Press, 1988), 3.

5. Kristin Roth-Ey, *Moscow Prime Time: How the Soviet Union Built the Media Empire That Lost the Cultural Cold War* (Ithaca, NY: Cornell University Press, 2011), 43–44.

6. See Eseniia (Meksika, 1971), Sovetskaia prokatnaia versiia, https://www.youtube .com/watch?v=MvwGodGKC74 (accessed July 7, 2023).

7. See "Theme Music from Yesenia" (1971), https://www.youtube.com/watch?v=mFV nrjyINOQ (accessed July 7, 2023).

8. As evidenced by various ads in the Mexican newspapers of the 1970s (more on this in chapter 4). See also Alfredo Gudinni, *El Castillo de las Estrellas* (Mexico: Grijalbo, 1996), 175.

9. Olivia Cosentino and Brian Price, eds., "Introduction," in *The Lost Cinema of Mexico: From Lucha Libre to Cine Familiar and Other Churros* (Gainesville: University Press of Florida, 2022), 1–2.

10. This included children's films (*Aventuras de un caballo blanco y un niño*, 1975; *Viaje Fantastco en Globo*, 1975), sex comedies (*Novios*, 1971), boxing films (*La Corona de un campeon* (1974), films dealing with Afro-Mexican history (*El Hombre de los Hongos*, 1976), and, especially, historical melodramas.

11. Marina Kosinova, "Prokatno-vozvratnyi mekhanizm sovetskoi kinematografii v period zastoiia," *Servis* 10, no. 2 (2016): 66.

12. The first review of the film was actually by Iuri Smelkov in the popular movie magazine *Sovetskii Ekran* (Soviet Screen), but it offered a very general lament on the enduring popularity of movies with "beautiful dresses and big passions." Iuri Smelkov, "Imeet uspekh . . .?" *Sovetskii Ekran* 15 (1975): 8–9.

13. Alexander Fedorov, *200 Foreign Leaders of Soviet Film Distribution: A Selected Collection* (Moscow: OD "Information for All," 2023); Alexander Fedorov, *A Thousand and*

One Highest-Grossing Soviet Movies: Opinions of Film Critics and Viewers (Moscow: OD "Information for All," 2023).

14. Her reflections on the film resulted in her first publication of an article on the problem of Soviet audience preferences: Maia Turovskaia, "Pochemu zritel' idet v kino?," in *Zhanry kino* (Moscow: Iskusstvo, 1979), 138–54.

15. Turovskaia, "Kinoprocess: 1917–1985," in *Zuby drakona: moi 30e gody* (Moscow: Act Corpus, 2015), 384. Translation mine. In the film, the rich heiress actually has a heart condition, but Turovskaia's mistake is entirely consistent with the long history of consumptive heroines in sentimentalist literature.

16. Turovskaia, "Kinoprocess: 1917–1985," 384.

17. *Churro* is a Mexican word referring to a bad and/or silly movie, literally a deep-fried piece of pastry. See Cosentino and Price, *The Lost Cinema of Mexico*.

18. The Soviet viewership of that telenovela far surpassed that of *Dallas*, which was on at the same time. See Kate Baldwin, "Montezuma's Revenge," in *To Be Continued . . . Soap Operas around the World*, ed. Richard C. Allen (New York: Routledge, 1995), 285–300.

19. Neepa Majumdar, "Disco Dancer and the Idioms of the Global-Popular," *Cultural Critique* 114 (Winter 2022): 90.

20. See Eleonory Gilburd, *To See Paris and Die: The Soviet Lives of Western Culture* (Cambridge, MA: Harvard University Press, 2018).

21. It was purchased in the Soviet Union almost ten years after the film's original release, as was a common practice for Soviet film imports, raising no objections from moviegoers habituated to a mix of newer and older films in cinemas.

22. This cultural modality is famously described by Alexei Yurchak in *Everything Was Forever, Until It Was No More: The Last Soviet Generation* (Princeton, NJ: Princeton University Press, 2005).

23. Roth-Ey, *Moscow Prime Time*, 93. Exactly the same intense emotional identification is evidenced in audiences' responses to *Disco Dancer*, as discussed in particular by Majumdar, which was sufficient for the fans to refer to the film as "realist." The same conclusion is reached in one of the few contemporary Soviet reviews of *Yesenia*, cited above: Smelkov, "Imeet uspekh . . .?" The critic compares *Yesenia* to romantic comedies from France and Japan and concludes that it's their lack of seriousness and strong emotions that makes them less popular with Soviet mass audiences, who prefer strong feelings and passions.

24. Roth-Ey, *Moscow Prime Time*, 43–44; Kosinova, "Prokatno-vozvratnyi mekhanizm," 64–72.

25. There were exceptions to this, of course, such as when *Gone with the Wind* (1939) premiered in Moscow in 1990 to enormous popular enthusiasm. The screening, arranged personally by Ted Turner, served as a clear marker of the US victory in the Cold War and the triumph of neoliberal ideology in Russia, making it considerably more overdetermined. Elizabeth Christie and Carey Goldberg, "A Popular Soviet Premiere: Film: 'Gone with the Wind' Comes to Moscow Courtesy of Ted Turner, and Soviet Moviegoers Give a Damn," *Los Angeles Times*, October 22, 1990.

26. For comprehensive accounts of this period, see José Agustín, *Tragicomedia mexicana, vol. 2: La vida en México de 1970 a 1982* (Mexico City: Planeta, 1992); Eric Zolov, *Refried Elvis: The Rise of the Mexican Counterculture* (Berkeley: University of California

Press, 1999); Louise Walker, *Waking from the Dream: Mexico's Middle Classes after 1968* (Stanford, CA: Stanford University Press, 2013).

27. Carl J. Mora, *Mexican Cinema: Reflections of a Society* (Berkeley: University of California Press, 1989); Charles Ramírez Berg, *Cinema of Solitude: A Critical Study of Mexican Film, 1967–1983* (Austin: University of Texas Press, 1992); Jorge Ayala Blanco, *La condición del cine mexicano* (Mexico City: Centro Universitario de Estudios Cinematográficos, 2018); Ayala Blanco, *La búsqueda del cinema mexicano* (Mexico City: Centro Universitario de Estudios Cinematográficos, 2017).

28. Ignacio M Sánchez Prado, "Alegorías sin pueblo: el cine Echeverrista y la crisis del contrato social de la cultura Mexicana," *Chasqui* 44, no. 2 (2015): 50.

29. Sánchez Prado, "Alegorías sin pueblo," 51.

30. David Maciel, "Cinema and the State in Contemporary Mexico 1970–1999," in Mora, *Mexican Cinema*, 197–214.

31. Eric Zolov, *The Last Good Neighbor: Mexico in the Global Sixties* (Durham, NC: Duke University Press, 2020), 290. On the longer history of Soviet-Mexican diplomatic relations, see Daniela Spenser, *The Impossible Triangle: Mexico, Soviet Russia, and the United States in the 1920s* (Durham, NC: Duke University Press, 1999).

32. Zolov, *The Last Good Neighbor*, 294.

33. Ilya Prizel, *Latin America through Soviet Eyes: The Evolution of Soviet Perceptions during the Brezhnev Era 1964–1982* (Cambridge: Cambridge University Press, 1990), 156; "SSSR—Meksika: Luchshe znat' drug-druga," *Latinskaia Amerika* 2 (1977): 159–71.

34. Maciel, "Cinema and the State in Contemporary Mexico 1970–1999," in Mora, *Mexican Cinema*.

35. Walker, *Waking from the Dream*, 121; Rodolfo Gamiño Muñóz and Yllich Escamilla, eds., *La Liga Comunista 23 de Septiembre: Cuatro décadas a debate: historia, memoria, testimonio y literatura* (Mexico City: UNAM/UATX, 2014).

36. On the Filmmakers' Union, see Masha Salazkina, *World Socialist Cinema: Alliances, Affinities, and Solidarities in the Global Cold War* (Oakland: University of California Press, 2023), chs. 1 and 4.

37. Beatriz Reyes Nevares, *The Mexican Cinema: Interviews with Thirteen Directors*, trans. Elizabeth Gard and Carl J. Mora (Albuquerque: University of New Mexico Press, 1976), 144–46.

38. There were ten Mexican feature films presented at the 1972 week of Mexican Cinema, and seven at the 1976 one, almost all of them directed by filmmakers associated with Olhovich's Marco Polo production company.

39. "Noticias: Rinden homenaje póstumo a director de Películas Nacionales," May 31, 2011, https://www.correcamara.com.mx/inicio/int.php?mod=noticias_detalle&id_noticia=2701.

40. Luis de la Hidalga, *Sonia Amelio, la Mexicana Universal* (Mexico City: Fundación Alejo Peralta, 2002), 37.

41. De la Hidalga, *Sonia Amelio*, 255, 257.

42. "Proxima Coproduccion Cinematografica Entre Nuestro Pais y la Union Sovietica," *El Nacional*, June 17, 1972, 6.

43. *Kino v bor'be za mir, sotsial'nyi progress i svobodu narodov: tvorcheskaia diskussia na III Mezhdunarodnom kinofestivale v Tashkente* (Moscow: Nauchno-issledovatel'skii institut teorii i istorii kino, 1974), 26–27.

44. Pimstein was also behind the original 1970 telenovela version of *Yesenia*, and would be responsible for the launch of telenovelas on Soviet and post-Soviet TV screens, beginning with *Los ricos también lloran*—more on him later in the chapter.

45. Semion Chertok, *Festival' trekh kontinentov* (Tashkent: Izdatel'stvo literatury i iskusstva, 1978), 159.

46. Chertok, *Festival' trekh kontinentov*, 163.

47. Fedorov, *200 Foreign Leaders*, 216.

48. German-born Crevenna's artistic trajectory in fact goes as far back as Gavaldón's. After he left the German UFA studio in the 1930s and ended up in Mexico, he was allegedly supposed to direct the 1943 version of *Santa*, a remake of the 1932 Mexican feature that became the template for the "melodrama of a fallen woman." With the exception of *Talpa* (1956, based on Juan Rulfo's story and entered into Cannes), most of his films were firmly rooted in the conventions of Mexican commercial melodramas of the 1950s, including several weepies he directed starring Libertad Lamarque and Marga López, but they never had as much popularity or critical acclaim, forcing Crevenna to turn to the increasingly "low" forms of genre cinema, such as *luchador* (Santo), horror, and historieta- and telenovela-based films. Rogelio Agrasánchez, "Jr. From the UFA to the Mexican Studios: Alfredo B. Crevenna," https://www.mexfilmarchive.com/documents/64.html; Interview of Alfredo B. Crevenna by Alejandro Pelayo. Mexico City: CONACULTA Cineteca Nacional: File E-00427.

49. For a paradigmatic take on this shift and its impact, see Alejandro Pelayo, "El Cine mexicano en la época de la presidencia de José López Portillo," in *A la sombra de los caudillos: el presidencialismo en el cine mexicano*, ed. Álvaro A. Fernández and Ángel Román Gutiérrez (Mexico City: Cineteca Nacional, 2020), 169–92.

50. "Los Chinos Prefieren el Cine Cursi Mexicano," *Avance*, July 23, 1976, 15.

51. Nikita Markov, "Sistema gosudarstvennogo upravleniia sovetskim kinematografom, 1963–1968" (PhD diss., Russian State Academic University of the Humanities, 2019), 181–91.

52. *Yesenia* in 1975 was in competition not only with the already-mentioned *How to Steal a Million* but also with *Oh Lucky Man* (UK, 1973), *Winnetou, the Warrior* (West Germany, 1963), *Bobby* (India, 1973), and several Egyptian melodramas.The highest-grossing among them, *The White Gown* (Al-Reda'a al-Abiad/ الرداء الأبيض, 1974) by Hassan Razmi, as well as the big Indian hit *Seeta and Geeta* (1972), would come out in 1977—but neither would match the success of *Yesenia*. See Fedorov, *200 Foreign Leaders*.

53. Markov, "Sistema gosudarstvennogo upravleniia," 302–03; Marina Kosinova, "International Relations of the Soviet Cinema in the Years of the Thaw," *Modern Research of Social Problems* 6, no. 50 (2015).

54. Roth-Ey, *Moscow Prime Time*, 62.

55. *El Nacional*, October 12, 1971, 8.

56. Emilio García Riera, *Historia documental del cine mexicano*, vol. 13 (Guadalajara: Universidad de Guadalajara, 1992), 243. The film earned $510,066.00. Mexico City: Cineteca Nacional, ARV F303.5 B36 v.6.

57. *Avance*, May 6, 1971. While Cano claimed she was being treated in the US for a heart condition, speculations about the real reason for her refusal to take the role ranged from her recovering from a plastic surgery to a powerful lover keeping her in a "golden cage." Gudinni, *El Castillo de las Estrellas*, 177.

58. Interview with Vargas Dulché in Beth Miller and Alfonso González, *26 autoras del México actual* (Mexico City: Costa Amic, 1978), 379.

59. García Riera, *Historia documental del cine mexicano*, vol. 13, 243.

60. For the effects of this crossover on female stardom, see Olivia Cosentino, "Starring Mexico: Female Stardom, Age and Mass Media Trajectories in the 20th Century," in *The Routledge Companion to Gender, Sex and Latin American Culture*, ed. Frederick Luis Aldama (New York: Routledge, 2018), 196–205.

61. Sofia Rios, "From Quinceañera to Miss XV: Coming of Age in Mexican Screen Melodrama," in *Children, Youth, and International Television*, ed. Debbie Olson and Adrian Schober (New York: Routledge, 2022), 232.

62. Tere Vale, *Valentín Pimstein: Una Vida de Telenovela* (Mexico City: Miguel Angel Porrua, 2016), 50–51. On the history of Televisa, see *Televisa: el quinto poder* (Mexico City: Claves latinoamericanas, 1985); Raúl Trejo Delarbre, ed., *Las redes de Televisa* (Mexico City: Claves latinoamericanas, 1988).

63. Claudia Fernandez and Andrew Paxman, *El Tigre: Emilio Azcárraga y su imperio Televisa* (Mexico City: Grijalbo, 2013), 93.

64. Televicine, the film production company within Televisa, would start making films in 1978, with content closely linked to the television programming, relying on musical and comedic acts. Trejo Delarbre, *Las redes de Televisa*, 142–43.

65. "Filmada en un plan de superproduccion que desmienten los feos colores, la desigual escenografia, sus apaticos actores y su aun mas apatetico y torpe director. . . . *Yesenia*, largo culebron con infinitos dialogos aclaratorios de parentescos conflictivos merece reproches mas aburridos que indignados." García Riera, *Historia documental del cine mexicano*, vol. 13, 243. Translation mine.

66. Andrey Shcherbenok, "Everything Was Over before It Was No More: Decaying Civilization in Late Stagnation Cinema," in *Reconsidering Stagnation in the Brezhnev Era: Ideology and Exchange*, ed. Dina Fainberg and Artemy M. Kalinovsky (London: Lexington Books, 2016), 77.

67. Felipe Gómez Gutiérrez, "Cómics femeninos y feministas en el México del siglo XX: de la representación a la autodesignación," *Descentrada* 2 (2018), e054, http://www.descentrada .fahce.unlp.edu.ar/article/view/DESe054.

68. Fernandez and Paxman, *El Tigre*, 162.

69. Incidentally, the 1990s remake of *María Isabel* featured Thalía, a Latin pop star whose own career was launched by Televisa—a perfect example of the integration of the music industry within Televisa and its telenovelas.

70. Tomás Perrín Escobar, "Impactos e impactotes," *Impacto*, April 14, 1971.

71. See Héctor Fernández L'Hoeste and Juan Poblete, "Introduction," in *Redrawing the Nation: National Identity in Latin/o American Comics* (New York: Palgrave, 2009), 5–6.

72. Anne Rubenstein, *Bad Language, Naked Ladies & Other Threats to the Nation: A Political History of Comic Books* (Durham, NC: Duke University Press, 2008), 15.

73. Rubenstein, *Bad Language*, 15–16.

74. For an in-depth investigation of this topic within the literary genres, see Alejandra Vela Martínez, "Cursi Feminists: Women's Magazines, Memory and Literary Canon in Mexico (1940–1980)" (PhD diss., New York University, 2021).

75. Harold Hinds and Charles Tatum, *Not Just for Children: The Mexican Comic Book in the Late 1960s and 1970s* (Westport, CT: Greenwood Press, 1992), 8.

76. Hinds and Tatum, *Not Just for Children*, 6.

77. Hinds and Tatum, 8.

78. Hinds and Tatum, 5.

79. Hinds and Tatum, 53.

80. Hinds and Tatum, 53; Joanne Hershfield, *Imagining la Chica Moderna: Women, Nation, and Visual Culture in Mexico, 1917–1936* (Durham, NC: Duke University Press, 2008), 5. For a recent discussion of the *chica moderna* archetype, see Dalton, "On Virgins, Malinches and Chicas Modernas," in *The Lost Cinema of Mexico*, 62–87.

81. Interview with Vargas Dulché in Miller and González, 383.

82. Interview with Vargas Dulché in Miller and González, 383.

83. Hinds and Tatum, *Not Just for Children*, 54.

84. Fernandez and Paxman, *El Tigre*, 162.

85. Hinds and Tatum, *Not Just for Children*, 5.

2. MEXICAN AND SOVIET WOMANHOOD, CIRCA 1970

1. Lauren Berlant, *The Female Complaint: The Unfinished Business of Sentimentality in American Culture* (Durham, NC: Duke University Press, 2008), 12.

2. Maria de la Paz Lopez, "Las mujeres en el umbral del siglo XX," in *Miradas feministas sobre las mexicanas del siglo XX*, ed. Marta Lamas (Mexico City: Fondo de Cultura Economica/Conculta, 2007), 101.

3. Gabriela Cano, "Las mujeres in Mexico del siglo XX: Una cronologia minima," in *Miradas feministas sobre las mexicanas del siglo XX*, ed. Marta Lamas (Mexico City: Fondo de Cultura Economica/Conculta, 2007), 54.

4. The exceptions were the Central Asian and Transcaucasian republics, where the percentage was significantly lower.

5. Elizabeth Brainerd, "Women in Transition: Changes in Gender Wage Differentials in Eastern Europe and the Former Soviet Union," *Industrial and Labor Relations Review* 54, no. 1 (2000): 138–62.

6. V. G. Kostakov, "Features of the Development of Female Employment," quoted in Gail Lapidus, *Revival: Women, Work and Family in the Soviet Union* (New York: Routledge, 1982), 192.

7. Gail Lapidus, "Introduction," in *Revival: Women, Work and Family in the Soviet Union* (New York: Routledge, 1982), 23.

8. Andrea Stevenson Sanjian, "Social Problems, Political Issues: Marriage and Divorce in the USSR," *Soviet Studies* 43, no. 4 (1991): 632.

9. Mary Buckley, "Women in the Soviet Union," *Feminist Review* 8 (Summer 1981): 79–106.

10. Michelle Murphy, *The Economization of Life* (Durham, NC: Duke University Press, 2017), 6.

11. Cano, "Las mujeres in Mexico del siglo XX," 55.

12. Lynne Attwood, *The New Soviet Man and Woman* (Basingstoke, UK: Macmillan, 1990), 5–7.

13. Celeste Gonzalez de Bustamante and Richard Cole, *Muy Buenas Noches: Mexico, Television, and the Cold War* (Lincoln: University of Nebraska Press, 2013), 239 passim.

14. Sarah Corona Berkin and Maria del Carmen de la Peza Casares, "La liberación sexual en tensión: las revistas femeninas de los años 1970–1980," in *Un siglo de educación sentimental. Los buzones amorosos en México*, ed. Sarah Corona Berkin and Maria del Carmen de la Peza Casares (Mexico City: Universidad de Guadalajara, 2007), 136; Alma Rosa Sánchez Olvera, *El Feminismo mexicano ante el movimiento urbano popular: dos expresiones de lucha de genero (1970–1985)* (Mexico City: UNAM/Plaza y Valdes, 2002), 113–31.

15. Eli Bartra, "Tres decadas de neofeminismo en Mexico," in *Feminismo en México, ayer y hoy*, ed. Eli Bartra, Anna M. Fernández Poncela, and Ana Lau (Mexico City: Universidad Autónoma Metropolitana, 2000), 45–81.

16. Jocelyn Olcott, *International Women's Year: The Greatest Consciousness-Raising Event in History* (London: Oxford University Press, 2017).

17. Olcott, *International Women's Year*, 141–43.

18. Olcott, *International Women's Year*, 142; Moema Viezzer, "El Comité de Amas de Casa de Siglo XX: An Organizational Experience of Bolivian Women," trans. James Dietz and Paula Tuchman, *Latin American Perspectives* 6, no. 3 (July 1979): 80–86.

19. For an overview of the position of the Socialist Bloc in these debates, see Jennifer Suchland, *Economies of Violence: Transnational Feminism, Postsocialism, and the Politics of Sex Trafficking* (Durham, NC: Duke University Press, 2015); Kristen Ghodsee, *Second World, Second Sex: Socialist Women's Activism and Global Solidarity during the Cold War* (Durham, NC: Duke University Press, 2019); Salazkina, *World Socialist Cinema*, ch. 4.

20. Karina Felitti, "De la 'mujer moderna' a la 'mujer liberada.' Una analysis de la revista Claudia de Mexico (1965–1977)," *HMex* 67, no. 3 (2018): 1346.

21. Carola García, *Revistas Femininas: La mujer como objeto de consume* (Mexico City: El Caballito, 1980), 35.

22. "Televisa Firma Intercambio con Rusia," *Radiolandia* 1544 (1977): 3.

23. Carola García, *Entre la tradición y la modernidad*, 80, 98–99.

24. "Love and Sex: Liberation or Subjugation?," *Kena* 217 (1972): 10.

25. Cover of *Kena* 217 (1972).

26. For an account of feminist contributions of these journals in this era, see Nathalie Ludec, "La fabrique du genre dans la presse mexicaine," *Nuevo Mundo Mundos Nuevos*, 2014, http://journals.openedition.org/nuevomundo/66404 (accessed July 25, 2023).

27. Inna Vasilkova, "La Twiggy rusa," *Kena* 157 (1970): 28–31.

28. "Angélica María tomo consciencia," *Claudia* (June 1970): 52–54.

29. "En la actualidad, de la misma manera que la mujer está exigiendo derecho al voto, exige derecho al orgasmo," *Claudia* (1974), quoted in Felitti, 1369.

30. "Los nuevos colores en la intimidad," *Kena* 209 (1972), 24–26.

31. *Kena* 203 (1972): 65.

32. *Edicion Super-femenina: Prohibida para Varones*, *Kena* 158 (1970).

33. Margaret Anderson, "Amor. Amor. Amor. La falsa mujer y la mujer mujer," *Kena* 158 (1970): 84–85.

34. On Anderson, see Elizabeth Francis, *The Secret Treachery of Words: Feminism and Modernism in America* (Minneapolis: University of Minnesota Press, 2002).

35. On Sand and the sentimental social novel, see Margaret Cohen, *The Sentimental Education of the Novel* (Princeton, NJ: Princeton University Press, 1999), ch. 3.

36. Benjamin Han, *Beyond the Black and White TV: Asian and Latin American Spectacle in Cold War America* (Rutgers, NJ: Rutgers University Press, 2020), 16.

37. *Kena* 156 (1970).

38. *Kena* 218 (1972).

39. *Kena* 178 (1970).

40. "La mujer de hoy y la de manana," *Kena* 218 (August 1972): 16.

41. Berkin and de la Peza Casares, "La liberación sexual en tensión," 177.

42. Berkin and de la Peza Casares, "La liberación sexual en tensión," 159.

43. Margara Millan, "En otro Espejo: Cine y video mexicano hecho por mujeres," in *Miradas feministas sobre las mexicanas del siglo XX*, ed. Marta Lamas (Mexico City: Fondo de Cultura Economica/Conculta, 2007), 405.

44. Nataliia Lebina, *Passazhiry kolbasnogo poezda. Etiudy k kartine byta rossiiskogo goroda, 1917–1991* (Moscow: Novoe Literaturnoe Obozreniie, 2023), 65–66.

45. For an exploration of the figure of an unruly woman, see Kathleen Rowe, *The Unruly Woman. Gender and the Genres of Laughter* (Austin: University of Texas Press, 1995); for a more recent discussion, see Maggie Hennefeld, *Specters of Slapstick and Silent Film Comediennes* (New York: Columbia University Press, 2018).

46. Cano, "Las Mujeres in Mexico del siglo XX," 56–57; Rosa Sánchez Olvera, *El Feminismo mexicano*, 115, 123–24.

47. For an in-depth exploration of this topic, see Niamh Thornton, *Tastemakers and Tastemaking: Mexico and Curated Screen Violence* (New York: SUNY Press, 2020).

48. See Hennefeld, *Specters of Slapstick*, 15.

49. Joanne Hershfield, *Mexican Cinema/Mexican Woman* (Tucson: University of Arizona Press, 2012); Julia Tuñón, *Mujeres de luz y sombra en el cine mexicano. La construcción de una imagen, 1939–1952* (Mexico City: El Colegio de México/Instituto Mexicano de Cinematografía, 1998).

50. For a recent elaboration of racial dynamics at play, see Arlene Torres and Norman E. Whitten Jr., "To Forge the Future in the Fires of the Past," in *Blackness in Latin America and the Caribbean: Social Dynamics and Cultural Transformations*, vol. 1, ed. Arlene Torres and Norman E. Whitten Jr. (Bloomington: Indiana University Press, 1998), 3–33.

51. Sergio de la Mora, *Cinemachismo: Masculinities and Sexuality in Mexican Film* (Austin: University of Texas Press, 2006); Jacqueline Avila, *Cinesonidos: Film Music and National Identity during Mexico's Época de Oro* (London: Oxford University Press, 2019).

52. Mark Pedelty, "The Bolero: The Birth, Life, and Decline of Mexican Modernity," *Latin American Music Review* 20, no. 1 (Spring/Summer 1999): 36, 40–41.

53. De la Mora, *Cinemachismo*, 24.

54. For two contrasting views of the *fichera* genre, see Sergio de la Mora, "'Tus pinches leyes yo me las paso por los huevos': Isela Vega and Mexican Dirty Movies," in *Latsploitation, Exploitation Cinemas, and Latin America*, ed. Victoria Ruétalo and Dolores Tierney (London: Routledge, 2009), 245–57; and Silvana Flores, "El cine de rumberas y ficheras: dos caras alternativas de una misma moneda," *Fonseca Journal of Communication* 20 (2020): 163–80.

55. Carlos Monsiváis, "One Suffers but One Learns: Melodrama and the Rules of Lack of Limits," in *Melodrama Unbound*, ed. Christine Gledhill and Linda Williams (New York: Columbia University Press, 2018), 151–83.

56. For an exploration of Soviet women's magazines' construction of Soviet femininity in the earlier period, see Lynne Attwood, *Creating the New Soviet Woman: Women's Magazines as Engineers of Female Identity, 1922–53* (Basingstoke, UK: Macmillan, 1999).

57. Daniel Gerould, "Russian Formalist Theories of Melodrama," *Journal of American Culture* 1, no. 1 (Spring 1978): 152–68; Semion Frendlikh, *Problema zhanrov v sovetskom kinoiskusstve* (Moscow: Znanie, 1974), 30.

58. Julie A. Buckler, "Melodramatizing Russia: Nineteenth Century View from the West," in *Imitations of Life: Two Centuries of Melodrama in Russia*, ed. Louise MacReynolds and Joan Neuberger (Durham, NC: Duke University Press, 2002), 55–78. See also Laura Engelstein, *The Keys to Happiness: Sex and the Search for Modernity in Fin-de-Siecle Russia* (Ithaca, NY: Cornell University Press, 1992).

59. Frendlikh, *Problema zhanrov*, 31.

60. Alexander Prokhorov and Elena Prokhorova, *Film and Television Genres of the Late Soviet Era* (New York: Bloomsbury Academic, 2017), 150–54.

61. Prokhorov and Prokhorova, *Film and Television Genres*, 173.

62. Christine Evans, *Between Truth and Time: A History of Soviet Central Television* (New Haven, CT: Yale University Press, 2016), 157.

63. Prokhorov and Prokhorova, *Film and Television Genres*, 162–64.

64. Iuliia Glushneva, "Sentimental Education across the Borders: Hindi Soap Opera and Translation Cultures on the Russophone Web," *Feminist Media Studies* (2023), in press.

65. Glushneva, "Sentimental Education across the Borders."

66. Attwood, *The New Soviet Man and Woman*, 4.

67. Natalia Baranskaia, "Nedelia kak nedelia," *Novy mir*, no. 11 (November 1969): 23–55.

68. *Pravda*, March 22, 1977, 2.

69. Mary Buckley, *Women and Ideology in the Soviet Union* (Ann Arbor: University of Michigan Press), 161 passim.

70. A. Kotliar and A. Shlemin, "Problemy ratsional'noi zaniatosti zhenshchin," Sotsialisticheskii trud, 1974, no. 7, p. 111, quoted in Lapidus, *Revival: Women, Work and Family in the Soviet Union*, 43.

71. Kotliar and Shlemin, "Problemy ratsional'noi zaniatosti zhenshchin."

72. Kotliar and Shlemin, "Problemy ratsional'noi zaniatosti zhenshchin."

73. Quoted in Attwood, *The New Soviet Man and Woman*, 143.

74. Marianna Muravyeva, "*Bytovukha*: Family Violence in Soviet Russia," *Aspasia* 8 (2014): 90–124.

75. Janet Elise Johnson, *Gendered Violence in Russia: The Politics of Feminist Intervention* (Bloomington: Indiana University Press, 2009), 23.

76. Johnson, *Gendered Violence in Russia*, 24.

77. Anna Rotkirch, *The Man Question: Loves and Lives in Late 20th Century Russia* (Helsinki: University of Helsinki Press, 2000), 68–76; Johnson, *Gendered Violence in Russia*, 24.

78. The rituals of *kul'turnost'* and romantic chivalry, however altered, were even visible within the Soviet subcultures, whether "dissident" or just nonofficial. Elena Zdravomyslova, "The Cafe Saigon *Tusovka*, One Segment of the Informal-Public Sphere of Late-Soviet

Society," in *Biographical Research in Eastern Europe: Altered Lives and Broken Biographies*, ed. R. Humphrey, R. Miller, and E. Zdravomyslova (Aldershot, UK: Ashgate, 2002), 141–77.

79. Rotkirch, *The Man Question*, 59–60.

80. On this shift, see Rotkirch, *The Man Question*; on the crisis of masculinity within Soviet melodrama, see Prokhorov and Prokhorova, *Film and Television Genres*, 151–54.

81. See Eliot Borenstein, *Overkill: Sex and Violence in Contemporary Russian Popular Culture* (Ithaca, NY: Cornell University Press, 2008).

82. Vladimir Semerchuk, "Smena vekh na iskhode ottepeli," in *Kinematograf Ottepeli*, vol. 2, ed. V. Troianovskii (Moscow: Materik, 2002), 154–55.

83. Marko Dumančić, "The Communist and Postsocialist Gender Order in Russia and China," in *The Cambridge History of Communism, vol. 3: Endgames? Late Communism in Global Perspective, 1968 to the Present*, ed. Juliane Fürst, Silvio Pons, and Mark Selden (London: Cambridge University Press, 2017), 422–47; Prokhorov and Prokhorova, *Film and Television Genres*, 151–53.

84. Dumančić, "The Communist and Postsocialist Gender Order in Russia and China," 425.

85. Christine Evans, "The 'Soviet Way of Life' as a Way of Feeling: Emotion and Influence on Soviet Central Television in the Brezhnev Era," *Cahiers du monde russe* 56, no. 2–3 (2015): 543.

86. Natalia Borisova, "'Liubliu i nichego bol'she: sovetskaia liubov' 1960–1980kh godov," in *SSSR: Territoriia liubvi*, ed. Stanislav Savitskii (Moscow: Novoe izdatel'stvo, 2008), 38; Prokhorov and Prokhorova, *Film and Television Genres*, 149–88.

87. Prokhorov and Prokhorova, *Film and Television Genres*, 174.

88. On the post-Soviet representation of sex and sexuality in popular culture, see Borenstein, *Overkill*.

89. For detailed discussion of this, see Rotkirch, *The Man Question*; Johnson, *Gendered Violence in Russia*, 24.

3. BETWEEN MEXICAN *CURSILERÍA* AND *RUSSIAN POSHLOST'*

1. Noel Valis, *The Culture of Cursilería: Bad Taste, Kitsch, and Class in Modern Spain* (Durham, NC: Duke University Press, 2002); Abraham Moles, *O Kitsch: A arte da ffelicidade* (São Paulo: Editora Perspectiva, 1971), 10.

2. Carlos Monsiváis, "La cursilería," in *Los ídolos a nado: Una antología global* (Barcelona: Debate, 2011), 14–15; Linda Egan, *Carlos Monsiváis: Culture and Chronicle in Contemporary Mexico* (Tucson: University of Arizona Press, 2001), 46.

3. Or "la elegancia históricamente posible en el subdesarrollo"; Carlos Monsiváis, "Agustín Lara: El harem ilusorio (Notas a partir de la memorización de la letra de 'Farolito')," in *Amor perdido* (Mexico City: Ediciones Era, 1977), 64.

4. Monsiváis, "La cursilería," 14–31.

5. "Los Chinos Prefieren el Cine Cursi Mexicano," *Avance*, July 23, 1976, 15.

6. Monsiváis, "Agustín Lara," 64.

7. Or "habitaciones amuebladas tipo Luis XIV aunque tercermundista; candiles, brocados, cortinajes; oficinas Chipendale"; Florence Toussaint, "Televisa: una semana de programación," in *Televisa: el quinto poder* (Mexico: Claves Latinoamericanas, 1985), 45.

8. Mark Pedelty, "The Bolero: The Birth, Life, and Decline of Mexican Modernity," *Latin American Music Review* 20, no. 1 (Spring/Summer 1999), 34.

9. Pedelty, "The Bolero," 32.

10. Alejandra Vela Martínez, "Cursi Feminists: Women's Magazines, Memory, and Literary Canon in Mexico, 1940–1980" (PhD diss., New York University, 2021).

11. Vela Martínez, "Cursi Feminists," 3.

12. Margaret Cohen, *The Sentimental Education of the Novel* (Princeton, NJ: Princeton University Press, 1999), 139.

13. See Sarah E. L. Bowskill, *Gender, Nation and the Formation of the Twentieth-Century Mexican Literary Canon* (London: Legenda, 2011).

14. Ignacio M. Sánchez Prado, *Strategic Occidentalism: On Mexican Fiction, the Neoliberal Book Market, and the Question of World Literature* (Evanston, IL: Northwestern University Press, 2018), 145.

15. Vela Martínez, "Cursi Feminists," 8–9.

16. Linda Williams, *Playing the Race Card: Melodramas of Black and White from Uncle Tom to O. J. Simpson* (Princeton, NJ: Princeton University Press, 2001), 36; Jane Gaines, *Pink-Slipped: What Happened to Women in the Silent Film Industries?* (Champaign: University of Illinois Press, 2018), 95–96.

17. For an example of analysis that supports such a summary, see Rafael Hernández Rodriguez, "Melodrama and Social Comedy in the Cinema of Golden Age," in *Mexico's Cinema: A Century of Film and Filmmakers*, ed. Joanne Hershfield and David Maciel (Wilmington, DE: Scholarly Resources Press, 1999), 101–23.

18. Vela Martínez, "Cursi Feminists," 2–3.

19. Discussion of La Cooperativa del Cine Marginal and films by Jodorowski, especially in the reviews and columns penned by José de la Colina, were present on the pages of *Claudia* throughout the 1970s.

20. *Kana* 184 (1971): 18. Esperanza Brito is a fascinating figure in her own right: a feminist, an activist for women's reproductive rights, and one of the founders of El Movimiento Nacional de Mujeres, she continued writing for popular women's magazines *Kena, Vanidades, Buenhogar*, and *Cosmopolitan* throughout the 1970s and 1980s.

21. "La gente pide churros: Pues si, ni modo, asi es: en Mexico no se hace buen cine," Jacqueline Andere, interview by Josefina King, *Claudia* (October 1969): 22–23.

22. Helen Krauze, "Tao Izzo y su mundo se asombro," *Kena* 209 (1972): 18–19.

23. "Mario Chávez Marion," *Kena* 184 (1971): 34–40.

24. See Florence Toussaint, "Otro mito de la television," *Fem* 4, no. 16 (1980): 67–68.

25. Vladimir Nabokov, "Philistines and Philistinism," in *Lectures on Russian Literature* (New York: Harcourt, 1981), 309–14.

26. Svetlana Boym, *Common Places: Mythologies of Everyday Life in Russia* (Cambridge, MA: Harvard University Press, 1994), 44.

27. Boym, *Common Places*, 29.

28. See Boym, *Common Places*, ch. 1.

29. Valis, *The Culture of Cursilería*.

30. Boym, *Common Places*, 45.

31. Monsiváis, "La cursilería."

32. Boym, *Common Places*, 45–46.

33. Boym, *Common Places*, 46.

34. Boym, *Common Places*, 41.

35. For a similar argument, see Andrew Ross, "Uses of Camp," in *No Respect: Intellectuals and Popular Culture* (New York: Routledge, 1989), 135–70.

36. Boym, *Common Places*, 65.

37. Alexei Yurchak, *Everything Was Forever Until It Was No More: The Last Soviet Generation* (Princeton, NJ: Princeton University Press, 2005); Peter J. Schmelz, *Sonic Overload: Alfred Schnittke, Valentin Silvestrov, and Polystylism in the Late USSR* (London: Oxford University Press, 2021).

38. Vela Martínez, "Cursi Feminists," 12; Schmelz, *Sonic Overload*, 91–92.

39. Peter Schmelz comes to a surprisingly similar conclusion in his discussion of Valentin Silvestrov's engagement with kitsch. Schmelz, *Sonic Overload*, 140.

40. M. Petrovskii, "Skronoe oboianiie kicha, ili Chto est' russkii romans," in *Russkii romans na rubezhe vekov*, ed. V. Morderer and M. Petrovskii (St. Peterburg, Russia: Geran', 2005), 5–74; Boris Iakubov, "Functioning of a genre-formative mechanisms of a 'cruel' romance," in *Filologicheskie nauki. Voprosy teorii i praktiki* 8, no. 38 (2014): 209–14.

41. Anna Fishzon, "The Operatics of Everyday Life, or, How Authenticity Was Defined in Late Imperial Russia," *Slavic Review* 70, no. 4 (2011): 795–818.

42. David MacFadyen, *Songs for Fat People: Affect, Emotion, and Celebrity in the Russian Popular Song, 1900–1955* (Montreal: McGill-Queen's University Press, 2002), 11.

43. Marina Trostina, "Zhestokii romans: zhanrovye priznaki, syuzhety i obrazy," in *Novye podkhody v gumanitarnykh issledovaniyakh: pravo, filosofiya, istoriya, lingvistika: mezhvuzovskii sbornik nauchnykh trudov, Saransk* 4 (2003): 197–202.

44. MacFadyen, *Songs for Fat People*, 36.

45. *Avance*, August 26, 1972.

46. See interview with Andrei Makarevich, a Soviet rock/pop musician and leader of one of the most popular groups of the 1970s and 1980s, Time Machine/Mashina Vremeni, in the TV film *Kiss Me Stronger or Operation Bésame Mucho* (*Tselui menia krepche ili operatsiia Bésame Mucho*, Maksim Vasilenko, 2005)

47. Quoted in David MacFadyen, *Red Stars: Personality and the Soviet Popular Song 1955–1991* (Montreal: McGill-Queen's University Press, 2001), 12.

48. *Bol'shoi tolkovyi slovar' russkogo iazyka*, ed. S. A. Kuznetsov (St. Petersburg, Russia: Norint, 1998).

49. For a historical account, see Jerrold Siegel, *Bohemian Paris: Culture, Politics, and the Boundaries of Bourgeois Life (1830–1930)* (New York: Penguin, 1987).

50. Emilio Lafuente y Alcántara in *Cancionero popular* (1865) states that "la palabra juncal, como cursi, guasa y otras tomadas del lenguaje gitanesco, tienen una significación difícil de explicar, por la vaguedad del concepto" (88). Quoted in Rusquin Chadez, "Epistemología de lo cursi: Género, sexualidad, identidad y nación en el mundo hispano, XIX–XXI" (PhD diss., University of Houston, 2018), 48. See also Valis, *The Culture of Cursilería*, 64–65.

51. Anna G. Piotrowska, "*Tsyganshchina* (цыганщина) and Romani Musicians in Tsarist, Soviet and Post-Soviet Russia: Change and Continuity," *European History Quarterly* 52, no. 4 (2022): 555.

52. Nicolay Bessonov, "Theatre Romen: Foundation and Creative Path," in *Roma Culture: Myths and Realities*, ed. Elena Marushiakova and Vesselin Popov (Munich: Lincom

Academic, 2016); Ivan Rom-Lebedev, *Ot tsyganskogo khora k teatru "Romen"* (Moscow: Iskusstvo, 1990).

53. For a thorough and nuanced exploration of this history, see Alaina Lemon, *Between Two Fires: Gypsy Performance and Romani Memory from Pushkin to Postsocialism* (Durham, NC: Duke University Press, 2000).

54. Edouard Chiline, "The Celluloid Drom: Romani Images in Russian Cinema," *Framework: The Journal of Cinema and Media* 44, no. 2 (Fall 2003): 34–41. See also Dina Iordanova, "Images of Romanies in Cinema: A Rough Sketch?," *Framework: The Journal of Cinema and Media* 44, no. 2 (Fall 2003): 5–14.

55. Anikó Imre, "Screen Gypsies," *Framework: The Journal of Cinema and Media* 44, no. 2 (Fall 2003): 16. My interpretation of the precise dynamics of this operation, however, differs from hers.

56. Timo Vihavainen, "The Spirit of Consumerism in Russia and the West," in *Communism and Consumerism: The Soviet Alternative to the Affluent Society*, ed. Timo Vihavainen and Elena Bogdanova (Leiden, The Netherlands: Brill, 2016), 25–26.

57. This forms an exception to the stage performances of Romen, which after 1940 were primarily done in Russian.

58. Oswaldo Andersen-Mundt, "El Cine sovietico se occidentalize," *El Nacional*, February 21, 1982, 26.

59. José Gallardo Saborido, *Gitana Tenia Que Ser: Las Andalucias Imaginadas por las Coproducciones Filmicas Espana-Latinoamerica* (Sevilla, Spain: Fundación Centro de Estudios Andaluces, 2010): 29–30. For more on this, see Eva Woods Peiró, *White Gypsies: Race and Stardom in Spanish Musicals* (London: University of Minnesota Press, 2012); Jo Labanyi, *Lo andaluz en el cine del franquismo: los estereotipos como estrategia para manejar la contradicción* (Sevilla, Spain: Centro de Estudios Andaluces, 2003).

60. Labanyi, *Lo andaluz en el cine del franquismo*, 12.

61. Inmaculada Alvarez and Maricruz Castro Ricalde, "Panhispanic Romances in Times of Rupture: Spanish-Mexican Cinema," in *Global Mexican Cinema: Its Golden Age*, ed. Robert McKee Irwin and Maricruz Castro Ricalde (London: British Film Institute, 2013), 155.

62. One of these, *Los Tres Amores de Lola* (René Cardona, 1956), mixes the flamenco and bolero with Agustín Lara's soundtrack, and Lara himself plays one of the three "loves" of Lola in the film.

63. Castro Ricalde, "Panhispanic Romances in Times of Rupture," 165.

64. Gallardo Saborido, *Gitana Tenia Que Ser*, 50–51.

65. Gallardo Saborido, *Gitana Tenia Que Ser*, 52.

66. Mariana Sabino-Salazar, "The Evolution of the Stereotype of the Gypsy Femme Fatale in Mexican Cinema (1943–1978)," paper presented at the Society of Cinema and Media Studies annual conference, April 2021.

67. Simon Morrison, *Bolshoi Confidential: Secrets of the Russian Ballet from the Rule of the Tsars to Today* (New York: W.W. Norton, 2016), 370.

68. "Proxima Coproduccion Cinematografica Entre Nuestro Pais y la Union Sovietica," *El Nacional*, June 17, 1972, 6.

69. Jose Lius Gutierrez Espindola, "La Industriazacion de la telenovela," in *Las redes de Televisa*, ed. Raúl Trejo Delarbre (Mexico: Claves latinoamericanas, 1998), 99–100.

70. Neyra Patricia Alvarado Solís, "Húngaros que no llegaron de Hungría: 'Gitanos' de México," *Cronica*, July 25, 2020, https://www.cronica.com.mx/notas-hungaros_que_no _llegaron_de_hungria_gitanos_de_mexico-1159692-2020.html (accessed January 8, 2024).

71. "Los Gitanos Autenticos Participaron en la Filmacion de Yesenia," *El Nacional*, July 8, 1971, 8. According to some accounts, the advisor on the scripts of both the telenovela and the movie was Pablo Luvinoff, the patriarch of the Romani community and head of the Pentecostal Romani Church of Mexico City (Iglesia Cristiana Gitana de México)—but it appears more likely that Luvinoff—who was brutally murdered in 2010—oversaw the subsequent, 1987 remake of the telenovela.

72. Alfredo Gudinni, *El Castillo de las Estrellas. La telenovela en todos los canales y en todos los países* (Mexico: Grijalbo, 1996), 177.

73. Héctor Ignacio Muskus Guardia, "Los Roma del Centro Occidente de México: Religión Pentecostal y Organización Social" (MA thesis, El Colegio de San Luis Potosí, 2012), 45–52.

74. Mattijs van de Port, *Gypsies, Wars, and Other Instances of the Wild* (Amsterdam: Amsterdam University Press, 2018), 153–54.

75. With the popularity of *Slave Isaura*, the equivalent Portuguese term *fazenda* entered Russian colloquial speech as a quasi-ironic way to refer to dachas, the typically rustic Russian summer homes, which, in the late 1980s and early 1990s, were frequently used for growing basic provisions during the time of economic collapse.

76. Jane P. Tompkins, *Sensational Designs: The Cultural Work of American Fiction, 1790–1860* (New York: Oxford University Press, 1985), xvi.

77. Lauren Berlant, *The Female Complaint: The Unfinished Business of Sentimentality in American Culture* (Durham, NC: Duke University Press, 2008), 40.

78. Neepa Majumdar, "Disco Dancer and the Idioms of the Global-Popular," *Cultural Critique* 114 (Winter 2022): 90.

79. "El feroz sentimentalismo encerrado en el ghetto de la cursilería prueba que un Sentimiento Puro es igual a cualquier Sentimiento Puro, si la sinceridad es la norma y no tiene por qué no serlo." Quoted in Brandon Bisbey, *Between Camp and Cursi: Humor and Homosexuality in Contemporary Mexican Narrative* (Albany, NY: SUNY Press, 2021), 22–23.

80. Piotrowska, "Tsyganshchina (цыганщина)," 566–67.

81. Bisbey continues by re-articulating Monsivais's position on underdevelopment: "This failure is predetermined—it is only by the exclusion of regions such as Mexico that the North is modern in the first place." Bisbey, *Between Camp and Cursi*, 23.

82. Michael Denning, *Noise Uprising: The Audiopolitics of a World Musical Revolution* (London: Verso, 2015), 2.

83. One could consider bolero an extension of Cuban *son*, which is certainly consistent with most musicologists' accounts—see, for example, Antonio Luis Bigott, *Historia del bolero Cubano* (Caracas: Ediciones Los Heraldos Negros), 59. On the other hand, Peter Manuel classified the Mexican bolero as part of the broader commercialization of what he terms the Mexican *Canción* with roots in Italian Bel canto—therefore decidedly unlike the kinds of musics described by Denning in *Noise Uprising*.

84. Denning, *Noise Uprising*, 101–02.

85. Boym, *Common Places*, 47.

86. Maia Turovskaia, *Zuby Drakona: Moi 30-e gody* (Moscow: Corpus, 2015), 410.

87. Turovskaia, *Zuby Drakona*, 411.

88. M. Kvasnetskaia, "Kak odolet' Eseniiu?," *Literaturnaia Gazeta*, July 21, 1976; Iulii Smelkov, "TK imeet uspekh," *Sovetskii Ekran*, no. 15 (1975): 8–9.

89. Neia Zorkaia, "Sovetskii kinoteatr, ili chto tam bylo na samom dele v proshlye gody," *Iskusstvo Kino* 11 (1995), 123.

90. Zorkaia, "Sovetskii kinoteatr," 122.

91. The tradition of *lubok* was in fact quite similar to prints by José Guadalupe Posada in Mexico, a comparison that did not escape the attention of Sergei Eisenstein during his stay in Mexico.

92. Zorkaia, "Sovetskii kinoteatr," 122.

93. Zorkaia, "Sovetskii kinoteatr," 122.

94. Bishnupriya Ghosh, *Global Icons: Apertures to the Popular* (Durham, NC: Duke University Press, 2011), 5.

4. THE PEOPLE, THE GRAY MARKET, AND THE BALLROOM GOWN

1. For an elaboration of this opposition, see Dlip Gaonkar, "After the Fictions: Notes towards the Phenomonology of the Multitude," *e-flux journal* 58 (October 2014), https://www.e-flux.com/journal/58/61187/after-the-fictions-notes-towards-a-phenomenology-of-the-multitude/.

2. Susana Draper, *1968 Mexico: Constellations of Freedom and Democracy* (Durham, NC: Duke University Press, 2018), 92.

3. Ravi Sundaram, *Pirate Modernity: Delhi's Media Urbanism* (New York: Routledge, 2010); Gordon Mathews, Gustavo Lins Ribeiro, and Carlos Alba Vega, eds., *Globalization from Below: The World's Other Economy* (London: Routledge, 2012); Joshua Neves and Bhaskar Sarkar, eds., *Asian Video Cultures: In the Penumbra of the Global* (Durham, NC: Duke University Press, 2017), 8.

4. Vijay Prashad, *The Poorer Nations: A Possible History of the Global South* (London: Verso, 2014); José Carlos G. Aguiar, "Estados de simulación: Piratería, contrabando, neoliberalismo y el control de la ilegalidad en América Latina," in *Metropolización, transformaciones mercantiles y gobernanza en los países emergentes*, ed. Carlos Alba Vega and Pascal Labazée (Mexico: Colegio de Mexico, 2015): 541–92.

5. Neia Zorkaia, "Sovetskii kinoteatr, ili chto tam bylo na samom dele v proshlye gody," *Iskusstvo Kino* 11 (1995): 121.

6. Nikita Markov, "Sistema gosudarstvennogo upravleniia sovetskim kinematografom, 1963–1968" (PhD diss., Russian State Academic University of the Humanities, 2019), 302–03; Marina Kosinova, "International Relations of the Soviet Cinema in the Years of the Thaw," *Modern Research of Social Problems* 6, no. 50 (2015).

7. The seminal text in this respect is Jane Gaines and Charlotte Herzog, eds., *Fabrications: Costume and the Female Body* (London: Routledge, 1990). For an overview of English-language scholarship on this topic, see Marketa Uhlirova, "Fashion in Cinema: Reframing the Field," in *The Routledge Companion to Fashion Studies*, ed. Eugenia Paulicelli, Veronica Manlow, and Elizabeth Wissinger (London: Routledge, 2022), 351–61.

8. For an example of explorations of fashion in historical dramas, see Pam Cook, *Fashioning the Nation: Costume & Identity in British Cinema* (London: British Film Institute, 1996).

9. For a historical emergence of this in the US context, see Michelle Tolini Finamore, *Hollywood before Glamour: Fashion in American Silent Film* (Basingstoke, UK: Palgrave Macmillan, 2013).

10. *El Informador*, May 7, 1971, 7; *El Informador*, May 14, 1971, 34. If you do an internet search for "Yesenia" in Russian, what comes up is an enormous number of beauty salons and boutiques with this name.

11. *El Informador*, May 6, 1971, 8c.

12. Ravi Sundaram, "Other Networks: Media Urbanism and the Culture of the Copy in South Asia," in *Structures of Participation in Digital Culture*, ed. Joe Karaganis (New York: Social Science Research Council, 2007), 48–73.

13. See David Desser and Garth Jowett, eds., *Hollywood Goes Shopping* (Minneapolis: University of Minnesota Press, 2000); and Sarah Berry, *Screen Style: Fashion and Femininity in 1930s Hollywood* (Minneapolis: University of Minnesota Press, 2000).

14. On Mexican middle-class consumption, see Louise Walker, *Waking from the Dream: Mexico's Middle Classes after 1968* (Stanford, CA: Stanford University Press, 2013), ch. 4.

15. Lilya Kaganovsky, "Between Pornography and Nostalgia: Valery Todorovsky's *The Thaw* (Ottepel')," in *Russian TV Series in the Era of Transition: Genres, Technologies, Identities*, ed. Alexander Prokhorov, Elena Prokhorova, and Rimgaila Salys (Boston: Academic Studies Press, 2021), 126–27.

16. See Natalya Chernyshova, *Soviet Consumer Culture in the Brezhnev Era* (London: Routledge, 2013). On Mexican middle-class consumption, see Louise Walker, *Waking from the Dream: Mexico's Middle Classes after 1968* (Stanford, CA: Stanford University Press, 2013), ch. 4.

17. A selective bibliography on this extensively covered topic includes Jean Thomas Allen, "The Film Viewer as Consumer," *Quarterly Review of Film Studies* 5, no. 4 (1980): 481–99; Maureen Turim, "Fashion Shapes: Hollywood, the Fashion Industry and the Image of Women," *Socialist Review* 13, no. 5 (1983): 78–97; Mary Ann Doane, "The Economy of Desire: The Commodity Form in/of the Cinema," *Quarterly Review of Film and Video* 11 (1989), 23–33; Jane Gaines, "The Queen Christina Tie-Ups: Convergence of Show Window and Screen," *Quarterly Review of Film and Video* 11, no. 1 (1989), 35–60; Anne Friedberg, *Window Shopping: Cinema and the Postmodern* (Berkeley: University of California Press, 1993); Stella Bruzzi, *Undressing Cinema: Clothing and Identity in the Movies* (London: Routledge, 1997); Sarah Street, *Costume and Cinema: Dress Codes in Popular Film* (London: Wallflower Press, 2001); Rachel Moseley, ed. *Fashioning Film Stars: Dress, Culture, Identity* (London: British Film Institute, 2005); Helen Warner, *Fashion on Television: Identity and Celebrity Culture* (London: Bloomsbury, 2014).

18. Ana M. López, "Our Welcomed Guests: Telenovelas in Latin America," in *To Be Continued . . . Soap Operas around the World*, ed. Richard C. Allen (New York: Routledge, 1995), 260; Heloisa Buarque de Almeida, "Melodrama comercial—reflexões sobre a feminilização da telenovela," *Cadernos de Pagu* 19, Campinas, 2002, 171–94.

19. Tolini Finamore, *Hollywood before Glamour*, 5.

20. Daniel Miller, "The Consumption of Soap Opera: The Young and the Restless and Mass Consumption in Trinidad," in *To Be Continued Soap Operas around the World*, ed. Richard C. Allen (New York: Routledge, 1995), 213–33. I thank Laura Zoe Humphreys for urging me to look more closely at this text.

21. Miller, "The Consumption of Soap Opera," 220–23.

22. Neia Zorkaia, "Mozhno li odolet' Eseniiu," in *Unikal'noe i tirazhirovannoe: sredstva massovoi informatsii i reprodutsirovannoe iskusstvo* (Moscow: Iskusstvo, 1981), 101.

23. Miller, "The Consumption of Soap Opera," 224–25.

24. Alexey Golubev, *The Things of Life: Materiality in Late Soviet Russia* (Ithaca, NY: Cornell University Press, 2020), 4.

25. Golubev, *The Things of Life*, 5.

26. Golubev, *The Things of Life*, 165.

27. Chernyshova, *Soviet Consumer Culture*, 88.

28. Chernyshova, *Soviet Consumer Culture*, 1.

29. Chernyshova, *Soviet Consumer Culture*, 133.

30. Chernyshova, *Soviet Consumer Culture*, 133–41.

31. Quoted in Olga Gurova, "The Art of Dressing: Body, Gender and the Discourse on Fashion in Soviet Russia in the 1950s and 1960s," in *The Fabric of Cultures: Fashion, Identity, Globalization*, ed. E. Paulicelli and H. Clark (New York: Routledge, 2009), 78.

32. Iuri Smelkov, "Imeet uspekh . . . ?," *Sovetskii Ekran* 15 (1975): 8–9.

33. Maia Turovskaia, *Zuby Drakona: Moi 30-e gody* (Moscow: Corpus, 2015), 391.

34. Maya Turovskaya [Maia Turovskaia], "Notes on Women and Film," *Discourse* 17, no. 3 (1995): 16.

35. Turovskaya, "Notes on Women and Film," 12–13.

36. Turovskaya, "Notes on Women and Film," 15.

37. We see this, for example, in Liudmila Gurchenko's memoirs, as well as many others'.

38. See Larissa Zakharova, "Dior in Moscow: A Taste for Luxury in Soviet Fashion under Khrushchev," in *Pleasures in Socialism: Leisure and Luxury in the Bloc*, ed. Susan E. Reid and David Crowley (Evanston, IL: Northwestern University Press, 2010), 95–120; Larissa Zakharova, "Soviet Fashion in the 1950s–60s: Regimentation, Western Influences, and Consumption Strategies," in *The Thaw: Soviet Society and Culture during the 1950s and 1960s*, ed. Denis Kozlov and Eleonory Gilburd (Toronto: University of Toronto Press, 2013), 402–35; Djurdja Bartlett, *FasionEast: The Spectre That Haunted Socialism* (Boston: MIT Press, 2010).

39. Jane Gaines, "Costume and Narrative: How Dress Tells the Woman's Story," in *Fabrications: Costume and the Female Body*, ed. Jane Gaines and Charlotte Herzog (London: Routledge, 1990), 205.

40. The critic of the film was perhaps not wrong in attributing its popularity to this aspect of the film, as it seems to be replicated by the more contemporary user comments on YouTube.

41. Natalya Chernyshova, "Philistines on the Big Screen: Consumerism in Soviet Cinema of the Brezhnev Era," *Studies in Russian and Soviet Cinema* 5, no. 2 (2011): 227–54, 232.

42. Parallel to this women's culture, bodybuilding culture, existing in a similarly informal "gray zone of Soviet sport," formed a masculinist counterpart to these shifts in gender conceptions and material practices. As Golubev explores, "Western bodybuild-

ing magazines, which were instrumental in the development of Soviet bodybuilding at its formative stage, helped to transfer the understanding of the masculine body as an individual aesthetic object to the Soviet cultural milieu. . . . When Soviet sports journalists and bureaucrats condemned bodybuilding as an 'ideologically alien' sport, it was the exhibitory and narcissistic nature of bodybuilding exercises and competitions and bodybuilding's alleged aversion to anything collective that sparked their most fervent reaction." Golubev, *The Things of Life*, 124–25. An interesting point of comparison for this would be the passions around Mexican (and American) wrestling culture.

43. The classic text in this respect is Mary Ann Doane, "Film and the Masquerade: Theorising the Female Spectator," *Screen* 23, no. 3–4 (1982): 74–88.

44. Cook, *Fashioning the Nation*, 3.

45. Alden Wicker, "The Fight to Strike 'Gypsy' from the Fashion Lexicon," *Vogue*, November 27, 2020, https://www.vogue.com/article/roma-activism-fashion.

46. Joe Ahern Zill, "Let Yourself Go Gypsy: Two Italian Models, Isa Stoppi and Mirella Petteni, as Gypsies," *Look* 31, no. 4 (February 21, 1967): 38–40.

47. "A Revolutionary Saint Laurent Showing," *New York Times*, July 28, 1976, 1; Genevieve Buck, "Rive Gauche Boutiques are Blossoming in Chicago," *Chicago Tribune*, March 14, 1977, B3.

48. H. Clarke, "Fashion at the Zenith of the Sun," *Vogue* 152, no. 10 (1968): 245–68.

49. Zolov, *Refried Elvis*, 137.

50. José Agustín, *Tragicomedia mexicana*, vol. 2, 15.

51. *Kena* 190 (June 1971), 24.

52. *Kena* 186 (April 1971), 28.

53. Bartlett, *FasionEast*, 121–26.

54. R. Kvietkevičiūtė, "Linas—Lietuvos pasididžiavimas," *Banga* (July 1967) (Kaunas: Leidykla Mintis), 6–7.

55. Edita Giedrimienė, "Mada—nauja ir tradicinė," *Banga* (August 1980), 2.

56. N. Barisienė, "Saulėtos vasaros dienoms No. 56," *Banga* (August 1980), 20–21.

57. Viacheslav Zaitsev, *Takaia izmenchivaia moda* (Moscow: Molodaia Gvardiia, 1983), 113.

58. B. Benešiūnienė, *Banga* 81 (1976), 27–28.

59. *Kena* 156 (1970), 38.

60. Iu. Khomiakova, "Knizhnoe kino," in *Posle ottepeli: Kinematograf 1970kh* (Moscow, 2009): 87–88.

61. For the changing meaning of *naco*, see Claudio Lomnitz, "Fissures in Contemporary Mexican Nationalism," *Public Culture* 9 (1996): 55–68. Lomnitz defines this taste regime as designating "an overassimilation to television and to the world of commodities" and, incidentally, among his examples he includes giving children foreign-sounding names and those that come from "comic books, magazines and soap operas"—consistently with the way the name Yesenia has been used in both Mexican and Soviet/post-Soviet contexts (57).

62. Sofia Rios, "From Quinceañera to Miss XV: Coming of Age in Mexican Screen Melodrama," in *Children, Youth and International Television* (London: Routledge, 2022), 213–32.

63. Julio Moreno, *Yankee Don't Go Home!: Mexican Nationalism, American Business Culture, and the Shaping of Modern Mexico: 1920–1950* (Chapel Hill: University of North Carolina Press, 2003).

64. Moreno, *Yankee Don't Go Home!*, 191.

65. *La Arte de la Idumentaria y la Moda en Mexico, 1940–2015* (Mexico: Fomento Cultural Banamex, 2016).

66. Louise Walker, *Waking from the Dream: Mexico's Middle Classes after 1968* (Stanford, CA: Stanford University Press, 2013), 125 (ibook).

67. Walker, *Waking from the Dream*, ch. 4.

68. Walker, *Waking from the Dream*, 258 (ibook).

69. Natalya Chernyshova "'The Great Soviet Dream': Blue Jeans in the Brezhnev Era and Beyond," in *Material Culture in Russia and the USSR: Things, Values, Identities* (London: Routledge, 2018), 165.

70. Djurdja Bartlett, *FasionEast*, 122.

71. Chernyshova in *Material Culture in Russia and the USSR*, 166–67.

72. Dalia Jurginienė, "Mada ir mes," *Tarybinė Moteris* 8 (1979), 332.

73. Agustín, *Tragicomedia mexicana*, vol. 2.

74. Dina Fainberg and Artemy M. Kalinovsky, eds., *Reconsidering Stagnation in the Brezhnev Era: Ideology and Exchange* (London: Lexington Books, 2016), 7.

75. See an extended anthropological analysis of this dynamic in Daniel Bertaux with Marina Malysheva, "The Cultural Model of the Russian Popular Classes and the Transition to a Market Economy," in *On Living through Soviet Russia*, ed. Daniel Bertaux, Paul Thompson, and Anna Rotkirch (London: Routledge, 2004), 25–52.

76. Alexey Golubev and Olga Smolyak, "Making Selves through Making Things: Soviet Do-It-Yourself Culture and Practices of Late Soviet Subjectivation," *Cahiers du monde russe* 54, no. 3–4 (2013), 517–41, 522.

77. Golubev and Smolyak, "Making Selves," 522.

78. Miriam Hansen, "Vernacular Modernism: Tracking Cinema on a Global Scale," in *World Cinemas, Transnational Perspectives*, ed. Natasa Durovicova and Kathleen Newman (New York: Routledge, 2010), 287–314; Michael Denning, *Noise Uprising: The Audiopolitics of a World Musical Revolution* (London: Verso, 2015).

79. Bishnupriya Ghosh and Bhaskar Sarkar, "The Global-Popular: A Frame for Contemporary Cinemas," *Cultural Critique*, no. 114 (Winter 2022): 1–22, 10.

80. Anna Kan, "Living in the Material World: Money in the Soviet Rock Underground," in *Dropping Out of Socialism: The Creation of Alternative Spheres in the Soviet Bloc*, ed. Juliane Fürst and Josie McLellan (Lanham, MD: Lexington, 2016); Marsha Siefert, "Entrepreneurial Tapists: Underground Music Reproduction and Distribution in the US and USSR, 1960s and 1970s," in *Music and Democracy: Participatory Approaches*, ed. Marko Kölbl and Fritz Trümpi (Vienna: mdw Press, 2021), 19–60.

81. See also Ana M. López, "Of Rhythms and Borders," in *Everynight Life*, ed. Jose Muñoz and Celeste Fraser Delgado (Durham, NC: Duke University Press, 1997).

82. Benjamin Han, *Beyond the Black and White TV: Asian and Latin American Spectacle in Cold War America* (Rutgers, NJ: Rutgers University Press, 2020), 77.

83. *Avance*, August 8, 1972.

84. Gerald Drews, *Los Paraguayos: eine Musiklegende geht um die Welt*, https://secondhandsongs.com/artist/112712/all.

85. Richard Stites, *Russian Popular Culture. Entertainment and Society since 1900* (Cambridge: Cambridge University Press, 1992), 173.

86. For an especially relevant discussion of the film, see Lilya Kaganovsky, "The Cultural Logic of Late Socialism," *Studies in Russian and Soviet Cinema* 3, no. 2 (2009): 185–99. One of the most interesting recent analyses of the film, however, centers not on Katerina but on her entrepreneurial and somewhat bawdy friend Liudmila, a character who provides the film with comic relief and is responsible for many of its most unforgettable and culturally resonant scenes. See Alexander Prokhorov and Elena Prokhorova, "Un/Taming the Unruly Woman: From Melodramatic Containment to Carnivalistic Utopia," in *Transgressive Women in Modern Russian and East European Cultures: From the Bad to the Blasphemous*, ed. Yana Hashamova, Beth Holmgren, and Mark Lipovetsky (New York: Routledge, 2016), 30–49.

87. Golubev and Smolyak, "Making Selves through Making Things," 540–41.

88. There are other characters who are similarly associated with specific kind of music: thus, for example, Antonina, the most traditional of three girlfriends, marries a similarly peasant-like young man, whose family gatherings are accompanied by Soviet songs from the period of the Great Patriotic War.

89. Natasha Roit, "Soviet and Chinese Copyright: Ideology Gives Way to Economic Necessity," *Loyola of Los Angeles Law Review* 6, no. (1986): 53–71, 59–60.

90. Consuelo Velázquez, National Prize for Arts and Traditions, Ministry of Public Education, Mexico, January 1, 2015, https://www.gob.mx/sep/acciones-y-programas/consuelo-velazquez.

91. Inna Vasil'kova, "Tselui menia krepche! Znamenitaia pes'na otmechaet shestidesiteletie, Vremia MN, Moskva, 21.04.2001."

92. "Ia potselovala ves' mir," *Ogoniok* 49, December 11, 2005, 17.

93. See interview with Mitrofanov in *Kiss Me Stronger or Operation Bésame Mucho* (*Tselui menia krepche ili operatsiia Bésame Mucho*) (Maksim Vasilenko, 2005).

94. For the development of this notion, see Ronald Radano and Tejumola Olaniyan, "Introduction: Hearing Empire—Imperial Listening," in *Audible Empire: Music, Global Politics, Critique*, ed. Ronald Radano and Tejumola Olaniyan (Durham, NC: Duke University Press, 2018), 1–25.

95. "Ia potselovala ves' mir," *Ogoniok* 49, December 11, 2005, 17.

96. See interviews in *Kiss Me Stronger*.

CODA: *YESENIA* IN CHINA AND THE ARRIVAL
OF TELENOVELAS IN THE SOCIALIST WORLD

1. "Los Chinos Prefieren el Cine Cursi Mexicano," *Avance*, July 23, 1976.

2. Mexican Film Week Pamphlet, Chengdu Film Company, 1979.

3. Cui Han-wen, "Analysis of the Image of Woman on Magazine Covers in Posteconomic Reform Era—Using Women of China and Rayli as Examples," 新闻研究导刊/ *Journal of News and Research* 5, no. 7, 151–52; Marko Dumančić, "The Communist and Postsocialist Gender Order in Russia and China," in *The Cambridge History of Communism, vol. 3: Endgames? Late Communism in Global Perspective, 1968 to the Present*, ed. Juliane Fürst, Silvio Pons, and Mark Selden (London: Cambridge University Press, 2017), 422–47.

4. Qing Yun, "Bye, Yesenia!" 电影评介/*Movie Review* 1984, no. 3, 36.

5. See https://baike.baidu.com/item/%E4%BD%B3%E7%89%87%E6%9C%89%E7%BA%A6/8610575 and https://blog.sina.com.cn/s/blog_4a4c1434010006tk.html (accessed July 20, 2023).

6. Esther Hamburger, *O Brasil antenado: a sociedade da novela* (Rio de Janeiro: Jorge Zahar, 2005); Memória Globo, "Bastidores," https://memoriaglobo.globo.com/entretenimento/novelas/escrava-isaura/noticia/bastidores.ghtml.

7. Paula Halperin, "Então Ela é Escrava? Escrava Isaura, Popular History and National Identity," *Significação: Revista de Cultura Audiovisual* 47 (2020): 162–83.

8. Raquel Kennon, "White Skin, Black Slavery: Bernardo Guimarães's *A escrava Isaura* and the Global Telenovela," *Studies in Latin American Popular Culture* 35 (2017): 138–59.

9. Gillian Tett, "What a Mexican Soap Star Taught Me about Globalisation," *Financial Times*, October 30, 2019. The plot of *Simplemente María* revolves around the title character's rise from a maid to an important fashion designer, thanks to her ability as a seamstress, and wherever the original Peruvian version of the telenovela was broadcast in Latin America, sales of Singer sewing machines skyrocketed (and, in fact, Singer ads often appeared before, during, and after its broadcasts). Everett M. Rogers and Livia Antola, "Telenovelas: A Latin American Success Story," *Journal of Communication* (Autumn 1998): 24–35, 30. As such, it provides yet another thematic link to our discussion of *Yesenia*'s relationship to homemade fashion. For a discussion of a related phenomenon within the contemporary Cuban context, see Paloma Duong, "*Postsocialismos de Bolsillo*: Women and Fashion in Secondhand Time," in *Portable Socialisms: New Cuban Mediascapes after the End of History* (Austin: University of Texas Press, 2023), 113–40.

10. See https://en.wikipedia.org/wiki/Natalia_Oreiro (accessed July 20, 2023).

INDEX

1968, events of, 10, 24, 63, 68, 69, 75, 139, 140, 178. *See also* Prague Spring; Tlatelolco massacre

ABBA, 18, 64
adaptation, 3, 11, 12, 16, 17, 28, 72, 77, 79, 81, 103, 105, 107, 114, 123, 130, 174, 176, 190n70. *See also* remakes
affective communities, 7, 8, 10, 11, 20–27, 56, 61, 67, 68, 114, 141, 171. *See also* cultural intimacies; sentimental communities
affinities: cultural, 5, 31, 33, 50; global, 20, 21, 23–26; political, 22, 24; transnational, 10, 14, 20, 22, 60, 164, 175. *See also* sentimental communities
Age of Love, The (*La edad del amor*), 37, 40–43, 47, 50, 51, 59, 60, 63, 132
Agustín, José, 9, 153, 162
Al Bano and Romina Powell, 18
Alcántara, Celia, 17, 79
Algeria, 3, 23
Allen, Robert, 28
Amado, Jorge, 28
Amelio, Sonia, 71–72, 130
Amelio García, Salvador, 72
Amphibian Man, The (*Chelovek-amfibiia*), 50, 55–57
anachronism, 16, 19, 20, 113, 114, 117, 119, 121, 124, 131, 136, 145, 148, 176. *See also* asynchronicity; temporality
Andere, Jacqueline, 64, 77, 82, 101, 117, 131, 173, 175
Anderson, Margaret, 92
anti-philistinism, 127, 148, 150, 151. See also *byt*

Appadurai, Arjun, 32
Argentina, 3, 4, 6, 12, 15, 17, 18, 19, 35, 36–37, 40, 41, 43, 45, 46, 50, 51, 53, 54, 55, 58, 59, 60, 62, 65, 79, 132, 162, 177, 187n13, 189n37
Artkino Pictures, 36
Askari, Kaveh, 19
Asturias, Miguel Ángel, 28
asynchronicity, 14, 17, 18, 117. *See also* anachronism; temporality
Attwood, Lynne, 9, 106
Azcárraga Milmo, Emilio, 77, 80

Baccara, 18
bailaora, 128
ball gown, 93, 147–51, 154, 157–59, 160, 161
ballroom dance, 52–55, 154
Bartra, Eli, 9, 85
Berlant, Lauren, 10, 28, 83, 134, 147. *See also* sentimental communities
"Bésame Mucho," 1, 2, 5, 6, 13, 19, 48, 124, 165–71
Bielousova, Gražina, 21, 184n62
black market, 8, 24, 122, 140, 141, 143, 146, 162, 163, 169. *See also* gray market; shadow economies
boho-chic, 151–57. *See also* ethnic fashion
bolero, 3, 5, 6, 13, 19, 32, 48, 51, 53, 54, 56, 80, 81, 95, 101, 113, 114, 115, 124, 125, 136, 166, 204n62, 205n83
Boney M, 18, 64, 167
bootlegging. *See* media piracy
Borenstein, Eliot, 7

Boym, Svetlana, 120–22, 136
Brazil, 3, 6, 8, 15, 29, 53, 54, 67, 68, 77, 131, 176,
    180n11, 192n105
Breckenridge, Carol, 32
Brezhnev, Leonid, 63, 105, 108, 127, 146
Brodksy, Nicholas, 41
Bulgakova, Oksana, 38, 44
But What If It's Love? (A esli eto liubov'?), 40
Byrne, Jeffrey, 23
byt, 112, 120, 121, 123, 146.
    See also anti-philistinism

cabaretera, 6, 100, 101, 102. See also *rumbera*
Canclini, Néstor García, 20, 30, 138
Cano, Fanny, 77, 101, 119, 131, 195n57
Cano, Gabriela, 9
Càrdenas, Làzaro, 26
Carnival Night, The (Karnaval'naia noch'), 38,
    46, 48
Carrà, Raffaella, 18
Cartas sin destino, 82
Cazals, Felipe, 69, 71, 74
Celentano, Adriano, 18
Chakraborty, Mithun, 10, 44
charro, 117, 128, 129, 131
Chávez Marion, Mario, 119
Chen, Kuan-Hsing, 31, 184n65
Chernyshova, Natalya, 9, 146, 150, 161–63
China, 2, 3, 11, 13, 17, 44, 65, 70, 74, 75, 102, 172–78
churros, 67, 118, 193n17
cinema, socialist, 29, 109
cinema of "independents," 69, 72
Claudia, 87–91, 93–96, 102, 116, 117, 119, 202n19
"Coimbra Divina," 49, 50, 59, 60
collectivism, 25, 26, 169
colonialism, 22, 23, 26, 32, 55, 132, 135, 136, 139,
    169, 178. See also postcolonialism
commons, 25–27, 50
communitas, 25, 26, 184n75
copyright, 19, 47, 168, 170. See also intellectual
    property
Corázon salvaje, 17, 172
Cortázar, Julio, 28
costume drama, 13, 16, 74, 133, 148, 151, 207n8.
    See also historical melodrama; period drama
*Courage of the People,
    The (El coraje del pueblo)*, 86
Cranes are Flying (Letiat zhuravli), 38, 40, 50, 167
Crevenna, Alfredo B., 2, 64, 74, 77, 80, 158, 159,
    195n48. See also *Yesenia*
Cuba, 2, 3, 14, 22, 25, 48, 54, 55, 70, 101, 130, 169,
    176, 205n83, 212n9

Cugat, Xavier, 48
cultural industries, 12, 30, 52, 53, 77, 79, 87, 133
cultural intimacies, 6, 7, 10, 11, 12, 20–22, 56,
    57–62, 65, 68, 143, 164, 178
cursi feminism, 116, 117, 119–21
cursilería, 113, 114, 116, 134, 136, 205n79.
    See also *lo cursi*

Dalida, 18
danzón, 101
Dark Rivers (Las aguas bajan turbias), 37
Dassin, Joe, 18
de Funès, Louis, 16
del Río, Dolores, 11, 100, 116, 118
Demare, Lucas, 36
Denning, Michael, 7, 135, 136
De Santis, Giuseppe, 48
deterritorialization, 8, 11, 20
Diamond Arm, The (Brilliantovaia ruka), 66
dictablanda, 4, 19, 140, 180n9
Dior, 44–47, 157, 189n44
Disco Dancer, 67, 193n23
distribution, 8, 16, 17, 19, 58, 68, 72, 73, 166, 168;
    of *Yesenia*, 12, 68, 74, 141
DIY, 5, 9, 13, 47, 50, 89, 141, 143, 159–65
dizi, 2, 177
Djagalov, Rossen, 14
D'Lugo, Marvin, 6, 7, 180nn12,14, 181nn16,21
domestic sphere, 9, 31, 41, 46, 89, 103, 120, 123,
    132, 143, 144, 146, 147, 150
Donskoi, Mark, 39
Dorsey, Jimmy, 48
Durbin, Deanna, 41
Dyer, Richard, 43

East Germany, 23
Echeverría, María Esther Zuno de, 153
Echeverría, Rodolfo, 69, 71, 72, 124, 166
Echeverría Álvarez, Luis, 61, 69, 70, 74, 75, 94,
    140, 143, 160
Egypt, 6, 8, 15, 29, 67, 68, 75, 136, 148, 195n52
Eisenstein, Sergei, 70, 166, 206n91
El encuentro de un hombre solo, 71
El Informador, 142, 143
Enamorada, 99
Epshtein, Mikhail, 40
españoladas, 37, 50, 51, 128, 129, 190n65
estrada, 47, 48, 56, 69, 125
ethnic fashion, 94, 101, 142, 151–57, 161–63
Eurovision, 18, 183n54
Evans, Christine, 7, 104
evening gown. See ball gown

evening-wear, 147, 148–51, 154, 157.
See also ball gown
excess, 29, 32, 49, 52, 54, 103, 113, 116, 120, 121,
124, 125, 133, 134, 148, 149, 178. *See also*
melodrama; sentimentality
exhibition, 3, 5, 8, 9, 12, 14–16, 21, 35, 56, 65, 66,
72–76, 83, 103, 130, 133, 141. *See also* festivals

fandom, 2, 3, 5, 12, 14–17, 33, 46, 47, 50, 57–62, 64,
65, 67, 132, 165, 169, 178, 182n35, 193n23
fashion, 11, 13, 36, 39, 44–48, 52, 61, 87–89,
91–94, 96, 97, 103, 105, 116, 119, 121, 125, 138,
141–49, 151–65, 167, 187n18, 188n20, 212n9;
DIY and self-fashioning, 50, 88, 91, 94, 143,
163; fashion industry, 3, 8, 64, 160; "gypsy"
and "ethnic" fashion, 4, 152, 153, 157, 162, 163
Félix, María, 11, 99, 100, 118, 119, 129
feminism, 9, 13, 27, 30, 31, 86, 89, 93, 100, 141, 144,
147, 151, 198n26, 202n20; in Mexico, 13, 82, 85,
86, 91, 96, 98, 102, 116, 117, 119–21; in USSR,
93, 147. *See also* cursi feminism
Fernández, Emilio, 32, 36, 72, 99
festivals: film, 14, 16, 36, 37, 42, 57, 58, 65, 70–75,
101, 130, 147, 175; Moscow International Film
Festival, 57, 58, 70–72, 74; music, 18, 38, 49,
53, 166, 167; Sanremo International Music
Festival, 18; Sopot International Song Festival,
18; Tashkent Film Festival, 57, 71–73, 101, 130;
World Festival of Youth and Students, 38, 49,
53, 166, 167. *See also* exhibition
fichera, 96, 101, 199n54
folk culture, 12, 18, 27, 29, 30, 37, 44, 48, 108, 137,
145, 147, 153, 154; folklore/folkloric, 18, 37, 44,
48 50, 52, 54 72, 73, 128, 137, 145, 154; folkloric
dance, 54, 71, 72, 154; folkloric fashion, 44,
94, 151, 152–54, 156; folk music, 44, 48, 54, 56,
72, 123, 128, 136, 154, 169, 192n105
Follow the Boys, 48, 165
Forty-First, The (*Sorok pervyi*), 38
Friedan, Betty, 86
Fuentes, Carlos, 28

Gaal, Franciska, 41
Gagarin, Yuri, 60
Gals (*Devchata*), 40
García Márquez, Gabriel, 28
García Riera, Emilio, 77, 78, 132
Gavaldón, Roberto, 74, 195n48
gender essentialism, 9, 13, 83, 85, 108, 116, 163
Gerasimov, Sergei, 72
Germany, 15, 35, 123, 147, 186n3, 195n48
Ghosh, Bishnupriya, 2, 10, 11, 17, 32, 33, 138, 164

Gilburd, Eleonory, 14, 191nn91,93
Gilda, 48
gitana, 128–31. *See also* "gypsy"
glamour, 12, 13, 26, 36, 37, 44, 45, 138, 144, 148
global 1960s, 7, 9, 10, 55, 56, 69, 102, 108, 109, 139
global icon, 10, 17, 44, 82, 111, 138, 144, 178.
See also stardom
globalization, 2, 4, 6, 7, 11, 19, 20, 24, 140, 141, 164,
175, 180n11; and neoliberalism, 2, 4, 7, 11, 19,
24, 140, 141, 178
global-popular, 2, 3, 4, 5, 12, 19, 25, 27–33, 134,
164, 177, 178. *See also* national-popular
Global North, 2, 8, 10, 11, 21, 27, 28, 135, 177, 178.
See also Global South
Global South, 2, 10, 24, 25, 67, 68, 131.
See also Global North
Globo, 3, 7, 77, 176, 192n10, 212n6
Golubev, Alexey, 9, 145, 163, 208n42
Goskino, 65, 71, 75, 145
graphic novels, 3, 5, 12, 17, 28, 69, 76, 79, 80, 102.
See also *historietas*
gray market, 140, 141
Gurchenko, Liudmila, 46–49, 208n37
Gutierritos, 77
Gypsies Are Found Near Heaven (*Tabor ukhodit v
nebo*), 123, 125, 127, 128
"gypsy", 4, 5, 11, 13, 20, 61, 66, 67, 94, 96, 97, 101,
112, 114, 123, 124, 125–37, 142, 146, 149, 151–53,
155, 157, 162; figure of, 4, 11, 20, 22, 97, 112, 114,
127–32, 134, 135, 190n65; "gypsy dance," 130;
"gypsy fashion," 4, 94, 96, 142, 149, 151–53,
155, 157, 162; "gypsy melodrama," 13, 61, 112,
124, 125, 146, 190n65; "gypsy music," 4, 5, 56,
123–25, 133, 135–37

Hansen, Miriam, 164
Hepburn, Audrey, 50, 93
Hepburn, Katherine, 93
Herzfeld, Michael, 22
Hirschfeld, Joanne, 81
historical melodrama, 3, 101, 108, 125–28, 149,
192n10. *See also* costume drama
historietas, 12, 17, 72, 79, 80–82, 88, 89, 92, 96,
102, 105, 112, 113, 130, 195n48. *See also*
graphic novels
Holidays in Prostokvashino (*Kanikuly v
prostokvashino*), 149, 150
How to Steal a Million, 67, 195n52
hybridity, 20, 41, 51, 54, 80, 136, 138, 164
hyper-femininity, 44, 95, 97, 101, 146, 181n28.
See also hypersexualization
hypersexualization, 101, 146, 181n28

identification, 24, 53, 67, 105, 109, 120, 123, 134, 139, 144; cultural, 8, 11, 53; emotional, 10, 67, 68, 193n23; and (mis)identification, 8

Iglesias, Julio, 18, 118

imperialism, 22, 23, 108, 126; and anti-imperialism, 23, 26, 68

import-substitution, 9, 141

India, 3, 6, 8, 10, 14, 15, 25, 28, 29, 31, 35, 40, 41, 42, 43, 44, 66, 67, 68, 75, 134, 136, 177, 189n40, 195n52

indigeneity, 22, 25, 36, 49, 94, 114, 117, 153, 157, 184n62; *indigenista*, 114

informal economies, 5, 9, 13, 15, 19, 21, 24, 50, 61, 64, 70–71, 75, 140–146, 159–65, 169, 171. *See also* black market; DIY; gray market; media piracy; shadow economies

ingenue (*la ingenua*), 37–40, 129. *See also* "modern girl" (*la chica moderna*)

Institutional Revolutionary Party (PRI), 4, 69, 170

intellectual property, 8, 49, 50, 61, 140. *See also* copyright

intelligentsia, 5, 23, 24, 27, 30, 63, 67, 69, 71, 75, 102, 108, 112, 120, 122, 123, 133, 136, 137, 148, 150, 151, 162, 167, 178

intermediality, 6, 12, 13, 28, 33, 69, 182n35

internationalism, 4, 9, 10, 24, 38, 49–51, 64, 127, 164. *See also* Third-Worldism

inter-referencing, 31

Intervision, 18, 183n54

intimacies: cultural, 10, 12, 20–22, 68, 178; transnational, 6, 7, 10, 11, 12, 56, 57–62, 65, 143, 164

Isaura (A Escrava Isaura). See *Slave Isaura, The*

Ivan's Childhood (Ivanovo detstvo), 38

Izzo, Tao, 118, 119

Jackson, Matthew Jesse, 20

Jacome, Aurora, 25

Jazz, 19, 47, 48, 51, 53, 55, 56, 135, 189n56

Jones, Andrew F., 7, 55

Kaganovsky, Lilya, 7, 46, 143, 211n86

Kapoor, Raj, 10, 16, 42–44, 57, 66, 131

Karush, Matthew, 7, 61

Kassabian, Anahid, 6

Kena (magazine), 87–96, 116–19, 153–55, 157, 160, 202n20

kitsch, 13, 111–13, 122, 170, 203n39. See also *lo cursi; poshlost'*

Kosinova, Marina, 15

Koster, Henry, 41

Kovalenko, Aleksandra, 46–48

Kriger, Clara, 41

Kristalinskaia, Maia, 46, 47

Krugozor (magazine), 18

Kulidzhanov, Lev, 71, 130

kul'turnost', 29, 38, 60, 103, 106, 107, 120–22, 157, 200n78

Kunakhovich, Kyrill, 23, 24

la bohème, 126, 129

La casa del Sur, 71

La Dolce Vita, 48

Lady of Camellias, The, 43

Lágrimas, risas y amor, 79, 81

Lahr-Vivaz, Elena, 32

Lamarque, Libertad, 36, 195n48

Lamarre, Tom, 8

Lamas, Marta, 9

Lapidus, Gail, 9

Lara, Agustín, 81, 101, 113, 114, 118, 166, 204n62

Larkin, Brian, 10

late socialism, 4, 29, 122, 151, 180n9

Latin craze, 53, 55

"Latin Pop Explosion," 7

Lautary, 123, 125, 127

Lavat, Jorge, 72, 74, 172

Leigh, Vivien, 50

lianhuanhua, 172

liberalism, 4, 10, 19, 22, 24–26, 31, 32, 36, 43, 74, 89, 93, 103, 104, 110, 122, 127, 138, 140, 148

literature, 26, 28, 79, 103, 117, 125, 151, 185n85, 193n15

Little Blue Flame, The (Goluboi Ogonek), 58–60

lo cursi, 13, 80, 81, 112, 144, 158, 167, 169, 203n50, 205n79; in relation to Russian *poshlost'*, 112–38. See also *poshlost'*

Lollobrigida, Gina, 16, 137, 174

Lomnitz-Adler, Claudio, 30

Look (magazine), 152

"Looking for Yesenia," 175

López, Ana M., 7, 28

López Portillo, José, 70

López Portillo, Margarita, 70, 74

Los Hermanos Coraje, 72

Los Panchos, 54, 166

Los Ricos También Lloran, 3, 67, 79, 176, 177, 195n44

Loteanu, Emil', 123, 125

"low" culture, 27, 69, 74, 75, 79, 104, 108, 118, 136, 169, 195n48. *See also* bad taste

lubok, 137, 138, 206n91
Lumpenproletariat, 128, 139

MacFadyen, David, 124
Magnificent Seven, The, 66
Marais, Jean, 16
María, 172
María Isabel, 79, 82, 196n69
Marshall, Niní, 36
Martín-Barbero, Jesús, 6, 7, 28, 30, 32, 53
Mathieu, Mireille, 18
media flows (and counter-flows), 2, 5, 6, 11, 16,
    19, 29, 68, 164, 175, 177
media piracy, 13 19, 33, 140, 143, 173, 178, 183n56.
    See also black market; gray market; informal
    economies; shadow economies
melodrama: and consumer culture, 144–51;
    general theory of, 5, 6, 14, 27, 134, 141; and
    global-popular, 27–33; in USSR, 13, 39, 103,
    104, 108–10, 123, 125–28, 166, 201n80
melodramatic media, 3–6, 13, 30, 61, 111, 144, 163,
    171, 175, 177
Mexican Golden Age cinema, 3, 11, 28, 30, 36,
    65, 69, 73, 74, 81, 95, 100, 102, 114, 117, 118,
    190n70
Miranda, Carmen, 48
"modern girl" (*la chica moderna*), 37–40, 81
modernization, 22, 23, 25, 30, 76, 86, 102, 128
Monsiváis, Carlos, 11, 28, 30, 101, 113, 114, 116, 120,
    121, 134, 136, 138, 205n81
Montand, Yves, 18, 57
Moreno, Zully, 36
Moscow Does Not Believe in Tears (*Moskva
    slezam ne verit*), 13, 128, 165–71
Moscow Film Institute (VGIK), 49, 71
multitudes, 24, 25, 27, 139. *See also* public sphere;
    "the popular"
Mundo Radial (magazine), 58, 59
Murphy, Michelle, 84
Mushroom Man, The (*El hombre de los hongos*), 74
musicarelli, 18

Nabokov, Vladimir, 120
national-popular, 19, 55, 61, 80, 129. *See also*
    global-popular
neoliberal feminism. *See* postfeminism
neoliberalism, 2, 4, 7–9, 11, 12, 19, 24, 25, 33, 61,
    85, 96, 116, 138, 140, 141, 143, 163, 178, 193n25.
    See also globalization
networks, 3, 6, 8, 9, 19, 21, 23, 36, 56, 58, 68, 143;
    informal, 21, 70–71, 145, 146, 164

New Latin American Cinema, 71, 86
nonassimilation, 127

obshchiny, 25
Olcott, Jocelyn, 9, 86
Olhovich, Sergio, 71–75, 194n38
Oreiro, Natalia, 177, 178
Orientalism, 21, 22, 26, 119, 127, 134
Ottawan, 18

P'ekha, Edita, 46, 49, 56, 60
Peliculas Nacionales, 72
period drama. *See* costume drama; historical
    melodrama
Perón, Eva "Evita," 36, 43, 177, 189n37
Perón, General Juan, 12, 36, 37, 41, 50, 51, 54,
    55, 58, 61, 132, 161. *See also* Perón, Eva;
    Perónism
Perónism, 19, 43, 51, 58, 61
personal care industries. *See* fashion
Peru, 17, 53, 79, 93, 212n9
Peter, das Mädchen von der Tankstelle, 41
petit bourgeois, 38, 121, 124
Pimstein, Valentín, 77, 79, 177, 195n44
piracy. *See* media piracy
Podalsky, Laura, 18
polystylist, 20, 94, 122
"popular, the," 9, 11, 14, 23, 27, 29, 30–33, 114, 121,
    127, 133, 137–40, 163. *See also* populism
populism, 5, 12, 20, 33, 36, 37, 40, 43, 54, 61, 69,
    127, 132, 141, 143, 178
poshlost', 13, 112, 120–123, 127, 135–37, 146, 150; in
    relation to Mexican *lo cursi*, 112–38. See also
    byt; lo cursi
postfeminism, 8, 9, 163, 178, 181n28. *See also*
    feminism; neoliberalism
postmodernism, 20, 79, 122, 153
postsocialism, 7, 13, 14, 20, 21, 24, 29, 110, 138, 175.
    See also post-Soviet
post-Soviet, 1, 8, 25, 31, 79, 107, 137, 138, 147, 171,
    177, 195n44, 201n88, 209n61
post-Stalinist period, 4, 18, 29, 50, 122, 124
Prague Spring, 10, 24, 63, 75, 139
Prasad, Madhava, 28
Presley, Elvis, 27, 51, 153
Princess on a Pea, The (*Printessa na goroshine*),
    107, 108
"private feelings," 40, 109, 122, 123
private sphere, 29, 32, 39, 43, 85, 106, 110
Prokhorov, Alexander, 7
Prokhorova, Elena, 7

public sphere, 10, 21, 23, 24, 32, 41, 80, 110, 126, 140. *See also* multitudes; "the popular"

¡Que viva México!, 70
quinceañera, 157–59
Quinceañera (film), 158, 159

Rabotsnitsa (magazine) 46
Rajagopalan, Sudha, 25
Rao, Rahul, 22
radio, 7, 17, 18, 28, 47, 48, 53, 56, 58, 70, 80, 81, 112, 113, 135, 145, 189n37. *See also* radio plays
Radiolandia, 59
radio plays, 17, 28, 81, 112
Rainbow (Raduga), 39
reception, 3–7, 40, 52, 61, 64, 67, 83, 105; Soviet reception of "Bésame Mucho," 165, 170; Soviet reception of *The Age of Love*, 42–44, 59, 111, 124, 129, 131–33, 138, 141, 144, 145, 147, 151, 164, 171, 172, 175, 176, 178, 180nn8,11; Soviet reception of *Yesenia*, 3, 56, 61, 65, 105, 110, 112, 120, 122, 127, 131, 136, 163. *See also* affective communities; fandom
Red Bells, The (Las Companas Rojas/Krasnye Kolokola), 70
remakes, 17, 79, 195n48, 196n69, 205n71. *See also* adaptation
remediation, 17, 83, 114, 119
Ricchi e Poveri, 18
rock and roll, 18, 19, 51, 64, 203n46
Roma, 4, 8, 26, 47, 76, 97, 98, 100, 102, 123, 125–28, 130, 131, 133–35, 152, 190n65, 205n71
Romani. *See* Roma
romansy, 5, 6, 13, 56, 123, 125
Rome, 11 o'Clock (Rome, ore 11), 48
Roth-Ey, Kristin, 7, 14
Rotkirch, Anna, 9, 106
Roussos, Demis, 18
Rubenstein, Anne, 9, 80, 81
rumbera, 100–102

Salazar, Antonio, 60
Sánchez Prado, Ignacio M., 11, 25, 30, 116
Saraceni, Julio, 36, 37, 44, 51
sarafannoe radio, 145
Sarkar, Bhaskar, 2, 33, 164
Schmelz, Peter, 19, 203n39
Second Franco-Mexican War, 2, 64
Second World, 20, 21, 24, 143
Senda prohibida, 77, 80
sentimental communities, 5, 10, 11, 20, 23, 62, 127, 134, 147. *See also* Lauren Berlant

sentimental culture, 4, 53, 83, 95, 104; "socialist sentimentalism," 40
sentimental education, 16, 28–29, 82, 105, 112, 168
sentimental media, 61, 83, 102
sentimental novel, 28, 92, 102, 116
sexual revolution, 9, 13, 83, 89, 96, 97, 105. *See also* global 1960s
shadow economies, 8, 24, 140. *See also* black markets; media piracy
sheet music, 19, 143
Sikora, Ruzhena, 48, 165
Simplemente María, 79, 138, 176, 212n9
Slave Isaura, The (A Escrava Isaura), 3, 67, 131, 176, 177, 205n75
soap opera, 3, 29, 32, 78, 144, 145, 179n7, 209n61. *See also* melodrama
Socialist Bloc (Soviet Bloc; Eastern Bloc), 2, 3, 6, 7, 8, 11, 14, 15, 20, 22, 23, 28, 33, 36, 49, 63, 65, 70, 71, 86, 87, 131, 198n19
socialist realism, 29, 38, 104
song covers, 19, 47, 165. *See also* copyright
Sovetskaia Kul'tura (newspaper), 48, 176
Sovexportfilm, 37, 75
Soviet-Mexican Cultural Association, 70, 130
Soviet-Mexican exchanges, 12, 25, 61, 65, 68, 70–75, 130, 194n31
Soviet Woman, 39, 147
Spanish Civil War, 47, 51, 55
Spring on Zarachnaia Street (Vesna na Zarechnoi ulitse), 38
Stagnation period, 63, 67
stardom, 4, 6, 12, 18, 36, 46, 47, 50, 56, 58, 65, 67, 88, 90, 93, 95, 101, 102, 118, 119, 123, 128, 144, 148, 177, 196n69; and fandom, 50, 57–62; of foreign stars in Soviet Union, 14–17, 42–44, 49, 50, 56–60; of Lolita Torres, 4, 12, 35–62; of Raj Kapoor, 42–44, 57; and transnational intimacies, 12. *See also* Lolita Torres; Raj Kapoor
state-socialism, 86, 138
structures of feeling, 8, 30, 53, 68
subaltern, 12, 24, 30, 33, 138, 139, 143, 169

tango, 3, 32, 41, 51–54, 124, 135
taste, 5, 32, 33, 35, 38, 41, 48, 51, 59, 80, 113, 118, 122, 136, 137, 138, 147; bad taste, 27, 54, 111, 113, 117, 120, 121, 125, 147, 158, 167; "good taste," 21, 29, 38, 121, 137, 151, 163; taste making, 18; taste regimes, 11, 111, 209n61
telenovela, 1–3, 6–8, 10, 11, 13, 17, 26–28, 53, 64, 67, 69, 72, 75–82, 88, 91, 92, 96, 101, 102, 105, 112–14, 119, 120, 130, 131, 138, 143, 144, 158,

171–78, 179n7, 180n11, 193n18, 195nn44,48, 196n69, 205n71, 212n9

Televisa, 3, 6, 7, 13, 17, 72, 77, 79, 81, 82, 85, 87, 88, 89, 114, 141, 158, 176, 196nn62,63,64,69, 198n22, 201n7, 204n69

television (TV), 1–3, 5–8, 13, 15–18, 28, 37, 52, 54–56, 58, 63, 64, 67, 68, 70, 72, 76–79, 81, 85, 87–89, 97, 102, 104, 105, 109, 113, 117–19, 127, 130, 131, 138, 143, 146, 148, 149, 160, 164, 166, 169, 171, 174–78, 188n20, 195n44, 196n64, 203n46, 209n61

temporality, 6, 15–20, 108, 117, 121, 145, 171, 176. *See also* anachronism; asynchronicity

Teresa, 77

Thaw period, 12, 35, 38–41, 44, 46, 50, 55, 56, 59, 61, 63, 64, 67, 75, 104, 108, 124, 132, 167

Third-Worldism, 10, 22, 23, 69, 86, 94, 114, 162, 164

Those Years (Aquellos años), 74

Thussu, Daya Kishan, 6, 181n17

Tlatelolco massacre, 10, 24, 69, 139

Torres, Lolita, 4, 5, 10, 12, 16, 17, 19, 35–62, 64, 65, 104, 110, 122, 124, 132, 178, 187n9, 189n50, 191n105

translation: linguistic, 23, 113; cultural, 56, 57, 114, 121, 146, 191n93; literary, 23, 28, 92; musical, 47, 49–52

transmediality, 8, 17, 28, 32

"trophy films," 35, 41, 130, 165, 186n3

tsyganshchina, 125, 126

Turkey, 2, 3, 29, 177. See also *dizi*

Turovskaia, Maia, 30, 65–67, 76, 134, 136–38, 147, 148, 150, 151, 193n15

ubiquitous listening, 6

Una mejor vida, 82

underdevelopment, 32, 57, 113, 114, 137, 205n81

United Nations World Conference on Women, 85–87

universalism, 5, 10, 11, 20, 25, 33, 38, 50, 60, 83, 91, 92, 120, 127, 133–35

Un novio para Laura, 37, 45

unruliness, 2, 12, 24, 26, 98, 100, 127, 136, 165; "unruly woman," 98, 100, 131, 145n199

Uruguay, 48, 177

Utesov, Leonid, 47–48

Vagabond, The (Awara), 42, 43, 55, 66, 131

Vanikoff, Isaak Argentino, 36

Vargas Dulché, Yolanda, 77, 79–82, 88, 115, 116, 130

Vasudevan, Ravi, 28, 31

Vega, Isela, 72, 101

Vela Martínez, Alejandra, 116, 117

Velázquez, Consuelo, 1, 51, 165, 168, 169, 170, 171

Velikanova, Gelena, 46, 47, 49

Verona, 94, 95, 153, 160

video, 3, 15, 19, 64

Vietnam, 22

Vogue (magazine), 152

Walker, Louise, 9

Walking the Streets of Moscow (Ia shagaiu po Moskve), 38

Welcome, or No Trespassing (Dobro pozhalovat', ili postoronnim vkhod vospreshchen), 38

White Gown, The (Al-Reda'a al-Abiad), 148

women's culture, 9, 13, 143, 144; in Mexico, 13, 80, 112; in USSR, 13, 89, 91, 102–12, 148, 208n42

women's liberation, 13, 73, 82, 83, 85–89, 91, 93–96, 102, 127, 144, 147, 151

women' magazines, 13, 80, 87–103, 112, 116–18, 143, 146, 153, 157, 160, 163, 200n56, 202n20, 209n61

Yesenia (character), 3, 11, 12, 17, 19, 26, 76–80, 82, 83, 91, 96–8, 100, 101, 121, 130–38, 142–44, 148, 149, 151, 157, 161, 173–75, 207n10

Yesenia (film), 2–6, 8, 10–13, 15, 17, 20, 25, 26, 30, 31, 33, 56, 61, 63–68, 72, 74, 76–80, 82, 83, 85, 91, 92, 98, 99, 101, 102, 105, 108–14, 116, 117, 119, 120, 122, 124, 127–34, 136–38, 140–43, 145, 147–49, 151, 153, 157, 158, 162–65, 171–78, 190n65, 193n23, 195nn44,52, 196n65

Yoshimoto, Mitsuhiro, 31–32

youth culture, 18, 38, 49, 52, 53, 63, 96, 148, 153, 166, 167

YouTube, 64, 67, 133, 208n40

Yurchak, Alexei, 14, 20, 122, 193n22

Zaitsev, Viacheslav, 157

Zakharova, Larisa, 44

Zarzosa, Agustín, 28

Zi, Li, 173

Žižek, Slavoj, 20

Zolov, Eric, 9, 153

Zorkaia, Neia, 30, 137, 138, 145, 151

9 780520 400757